THE ELLORA MONOLITHS

THE ELLORA MONOLITHS

(Rashtrakuta Architecture in the Deccan)

by

K.V. SOUNDARA RAJAN

Additional Director General (Rtd.) Archaeological Survey of India

GYAN PUBLISHING HOUSE

New Delhi - 110002

THE ELLORA MONOLITHS

RASHTRAKUTA ARCHITECTURE IN THE DECCAN

ISBN : 9788121201179

PRICE- 900

K.V SOUNDARA RAJAN

Published in 2015 in India by
Gyan Publishing House
23, Ansari Road, Daryaganj,
New Delhi - 110002
Phones : 23261060, 23282060 Fax : 23285914
e-mail : books@gyanbooks.com
website : gyanbooks.com

Laser Typesetting at : Vinayak Printers, Delhi
Printed at : Salasar Imaging System, Delhi

Preface

THERE are some spectacular and profound groups of monuments in India which, by their richness, evocative aesthetic appeal and prodigiousness, are well nigh unparalleled. Ellora caves are one among these choice few. Among even these array of cave art specimens, the monolithic creations touch a new peak of grandeur, for the achievements of the master masons and sculptors who designed them. Ellora has as many as *five* of them and all of them are the proud patronage of the Rashtrakutas of Ellora. This, by itself, would single them out as the fit topic for detailed examination. *Rashtrakuta* art at Ellora was destined to be immortal with the *magnum opus* of Kailasa monolith of Krishna I, but certainly to the art-historians, all the five monoliths would open out windows on the development of architecture, blossoming of vigorous religious art, and the multitudeneus but patternised interaction of cults, not to mention the sheet designing of these 'cheese-cake' marvels.

It is extremely difficult to satisfy all interests in such a situation. The author's chief if not the sole aim was to give an authentic presentation of these wonderful models—which they truly are of structural temples of coeval age on perishable materials which are lost to us—from an architect's and art-historical view point and to graft into the study, an analytical summation of what role these monoliths played in the overall comparative picture of other monoliths of other regions and both earlier to and later than them—as in the case of the celebrated Pallava monoliths or 'rathas' at Mahabalipuram, and the Pandyan solitary splendour at Kalugumalai. The author would like to think that the scheme of study and the integrated assessment of the constituent art-elements of these monoliths in the main stream of Indian pre-mediaeval art, has not been presented so far in the manner preferred in this book.

The author would be failing in his duty if he does not mention that several colleagues and scholars in seminar meetings and elsewhere, had looked at these art creations at Ellora from many angles, and had indirectly created an urge in the author to render justice to them in the manner understood and appreciated by him, notwithstanding the numerous tomes written on these for more than a century, from Ferguesson to Percy Brown and other later young scholars.

The photographs illustrating these monuments and their features are by courtesy of the Archaeological Survey of India, which the author gratefully acknowledges. A necessary and sufficient set of line drawings has been provided to reveal what often human vision cannot take in, at one sweep.

The author wishes to thank his wife, Kumuda, for having been the silent stimulus in his studies on Ellora during some of which she had also accompanied him.

Thanks in ample measure are no less due to Smt. B.P. Garg of Gian Publishing House for her good and cordial efforts towards the format and design of the book.

The author wishes to dedicate the book to the cosmic and etherial presence of Lord Siva over the hill range at Ellora caves where scores of unknown artisans had themselves dedicated their skills.

Ashada Purnima 1987
New Delhi.

K.V. SOUNDARA RAJAN

List of Plates

parapet and without any central miniature shrine crest or the animals in the round on the periphery.

Plate XII—Ellora : Chota Kailasa—Showing the south-eastern corner of the tower and the unfinished lower levels.

Plate XIII—Ellora : Chota Kailasa—Sukanasa front with the Sankha and Padma nidhis and with the tower scheme below. The Sukanasa contain a sub-shrine within it.

Plate XIV—Ellora : Chota Kailasa—View of the *Mukha*-chatushki porch of the front entrance.

Plate XV—Ellora : Chota Kailasa—View of the entrance from south-west, showing a part of the cloister and front flat-roofed dvaramandapa exterior also.

Plate XVI—Ellora : Chota Kailasa—Details of the triangular udgamas, pilaster scheme and the *Vidyadhara* couple.

Plate XVII—Ellora : Chota Kailasa—View of the Superstructural tower and the Sukanasa on the roof.

Plate XVIII—Ellora : Chota Kailasa—Roof of the Sabha mandapa with Sukanasa projection leading to the upper storey shrine within, and the damaged main tower of the monolith.

Plate XIX—Ellora : Chota Kailasa—General view from south-western side showing exterior of dvaramandapa, view of the inner temple and its tower against the steep hill scrap.

Plate XX—Ellora : Chota Kailasa—Carved detail of the *Padma-nidhi* type on the flanks of the *mukhapatti* of the *Sukanasa*

Plate XXI—Ellora : Chota Kailasa—Carving on the upper *tala* wall of the tower—a mithuna pair seated.

Plate XXII—Ellora : Chota Kailasa—General view of the south-western corner of the monolith.

Plate XXIII—Ellora : Cave No. 32—(Indrasabha)—General view from outside showing the *prakara*, *dvarasala* and the inner *chaumukh* tower.

dvarapalas on either side. The lotus tank in front of Lakshmi is a magnificant relief work.

Plate XXXVII—Ellora : Cave No. 16 (Kailasa)—Gajalakshmi panel in the lower level passage porch, with its lotus tank depiction in foreground.

Plate XXXVIII—Ellora : Cave No. 16 (Kailasa)—Southern court-figure of monolithic elephant and the barrel-vaulted cave front on the south wall scrap.

Plate XXXIX—Ellora : Cave No. 16 (Kailasa)—Detailed view of the southern wall of the front mandapa, showing the panel sculpture of Tandava Siva in the central part and shrine reliefs of smaller size on the sides.

Plate XL—Ellora Cave No. 16 (Kailasa)—Mid-level view of the emerging stairecase with the mukhamandapa and the twin-bhumi level wall section on the plinth.

Plate XLI—Ellora : Cave No. 16 (Kailasa)—Axial view of the upper level set-up, from south-west, showing part of Nandimandapa, Mukhamandapa, Southern porch (bhadravalokana) and the superstructural tower and the *hara* system besides part of the monolithic banner pillar on the south-west courtyard.

Plate XLII—Ellora : Cave No. 16 (Kailasa)—South side porch (bhadra-valokana)—Details.

Plate XLIII—Ellora : Cave No. 16 (Kailasa)—Details of the massive plinth and the parivara monolith sub-shrines at the upper level on the northern side.

Plate XLIV—Ellora : Cave 16 (Kailasa)—General view from south-west, emphasizing the deep sheer pit, shaft sunk into the hill top, for carving out the central monolithic tower.

Plate XLV—Ellora : Cave No. 16 (Kailasa)—South court, south western corner showing monolithic column, door leading to the upper level, with planking Ramayana panel and the rise of the upper sides of the Nandimandapa porch and the corner wall shrine relief.

Plate XLVI—Ellora : Cave No. 16 (Kailasa)—General view from the north-western corner of the court.

Plate XLVII—Ellora : Cave No. 16 (Kailasa)—Mukhamandapa porch poised over the ground *tala* high plinth, with massive *hora* parapet, and gaja-munda vedi for the porch itself. Ramayana panel narration on the exterior of the hidden staircase south face, is also seen.

Plate XLVIII—Ellora : Cave No. 16 (Kailasa)—Full view of the main scheme from top to bottom, from the south-western side showing monolith pillar, massive plinth, upper mandapa porch and the tower above.

Plate XLIX—Ellora : Cave No. 16 (Kailasa)—Nandimandapa exterior north-west corner showing supporting pillar scheme wall details and the monolithic banner column in the north-west court, side wing.

Plate L—Ellora : Cave No. 16, (Kailasa)—Roof centre of the Nandi-mandapa showing inter-locking mahanasika barrel in a *tri-ratha* layout carrying divinilty within the *kudu*.

Plate LI—Ellora : Cave No. 16 (Kailasa)—Close view of the main shrine tower and its *sukanasa*.

Plate LII—Ellora : Cave No. 16 (Kailasa)—Main *vimana* tower-south face, showing the liner storeyed pattern and the well-projected *sukanasa* on front.

Plate LIII—Ellora : Cave No. 16 (Kailasa)—Parivara shrine monolith on the north-east corner-frontal view.

Plate LIV—Ellora : Cave No. 16 (Kailasa)—General view of the monolithic parivara sub-shrine on the north-west corner which faces south.

Plate LV—Ellora : Cave No. 16 (Kailasa)—Inner cloister—details of the lower part of Andhakasura vadha murti, with seven *matrs* and ganas-the foot of Siva planted on two gana heads; Kalabhairava (emaciated) dancing near by.

Plate LVI—Ellora : Cave No. 16 (Kailasa)—Panel of Somaskanda seated on Nandi Bull, with attendants.

Plate LVII—Ellora : Cave No. 16 (Kailasa)—Eastern court of the monolith at ground level, with the running sides of square sectioned pillars fringing the cloister walk, over a vedi parapet relief.

Plate LVIII—Ellora : Cave No. 16 (Kailasa)—Wall panels of the Sabhamandapa exterior showing also the hara above and the frowning lion on the mukhamandapa roof edge. The major panel here is of Jatayu's fight with Ravana.

Plate LIX—Ellora : Cave No. 16 (Kailasa)—Wall details on the main mandapa exterior, south side, showing panels of Lakulisa (in niche shrine), Ravana fighting Jatayu etc. and the south side porch and the *hara* scheme above it.

Plate LX—Ellora : Cave No. 16 (Kailasa)—Main temple bridge porch below Nandimandapa, showing the Ramayana panel.

Plate LXI—Ellora : Cave No. 16 (Kailasa)—Panel figure of Surya with elaborate makara torana, with Aruna and attendants relieved out of the makara motif.

Plate LXII—Ellora : Cave No. 16 (Kailasa)—Side walls of the front porch in the court;-Parvati wearing *channavira* and mirror in left hand seen, with vidyadhara hovering above.

Plate LXIII—Ellora : Cave No. 16 (Kailasa)—Wall of sabhamandapa (exterior upper level) mithuna in 'direct kiss pose.

Plate LXIV—Ellora : Cave No. 16 (Kailasa)—Inner cloister—Wall face of the sabhamandapa exterior south—Mithuna in *kapola-chumbana* pose.

Contents

1

Introduction

THE great Kailasa monolithic complex (Cave XVI) at Ellora is undisputedly one of the most ambitious rock-architectural projects ever undertaken anywhere and brought to a successful conclusion. Considered by any standards of temple modelling, it deserves the prime place by its aesthetic balance, formal majesty and iconographic profundity. That it should have been conceived and carried out at a time when structural architecture in the stone medium had already been developed to an impressive stage makes this *magnum opus* of the rock-art of the Rashtrakutas all the more magnificent. It is also to be noted that except for the Pallava monoliths at Mahabalipuram there was no contemporary achievement to take immediate inspiration from. The indescribable power of suggestion instinct in the remarkable array of cave temples at Ellora of the Chalukyas and of Dantidurga Rashtrakuta, should have cried out for a bold and novel experimentation of a free-standing model frozen in rock; and Krishna, the second monarch to sit on the throne of the Rashtrakutas, in the capital, perhaps located near Ellora itself, rose equal to the situation. The craft potential of the place should have already reassured him of the success of the venture. But it is certainly indisputable that a new spirit of religion and resurgent art was invoked by the royal patron in creating this miniature Kailasa—the model of the macrocosm. If the body mass of Deccan trap rock had thus been preservingly reduced by an uncanny vision of the royal patron to a sanctuary of impeccable rhythm, the vesture of legendary, mythical and canonical iconography that clothed the shrine model was the expression of the unsurpassed god-mindedness of the craftsmen and clergy. But Kailasa was not certainly born in a day. It shows the assimilation of the most notable trends in formal architecture, both functional and ritual, and anticipates the creations of the same dynasty at the self-same place, as in the Chaumukh of Indra Sabha and Chhota Kailasa (both of the Jain creed). Its atypical precursor and successor were Dantidurga's *mandapa* in front of Dasavatara cave, carrying the inscribed record of that king and the panchayatana lay-out displayed on the southern upper ledge of the Kailasa pit. But the distinction in style between the two aforesaid specimens and Krishna's Kailasa is well taken because they show between a convincing familiarity with the 'northern' as well as 'southern' architectural modulations, the parallel developments of which had been the most notable events of the art under the Chalukyas gone by. Together, thus, with the two Jain monoliths mentioned earlier, they form a most substantial contribution in the monolithic rock art of free-standing temple style and would deserve a separate and detailed attention. It is needless to add that the compressed architectural and plastic idioms, themes, and motifs that represent the otherwise inert rock-mass of these creations would stand close scrutiny. If the medium adopted—namely a monolithic rock-scoop was a shade retrograde for the age, the magnitude of sculptural vigour and *elan* implicit in it could not have been more convincingly presented against a less colossal back-drop. As the finite expression of an unshakable faith and resolute action in the religious plane of contemporary Deccan, Kailasa was indeed a *non-pareil.*

At the time of the inception of the Rashtrakuta monoliths at Ellora, as already stated, there were only the '*Rathas*' of the Pallavas at Mamallapuram, as the fore-runner. But a fairly well distributed patronage favouring monolithic models was observed by the late eighth century A.D., and the one following, and these largely followed the prevalent local composition in style. The earliest of these, would be Vettuvankoil at Kalugumalai in the Pandyan country, datable around 800 A.D.; followed by Dhamnar in Madhya Pradesh (displaying a reasonably complex *Astaparivara* shrine-complex of the curvilinear northern type, datable to mid-ninth century A.D.); the *Charbhuja* Vishnu temple on the brim of Gwalior hill, of the late ninth century A.D.; the series of seven monoliths at Masrur in Kangra valley of about the same time; and the small but variant rectangular shrine (unfinished) with wagon-top *sikhara* at Coglong in Bihar, of perhaps the same time, or somewhat later. Ellora's contributions thus, alike in quality as in quantity, were more than adequate. Its reasonable homogeneity in style and contemporaneity with stylistic modes elsewhere would seem to make them form a compact Rashtrakuta *milieu*, and thus of intrinsic importance. That they should have been so equally divided between Hinduism and Jainism in their affiliation would also tend to show the discerning art-patronage of the Rashtrakuta monarchs and the competitive role of Jainism in the then Western Indian scene. The order in which these monoliths would be dealt with would be: Dasavatara *mandapa* with inscription of Dantidurga, Kailasa complex, Monolith on the roof of the south bank of Kailasa, Indra Sabha Chaumukh, and Chhota Kailasa Admittedly, Kailasa would command a central place, but the treatment would exclude 'Lankesvara' and river shrines to its north, and the double-storeyed excavation, the Surya, the 'Saptamatrika' mandapa and the apsidal scooped corner shrine to the south side, all of which have already been covered in the previous volume on the 'cave temples of the Deccan'.

2

Architectural Traditions

THE accession of knowledge and heritage of temple forms at the time of the creation of the monolithic marvels at Ellora would have to be divided into two classes, the northern and southern styles, for a better correlation with the Ellora examples. As already noted, only the Dasavatara *mandapa* and the roof brink excavation display recognizable northern architectural features. Of the former, owing to the fact that this *mandapa* happened to be the rather desparate appendage to the main shrine in the upper storey, it was not able to show any characteristic profile or superstructure. Without going into the details of the *mandapa* (which will follow under the appropriate section) one may note that while its top has some features which resemble somewhat the corresponding ones on the *maha mandapa* roof of Kailasa, it has one element that is lacking in Kailasa, namely the slightly sloping exterior profile of the roof—the interior alone being shown as a flat ceiling. The slopy roof, further characterised by a slightly raised clerestory central part is seemingly influenced by the Ladakhan type and is truly a Chalukyan vestige, and since this *mandapa* is considered as Rashtrakuta and of Dantidurga mainly from the valuable inscription on its porch wall, it could not be firmly asserted that it was carved only during Dantidurga's reign and not slightly earlier. The possibility thus of a late Chalukya monolith which was inscribed upon by Dantidurga could not entirely be ruled out. The side walls of the *mandapa*, boldly introduce niches with *udgama* tops—a feature so characteristic of the *rekha-nagara sikharas* of the Chalukya temples in the Deccan. The modulations of these *udgamas* with their tendency to be somewhat elongated and of clear *jalaka* patterns almost of the *latina* type would seem to suggest a broad affinity with the contemporary Gurjara-Pratihara art idiom in Madhyadesa and Rajasthan.

It is not clear if the *mandapa* was intended as the *nandi*-pavilion, since its interior evidence is against it. Further, it is closed from the west although there is a portico attached to it. This might have been by accident and due to incompleteness also. It is thus equally likely to be a *bhoga* or *nata mandapa*. It is interesting that it has only a door facing east. Its accent, in its carvings on *mithunas* would suggest that it might have served as a *nata* and *bhoga mandapa*. If so, do not have any parallel to it in this region. Open triple or four porched *mandapas* are more common in this period, as indeed reflected in the Kailasa monolith *maha mandapa*, and the Chhota Kailasa vestibule. But if its detached character slopy roof and its closed walls are its most significant features, we should perhaps be inclined to take it as having served as the *Nandi-mandapa*, on the strength of the 'Kailasa' analogy, if indeed this did not form a separate shrine by itself.

The other roof brink '*panchayatana*' shrine is even more interesting since it combines northern and southern features the false *sarvatobhadra* character with porches on the cardinal points and the four corner subsidiary shrines of the *ekatala*, *alpa vimana* type, seeing the elements of the former and the provision of the four *gopura dvaras* (of single floor in three of them apparently and double storeyed on the eastern side), the *prakara* walls connecting them with corner sub-shrines, and the prevailing tiered 'southern' architectural form of the main as well as the corner sub-shrines, being the elements of the latter style. It is rather disadvantageously located, from the point of view of drawing wide attention and by the fact that it rests almost squarely upon the double storeyed shrine on the south court of Kailasa would indicate that it was not very far removed in time from it and most probably succeeded it. That they were not part of the same scheme, is, however, evident, by the disparity in style between them. The *panchayatana* from alike in structural style as in the monoliths was not represented in the Deccan before this example at Ellora.

The most outstanding feature of the Kailasa monolith is its elevation, acquired by a solid foundational ground *tala*. This is not a casual or purely functional arrangement, but one implying known architectural formulae. We know that in providing for the foundation or base of a temple, we have two variant methods of achieving this. The first is the provision of the *upapitha*, as in southern usage, or the *jagati* terrace as in the northern. It is obvious that the northern usage is inapplicable in Kailasa. The other variant arrangement is the provision of a solid (*ghana*) ground *tala*, complete with base (*adhisthana*), wall (*pada*) and entablatures (*prastara*). It is in this that has happened here. This automatically necessitated a stairway access to the upper floor and in order to make it symmetric and 'L'-shaped flight of steps was provided on either side of the court at the front angle of the *Nandi-mandapa* with the inner unit. We find the utilisation of this solid ground floor arrangement, essentially in two dissimilar contexts elsewhere in the Deccan and the deep south. Firstly, in the Chalukyan period, the Durga temple at Aihole is a plausible example of this, although here the lower plinth tends to become almost an *upapitha*. We should, however, not fail to note the provision of a short '*pada*' part in the form of a '*kantha*' followed by a solid '*vedi*' capped by a functional '*vedi*' parapet around the upper shrine. This example, however, precedes the 'Kailasa' of Ellora by more than a century and is indeed incipient, to a degree, in its characteristics. The other examples occur in the Chandraprabha temple at Tirupparuttikunram (Jina Kanchi) just outside Kanchipuram in the north Tamil Nadu, Saumyanarayana temple at Tirukkositiyur in Ramanathapuram District, Umamahesvara shrine, near Nataraja Sabha in the temple-complex at Uttarakosamangai, Ramanathapuram District, all in Tamil Nadu. On present evidence, the range of the age of these shrines could be from 800-900 A.D., and it may be stated that they succeed the Kailasa monolith. To this extent, the experimentation accomplished at Ellora is one of the earliest examples of this kind mentioned in the Silpa texts.

Another architectural innovation is the designing of the *Sabha mandapa* in the Kailasa and Chhota Kailasa. They have two side balconies in the former, and a front *agra mandapa* porch in the latter. In the Chalukyan temples, upto the mid-eighth century A.D., we have examples of a separate *agra mandapa* porch attached to the main door vestibule (of the shrine) which latter will have the main frame of ingress. The other two or three points of the compass are generally closed either in solid masonry or sometimes provided with *ghanadvaras* or large false grill-window frames with a *praggriva* like porch outside borne on two pillars or pilasters or both. The provision of a front porch as well as side porches of an open type in continuation of the main vestibule occurs in Chalukyan features for the first time only in the Virupaksha temple at Pattadakkal and is almost a solitary example in the Chalukyan group. These are, on the other hand, a common feature noted in the 'nothern' style temples of Upper India where they form integral parts of the *Ranga mandapa* or *Navaranga*, as *chatushkis* and are in the form of parapets with seat-backs (*kakshasana stones*) supporting dwarf pillars which in turn support the ceiling. Here, they have been employed by the Rashtrakutas in a truly southern (or *Dravida*) *vimana* type which usually has a level and plain roof in its vestibule. It is reasonable to presume that Krishna would have drawn his inspiration for such features, to a greater degree from the Chalukyan example at Pattadakkal (owing to its great nearness in time with the beginning of Kailasa monolith), and to a lesser degree from the Central and Northern Indian examples (which he would have been familiar with, owing to nearness in location and due to his peripatetic military campaigns). It is usually held that Pattadakkal Virupaksha temple formed the model for Krishna. But it is well to remember that the kinship between these two, on scrutiny, is not all so close to one tends to believe. For instance, Virupaksha temple has a square *sikhara* whereas Kailasa has a truly octagonal *sikhara*. Virupaksha is *sandhara* and Kailasa is *nirandhara*. Kailasa is an *astaparivara* unit, while Virupaksha almost a sixteen *parivara* unit. Kailasa *nandi-mandapa* is a closed hall, while Virupaksha *nandi* shrine is a simple, open pillared *mandapa*. Virupaksha has two *gopuradvaras* (on the front and on the rear), while Kailasa has only one on the front. Kailasa, however, has a closed cloister walk and an open *pradakshina patha* while Virupaksha has only one and at level with the sub-shrines. Virupaksha *linga pitha* is square, while at Kailasa it is circular. All the same, it has a similarity in its longitudinal lay-out with Kailasa, and, besides, has a *sukanasa* attached integrally to the first *tala* and rising upto the second, which in its *sala* superstructure, has a convincing similarity to the Kailasa *sukanasa*. The art motifs, the sculptural panels, the animal designs and the parapet or (*hara*) over the *maha mandapa* of both are strikingly similar, through somewhat more developed at Ellora. It is interesting that Krishna should have scanned Pattadakkal for his model, located deep in lower Karnataka (and even perhaps Kailasanatha temple at Kanchi in Tamil Nadu), while the location of his own imitation was so far, north, in the upper Deccan. Two explanations might be offered for this. Firstly, Krishna and most probably, Dantidurga, had their capital at Elapura (Ellora) itself, and this explains their most magnificent efforts being confined to this place. Secondly, the sway of the newly founded Rashtrakuta empire would have extended over the regions of the erstwhile Chalukyas of Badami, particularly at Aihole and Pattadakkal (and at one time during the reign of Dantidurga, touched Kanchi also where he struck a favourable deal with Nandivarman II by marrying his own daughter Reva to the Pallava monarch) and it is no wonder that Dantidurga and Krishna should have prestigeously taken hold of Pattadakkal and Aihole and Kanchi as a mark of their temporal supremacy over the Chalukyas and Pallavas, and in this process had an opportunity to take a good and meaningful look at the Chalukya and Pallava gems of structural architecture at these three places, particularly Pattadakkal and Kanchi. By this time, the former had become known that name, and not Raktapura or Kishuvolal—its original name—and the halo of this royal association with this place was not lost on the Rashtrakutas.

Even so, the fact remains that the interior lay-out of the Kailasa is as different from Virupaksha as one can make it. For in the latter, it was not a *navaranga* type but one resolving itself into a well defined central nave with clerestory and side aisles—a truly Chalukyan character. Nor was any scope existing for an *ardha mandapa* owing to the *sandhara* shrine at Pattadakkal, as indeed found in the *nirandhara* shrine at Kailasa. This is, of course, the direct consequence of the *sandhara* character of the former and the *nirandhara* type of the latter. It is thus not an easily reconcilable idea to make Kailasa an unreservedly imitative copy of Virupaksha and one would have it rather it was the amalgam of the most notable trends at the time Krishna embarked on his ambitious assignment. What more, the central theme of Krishna's labours was indubitably in favour of a truly southern 'Dravida' architectural model, of the *astaparivara* type, without any element that would detract from its Dravida style and stamp. Thus, if one were to be asked which was the most characteristic and comprehensive essay in the 'Dravida' temple design in the Deccan in the third quarter of the eighth century A.D., the answer could have been unhesitatingly in favour of Krishna's Kailasa and none else, and therein lies its special merit.

It is equally unnecessary to consider Kailasanatha of Kanchi by Rajasimha Pallava as having been the arche-type for Virupaksha temple and that this itself in turn served the same purpose for Krishna's Kailasa. Undeniably, all the three are of the same genre—the southern architectural style—but perhaps the resemblance almost ends there. The integrally constructed seven subsidiary shrines of identical shape (all *sama-chaturasra ekatala prasada* primarily, notwithstanding the varying *kuta* or *sala* that roof them), built in the thickness of the wall around the central shrine of Kailasanatha each not only showing *identical* god-head within, namely, the Somaskanda panel, but also having only a restricted eastward or westward orientation and not at all having any front vestibule beyond its transept passage as one emerges from the cella, is so completely and drastically different from the phraseology implicit in the Virupaksha and the one manifest in the Kailasa. The *nata* or *bhoga mandapa* at Kanchipuram was a construction of Chalukya Vikramaditya as shown by its pillar inscription, and it was an open pillared *mandapa* detached from the main shrine unit. At the time of its completion and when Vikramaditya saw it, Kailasanatha would have comprised only the innermost square unit with its seven sub-shrines in wall thickness, and with its *chatustala* stature. It was also patently without any *sukanasa*—as befitted its regional ilk. Its pseudo-*sandhara* ground tala structure was itself a feature demanded by the magnitude of its superstructural dimensions and is merely a very narrow, non-ritual, cellular arrangement for the *kadalikakarana* process of astylar corbel-vaulting of its *alindra* roof. It becomes truly ritual and well defined only in the Vaikunthaperumal temple at the same place, of Nandivarman II nearly half a century later. It would thus be futile to compare its layout with either Virupaksha or with Kailasa in which latter place the sub-shrines had become separate and individualistic entities of square or rectangular forms, as called for by the canonical rules, for the deities which are to be enshrined in them. Nor would it be facile to consider "the differences that are noticed between Virupaksha and Kailasa as, in a large measure, due to the necessities of the rock hewn technique" in the latter. It would perhaps be, more meaningful to take the Kailasanatha superstructure—particularly the last *tala* with its *sikhara* (forming the *alpa vimana* or primary unit) as having strongly influenced and impressed Krishna's *sthapatis*, as the most emphatic core of the prevailing 'Dravida' temple model, which they unhesitatingly accepted for Kailasa. This cannot be said of Virupaksha whose *sukanasa*, however, found immediate response in the *sukanasa* of Kailasa, owing to its being a truly regional stylistic component that Krishna's craftsmen took Kanchi Kailasanatha model for the *prakara* wall design, together with the incipient *ekatala sala sikhara gopura dvara* as well, is perhaps a sustainable proposition. In the sequel, we would be nearer the truth, if we consider that in having fully studied and analysed the constituent architectural components of the Virupaksha temple at Pattadakkal and Kailasanatha temple at Kanchipuram, for organising his own architectural *piece de resistance*, Krishna had flattered both these creations but arrived at entirely his own conclusions for his Kailasa master-plan, and had hand-picked the elements of these reigning masterpieces but most adroitly blended them with the unquestionably contemporary trends in temple style of his day and reign, and by the wisdom of this decision to make his creation the real product of the ritual, deliberately carved out Kailasa—the most faithful monument to southern school of architecture of late eighth century A.D., in the Deccan.

A look at Kailasa from different angles, from lower as well as upper levels, would probably bring out one common reaction to its profile namely that its elevation, above the cornice of its main shrine is not commensurate with its total height of its solid plinth and main floor wall. This is indeed a spontaneous response to its basic 'pit-layout' as was but inevitable. In fact, it was by a consummate skill in the maximum utilisation of the rock-mass, differentially eliminated, that the maximisation of dimension of this monolith has beenaccomplished. It is this techniques that has given the rising crescendo—elevation to the constituent front *mandapas* along the axis of the main *vimana* proper, by which process the *dvara gopura* being the westernmost and outermost unit is at a lowest range of height from the prevailing ground level around, the *nandi-mandapa*, attaining the next elevational stage; the *mukhu mandapa* the next higher, and the *Ranga mandapa* the further stage, reaching the superstructure of *sukanasa* over the cella and *ardha mandapa*. This was the best that could be made of the hemmed in and entranched character of the space selected for the Kailasa monolith. (*Plate I*) This does not, however, explain why despite the solid and massive basement plinth provided for it, the profile of the temple is still of a subdued character. We may deal with this issue at some length owing to its intrinsic interest. Firstly, it is to be noted that, had not the solid basement been given to the temple, the stature of the shrine would have been still more stunted, and it would have involved a purposeless cutting away of solid rock. The technique that was actually employed, raised the level of the temple by a fixed height and operating at that level, successively reduced the wall heights along the axis, to follow as closely as possible the contour of the hill slope, consistently with the full elimination of the weathered outer rock-rot. From the point of view of labour, this was a clever and heartening device. But it was not certainly a matter of reduction in the quantum of rock-dissipation alone. The design that Krishna's master-masons had on their blue-prints involved a main shrine with its *ardha mandapa*, and outer *pradakshina patha* and sub-shrines on the fringe of the *pradakshinapatha*, a *maha mandapa* with flanking porch projections on three directions, reaching beyond the limit of the main shrine complex, with a gap all around almost equal to the *nandi mandapa* of the first floor, and followed by the *dvara gopura* which would have the same thickness axially as the cloister walk elsewhere around the main shrine complex at ground floor level. Thus, the entire width of the shaft pit intended for the enterprise had to be divided into five parts with all the lateral parts of almost equal dimensions, and the central part about twice that of any other part. This naturally restricted the block of rock that would ultimately be available for the shrine proper to a minimum, and thus the improvisation of a solid basement plinth was quite expedient, and had highlighted the monolith. The question arises, however, as to why the architects could not have raised the dimensions of the superstructure of the *vimana* itself, in relation to its working level and the solid basement plinth. It is here that the motivating factor that was at the root of the entire performance unfolds itself.

The creation of a monolithic marvel at Ellora, commenced by Krishna (if not by Dantidurga himself) was not for any self-satisfaction or vain glory, but to crystallise in stone, the accepted principles and ritual confines of the religious architecture of the times of which the king was an enthusiastic patron. The superstructural rhythm (or *tala-chhanda*) was not one to be ordained by a royal *fiat*, but to receive the mandate of the canonical pandits and the clergy well-versed in this. The period to which Kailasa would pertain was still labouring under the limitations of the *jati vimana* norm, with a four-*tala* maximum, the *mukhya vimanas* that could stretch their stature to 12 *talas* maximum, had yet to be. Otherwise, it would indeed be anomalous that such a stupendous feat in the monolithic medium should have satisfied itself with a modest *chatustala vimana*. The Kailasanatha (Kanchi) analogy was before Krishna, and the *silpa* texts could not permit the erection of a more numerically ambitious storeyed superstructure than *chatustala*—which was a rigid limit followed most loyally by all the patrons, as in the Vaikunthaperumal temple, Kanchi, Shore temple, Mahabalipuram, Virupaksha temple and all other temples at Pattadakkal. Temples with lesser storeyed superstructure had been extant, but not greater. In these circumstances, the only way in which the Kailasa *vimana* could have been given a face-lift was by disciplining the *talacchanda-mana* itself, to eke out the maximum stature. The *Kasyapa silpa*, contains perhaps the best arrangement by which, even subject to the *chatustala* limitation clamped on the temples, it was possible to get a slenderness of storeyed eminence. This was perhaps not yet in vogue and would have been essentially a late tenth century or slightly later compilation, since at that period we actually find its application by Rashtrakutas themselves, to great advantage raising even *dvitala vimanas* to considerable height. This formula indeed became a diagnostic trait of the Rashtrakutas and western Gangas by this time, all over the South. *Mayamata* and *Isanasivagurudevapaddhati* envisage a progressively diminishing storeyed level for the superstructure, which is indeed what has been applied both at Kanchi and at Ellora. Thus the canonical discipline under which Krishna's craftsmen were functioning could not have produced a more balanced main *vimana* than what we see at Kailasa, and thus the raising of the height by a solid *tala*, as a plinth, was itself truly an innovation of its times. Indeed, it could be seen that the device that could raise the height of the *vimana* without raising the number of *talas* has already been displayed in an inchoate stage on Kailasa, by the multiple mouldings of the *prastara* (entablature) of the *talas* horizontally emphasised, but primarily tending to it the second *tala* level adventitiously, in the rock-cut model.

One of the most interesting elements of this *vimana*, however, is the octagonal *sikhara*. It is clear that the regional model, as pursued by the Chalukyas, had already shown a bias for a *chaturasra vimana* and the *astasra* type had been its own earlier precursor. The Chalukyan *vimanas* after the mid-seventh century, rarely, if ever, sport the octagonal *sikharas*, whereas the Pallava *vimanas* from the time of Mamalla upto the time of Rajasimha were largely restricted to the octagonal form, the square making its appearance fleetingly in the latter king's regime, and getting superseded in favour of the circular *vimana* from the third quarter of the eighth century A.D., in the reign of Nandivarman II. The Rashtrakutas, thus, had largely been leaning upon the southern usage in the shape of the *sikhara*, but nearest to the square Chalukyan *sikhara*, after the last quarter of the eighth century A.D. The only other southern dynasty that follows this Chalukya-Rashtrakuta preference for the octagonal and the square type of *sikhara*, to the exclusion of the circular, is the Pandyan, as at Kalugumalai and many other places in the south Pandyan country, which would thus establish its art-nexus, directly with the Deccani traditions, without being inhibited by the contemporary Pallava-Chola usage in their own region.

An eye-catching device adopted at Kailasa was the monolithic erection of two pillar-standards in the centre of the south-eastern and north-eastern open court around the main *vimana*, accompanied also by two massive elephants facing inwards from the south and the north respectively. The elephant, was perhaps, the most favoured animal cognizance for the Rashtrakutas since they excelled in their elephants brigade for many generations. But these two banner pillars that serve, as it were, the measuring rods of the temporal fame of the great Rashtrakuta monarch, should certainly have had some specific significance. By their very alignment and number, they are not to be taken as *dhvajastambhas*. They are too widely set and obstructed by other structural forms in between, to have served as *Toranastambhas*. Their massive character and height show them to be a purely artistic motif, as colossal as the main monolith they serve to embellish. What then would have been their inner meaning? A partial clue is afforded by the display of the same device, apparently by one of Krishna's successors in the late ninth century A.D., in the Indra Sabha (Cave XXXI) wherein by the side of the Chaumukh and within a *sala-gopuradvara*, and in the open court is to be found a banner shaft, which unfortunately fell down late last century and the blocks have been assembled by masonry fittings. If this persistence of the pillar shaft device should have any meaning on the basis of its own internal evidence, it is by the fact that the design of the pillars themselves vary, as between the Kailasa examples, and the Chaumukh specimens. No doubt, the lapse of more than a century would have resulted in an evolution of the art-design as well. But this very fact appears to provide a clue to the character of these shafts. It would mean that these shafts served mainly to represent the pillar 'order',—essentially southern and Deccani—that prevailed during the respective period represented by the monuments where they occur. If this be so, they are the most meticulous representations or models of the main 'pillar' order utilised in Kailasa, showing all the mouldings of the pillar from the '*oma*' or '*pitha*' to the *padma* and *phalaka*. On the top of the *phalaka*, however, a '*trishula*' or a '*suladeva*' appears to have been surmounted as a measure of consecration of the temple. The design had varied at Chaumukh and had indeed become somewhat more gorgeous, while the pillar design of Kailasa shafts is informed by a prevailing plainness of surface decoration and emphasis of the modulations of the constituent parts and their proportionate and relative dimensions. Thus, they served to typify the contemporary pillar order primarily, and function as '*mana-dandas*' of the rock-cut monuments in whose propinquity they occur.

It is observable that the Chalukyan structural style well preceded the Rashtrakuta monolithic enterprise at Ellora. It is a moot point whether Chalukyans were unequal to this task in which the Rashtrakutas later showed their special talent. But the very fact of the earlier inception of the Chalukyan structural style would attest to the fact that in so far as the technical and cultural impetus was concerned, the Chalukyans had an edge over the Rashtrakutas. Thus the absence of a corresponding monolithic creation by the Chalukyas need not occasion any surprise and might be explained away by the fact that they did not have any suitable spot in the sandstone crage for a monolith. That they had left vestiges of such, in combination with structural pavilions at Badami itself, as on the lower benches of the Upper Sivalaya cliff overlooking the village would suggest that monolithic technique was neither unknown to them nor beyond their capacity. But having already gained an early start in the structural media they did not feel inclined to revert to the non-functional monolithic medium, but continued to stabilise and elaborate the free-standing structural temple. Perhaps also they did not have any monolithic model then to take specific inspiration from. The '*rathas*' of Mamallapuram were to appear only in the middle of the seventh century A.D. well after the inception of the Chalukyan style although they had their cave style continuing upto the end of the seventh century A.D. With the Rashtrakutas it was all different. The political set-up calling for a challenging and novem programme, with the cultural precedent found already at Mahabalipuram of the Pallavas, the technical inheritance that had been well displayed in the cave temples of both Chalukyas and Rashtrakutas at Ellora and which had almost exhausted itself in that direction – all these made the context most ripe for the new turn in the Rashtrakuta rock-art—the monolithic models.

3

State of Canonical Art

IT is to be appreciated that the period which culminated in the Kailasa monolith was a period of great artistic and religious ferment. The devolution of the classical Chalukya art idiom into a robustly sectarian mould was one of the most notable transformations of this stage. The Brahmanical temple worship was steamlined by a vigorous and purposeful clergy and the *agamic* and canonical formulae for the integration of glyptic art with mythical and Puranic functional bias was achieved. Specifically the stage was more or less set for the parting of the ways between Saiva and Vaisnava creeds, and within half a century temples almost exclusively start representing Saiva or Vaisnava iconography whose only loose link was the adaption of Visnu or Brahma ubiquitously. This polarisation, however, was achieved in stages. The Rashtrakutas continued the late Chalukya mode of isolating Saiva and Vaisnava iconography in the wall panels, and in the emphasis of the Saiva themes in even comparatively less conspicuous places like the miniature *nasikas* on the cornices etc. The Kailasa monolith, thus was to be the first important stage in the depiction of cult-leanings on the temple fabric in a truly representative character, owing to the monolithic form of the shrine. It is not clear what, particularly impelled Krishna to call it 'Kailasa'. Perhaps, the lofty stature of the monolith basing the classical poetic imagery tempted him to affix the name of the snow bound Empyrean on the Himalayas. Or, the depiction of the famous theme of Ravana shaking Kailasa, shown almost in the form of a tableaux than of a panel, on the southern wall of the basement storey, made the affixation of this name appropriate in popular mind. Anyway, from a purely cannonical angle, it would seem that this name has no *prima facie* connotation, since Kailasa should represent circular shape of *sikhara*, among the five basic shapes of ancient *silpa* texts, (the square (*Vairaja*), circular (*Kailasa*) elliptical (*manika*), the rectangular (*pushpaka*) and the octagonal (*trivishtapa*). The shape of its *sikhara* was octagonal and not circular. However, probing deeper we see that the shrine was one of the very first at Ellora wherein the *sanctum sanctorum* carried a circular *linga-pitha*, and if this was the basis, upon which the term Kailasa had been applied for it, we see that it was most apposite, since once the circular *linga pitha* came into being, there was practically no looking back and using other variant forms, namely, the square and the octagonal and throughout South India, and also perhaps in many parts of the north, the circular *linga pitha* became ubiquitous. This was perhaps the canonical significance of the term '*Kailasa*'. No Chalukyan cave or structural temple was a circular *linga pitha* which is almost always square therein.

In the case of Kailasa shrine, it is also seen that the *linga* is detachable from the *pitha* although the material of the *linga* is the same as that of the *pitha*. We have to note that almost all the Rashtrakuta cave temples at Ellora also follow this principle while in the Chalukya it was sometimes of the monolithic type as well. It has sometimes been contended that the Kailasa shrine should be taken as having had a *svayambhu-linga*. Since the *pitha* itself is rock-cut and not natural and on top of it, the *linga* is a portable piece, the *svayambhu* category would not scientifically be applicable to this *linga*.

Also for the first time, the projection of the *nala* of the *linga pitha* into a regular *pranala*, upto and beyond the cella wall making it, peep out on the exterior plinth of the cella, is noticeable. This is in line with the device adapted in structural temples wherein the water of *abhisheka* in the cella is collected and drained off by the provision of (*a*) a *varimarga* or channel slab placed on the floor in such a way as to reach upto the middle of the thickness of the side wall of the cella and (*b*) a *pranala* or projecting spout-channel sligned to the *varimarga* and carrying the channel passage forward and discharging the water off its tip. This feature has been carefully dealt with and its specifications fixed in almost all southern canonical texts. Thus, this *varimarga* and *pranala* should be on the northern side of *linga*. They should be inserted as a separate piece fitted to the moulded stones of the *adhisthana*, and not arbitrarily interposed by cutting the mouldings of the *adhisthana* after their lay-out. Many other interesting injunctions detailing the relationship between the types of *adhisthanas* that can be so cut for the placement of the *pranala* are also to be found in the *silpa* texts. In the case of Kailasa it is significant that, unlike the cave temple types (earlier and indeed even the later ones) wherein the exterior plinth or *pradakshina patha* is not available owing to the excavated character of the shrines), the *linga pitha* carries its protruding *pranala* forward piercing the wall and peeping out, thus forming a landmark in the adumbration of such a ritual usage in structural temples. It is, however, seen that in the almost contemporary structural temples of the Chalukyas, this method had not been adopted and only a drain channel had been fixed under the wall, and led away due north beyond the outer plinth base of the temple premises proper. The corresponding southern usage under the Pallavas and the Chola-Pandyas was also different wherein the regular *varimarga* channel and the *pranala* (spout external) were both available and the difference largely exists in the particular moulded level of the *adhisthana* that the insertion is found fitted. Thus, the projection of the *linga pitha's nala* itself to serve as the *varimarga-cum-pranala* is rather an incipient stage and fully bears out the transitional character of Kailasa temple in the ritual organisation of Brahmanical religion in the Deccan and its general leaning towards the southern usage as found in the texts.

The iconography of the temple fabric again represents a definitive stage in the formation of the sub-shrines. Elsewhere in Ellora, owing to the cave-temple matrix of the examples, niche panel sculptures stood for regular subsidiary shrines and signified the iconic fixation of each divinity in the context of the main shrine affiliation. But in the Kailasa monolith, the lay-out itself had been planned as an *astaparivara* complex and, thus, the need for the panel sculptures which would occupy the appropriate positions on the walls did not arise. Thus, there was a supercession of the usual arrangement of having Ganesa in the *ardha mandapa*, on the side (north) wall and Karttikeya (south wall), Saraswati (on the north side) and Gajalakshmi (on the south side) on the cella exterior (facing front) on either side of the door of *ardha mandapa*, and further showing on the north-east corner of the *ardha mandapa* Parvati in penance and corresponding south-east corner Durga. In its place, the provision of Siva-Parvati (or Uma-sahita Siva) in Kailasa shrine has been carved on the side walls of the *ardha mandapa*. The seven *parivara* sub-shrines around the temple were presumably to have contained Surya, Karttikeya, Saptamatri, Ganesa, Durga, Jyestha and Chandesa variously. Of these, the Saptamatrika shrine would have been the rectangular one, and the south-west and north-west corner shrines would have been those of Ganesa and Karttikeya and the north-east shrine would be that of Chandesa the corresponding south-east being that of Surya.

This is why in Kailasa, we find the *maha mandapa* so completely free from figure sculpture, whereas in a corresponding Rashtrakuta cave temple type, almost contemporary with (but slightly earlier than) Kailasa, such as Lankẹsvara cave to the north of Kailasa, in the upper flank, is so full of panel carvings of divinities. At Kailasa, further, there was an outer *prakara* cloister also, with the result that the disposition of the divinities was mainly confined to the outermost cloister walk of the main complex at ground floor level, exterior wall of the inner shrine, and the sub-shrine groups.

One of the most interesting icons of the closed ground floor cloister is the Lingodbhava. This is to be found in almost the centre of the eastern corridor, facing the monolith and its cella. This depicts Siva, as emerging from the massive pillar-like staff, with Visnu and Brahma standing on either side and offering salutation. This is rather a peculiar variant of the usual type depicting a lenticular vertical cavity in the shaft wherein Siva is shown. This, nonetheless by its location and orientation, suggests that at the time of the erection of Kailasa, the usage of having Lingodbhava on the back wall of the shrine was fully in vogue and that was why, it had been aligned and oriented in that fashion. Thus, it gives a broad iconochronic stage applicable for a wide area in South India, including the regions of the Pallava and Chola kings, and becomes useful. It is seen that at a slightly later period, in place of this Lingodbhava, Visnu comes to occupy the rear wall niche and Brahma becomes a fixation on the northern wall, the corresponding southern wall being occupied by Dakshinamurti. The *ardha mandapa* outer walls are to carry from this period onwards Ganesa, to the south and Durga to the north. Thus, in relation to the position of Lingodbhava in Dasavatara cave, it could be said that Kailasa crystallised a more specific and typical stage of ritual iconic fixation in a Saiva shrine. It is also to be noted here that Lingodbhava is not found in Lankesvara cave, thus attesting to its relatively earlier age to both Dasavatara and Kailasa.

Another interesting iconographic theme employed in more than one place in Kailasa itself is the depiction of Siva bearing on his left shoulder a replica of *linga* itself, and holding it by two of his hands. This *lingadhara-Siva* is unique in Saivite cult forms, but not occurring for the first time in Kailasa. Its earliest occurrence is in the early Chalukyan temples at Aihole, as seen in the Prince of Wales Museum, Siva-Parvati panel from Aihole.

In Aihole itself, it is seen repeated at a number of places. It occurs at Pattadakkal in the Virupaksha temple and at a few other places. It occurs at Ellora, in the Kailasa, as is being discussed. Its provenance extends over a wider area than is suggested by the Chalukya-Rashtrakuta kingdoms, and its chronological range also would suggest that it continued to be in vogue upto the tenth century A.D. The various other places, where it has now been observed by the author as occurring, include the Eastern Chalukyan tract (Nagarjunakonda valley—Hyderabad Museum figure from State excavations, across Krishna, in the Yellesvaram valley), where it is further enriched by a full Siva *parivara* group comprising Parvati, Karttikeya and Ganesa. The eastern Chalukyan stamp of this and other similar sculptures of Harihara, Ardhanari etc., inside miniature shrine models excavated here, is reinforced by the inscription of Vijayaditya of the Eastern Chalukyan line on one of them. Further south, in Tondaimandalam or the traditional Pallava tract of Tamil Nadu, the most persuasive example of this *Lingadhara-Siva* is from the very Pallava capital, Kanchi in the Muktesvara temple, apparently of the time of Nandivarman Pallava Malla II, by its appellation in its records as Dharmamahadevisvaram, datable to the close of the second half of the eighth century A.D. Proceeding still southwards, we have two examples of this known till now, one in the temple at Kilayur (Agastisvara temple) or Irukkuvel style and ascribable to the end of the ninth century A.D., and the other at another but earlier celebrated Irukkuvel centre of architecture at Kodumbalur datable to c. 657 A.D., where, in the so-called Muvarkoil, the middle temple has a most gracious carving of this type of Siva (as the *Vimanadevata*) in the southern niche of the upper *tala*. Thus, the importance and the quick and ready dissemination of this cult-image is well substantiated, ranging from the early seventh to the late ninth century A.D. There are only two aspects of this image that would detail us now. The source of dispersal and the inherent significance of this form. We know that at early culture stratigrahpic level, there is the Mathura terracotta of Siva carrying *linga* on its head belonging to the early centuries of our era. Thus, we may even consider as essentially a *mukha linga* and nothing much more. But further down we have literary references to the Bharasivas and their special cult leanings in the Vakataka inscriptions, the most spectacular feature of which is that Bharasivanagas won distinction by the indefatigable consistency with which they carried the idol of *linga* on their shoulders, to the extent of pleasing Siva by this act and getting his blessings. Thus, the act of carrying *linga* on one's shoulders had been a special act of veneration and a standard diagnostic characterisation of certain Saiva groups in this period. This should have been given further boost during the expansion of the Pasupata-cult, before its Kalamukha and Kaula varieties of the early mediaeval times. These perhaps took the stamp of such a ritual carriage of *linga* as their credo and even so much identified this with Saivism that Siva himself has been depicted in that act. The inner meaning of this icon, however, might perhaps have been that the *linga* as a symbol of Saiva iconism of the *arupa-rupa* variety, primarily connoted the pillar or shaft of fire or sacrificial pole that it originally derived itself from, and had nothing to do with the latter day inculcation of male-organ analogy to it functionally and structurally, although it might perhaps be conceded that the metabolism of Saivite cult ramifications logically led to such a postulate eventually. Thus, this *linga*-bearing cult is sharply different from the other and equally misunderstood *pasupata* sectarian group, namely; that of Lakulisa with his *membrum virile*. The *urdhvaretas* character of Lakulisa, it should be noted, certainly had no direct bearing upon the *linga*-theory and was a symbiosis, in itself, of the Siva-Karttikeya nexus, wherein Siva's *urdhvaretas* was taken to have been collected and garnered and nourished by Agni into the Kumara embryo. We realise that the *linga-dhara*-Siva should give an effective quietus to the *linga-yoni* theory, particularly due to the widely diffused character of this iconigraphic form, as shown above, and the Kailasa example would tend to spotlight the great centre that Ellora should have been of the esotheric Saiva sects in the eighth century A.D.

The interesting additions to the main Kailasa complex are the shrine for the river goddesses located in the north-west corner of the outer court and a corresponding shrine at the south-west corner. It is well-known that river goddesses formed an integral part of the temple iconography even in the earlier Chalukyan periods and under the Guptas in the north, as reflected by their ubiquitous usage on the door frames, jambs, and dvarapala units. But, this is certainly remote and unconnected with a separate shrine for the river-goddesses. Further, while traditionally only Ganga and Yamuna alone are displayed, this Kailasa sub-shrine for river-goddesses would seem to contain three persons, perhaps including river Saraswati as well. If we might hazard a guess, this idea could have gained ground in the Rashtrakuta royal patrons only by a direct association of Triveni or Prayaga with their invasions. We note that Dhruva, the younger son and successor to Krisna I actually had a successful expedition into the Doab where Pala king Dharmapala was poised for an attack. In the ensuing battle, Dharmapala was routed and had to flee from the battle-field leaving behind his white royal umbrella—an insignia of authority. Dhruva spent some weeks on the banks of Ganga and Yamuna and as a memento, these rivers were incorporated in the Rashtrakuta imperial banner. His son Govinda III did one better by his tempestuous expedition and victories in the entire northern plains upto Himalayas and it is but proper therefore to think that the idea to erect a separate shrine for the three river goddesses was essentially the outcome of Rashtrakuta invasions into the Gangetic valley during the reigns of the above two kings, and accordingly, the excavation of this sub-shrine itself should perhaps be placed between 773-802 A.D. This river goddess temple was designed to be erected, perhaps, as a monolith, two-storeyed of the *Gajaprishtha* or apsidal type of *vimana*, as could be seen from the engraved outlines of this profile on the face of the cliff above the balconeyed upper storey scheme of this shrine. A similar apsidal barrel vault type has actually been partially scooped out at the diametrically opposite southern corner of the Kailasa court. It is unfortunate that both of these were left unfinished in their full exterior stature.

4

Early Monoliths Vimana Architecture— Formal Analysis

FROM a broader art historical context it may be appropriate to categorise the Rashtrakuta art as essentially pre-mediaeval while the corresponding early Pallava art was both post-classical and pre-mediaeval. It is, however, relevant that vigorous nature of Rashtrakuta art, their realistic sculptural modulation of the face and the body while somewhat accentuated still do not under any circumstances become either stylised or repetitive. Their range of iconographic depiction was certainly varied with equal facility of depiction on the Saiva, Vaisnava and Sasta side and as could be seen from their sculptures other than in trap rock, like sand stone, granite etc., it would appear that this flair was kept unimpaired by the Rashtrakutas.

The Rashtrakuta efforts in monolithic architecture had been preceded by the Pallava creations at Mamallapuram. These creations range roughly between the first quarter of the seventh century A.D. to the second quarter of the eighth century A.D. and thus it would be worthwhile to compare the formal characteristics of either delineation in respect of specific features of *vimana* architecture they have sought to reveal. These could be conveniently distinguished in the following categories :

(*a*) *tala*;

(*b*) whether it is *sandhara* or *nirandhara*;

(*c*) correspondingly whether it is of the *arpita* or *anarpita* type;

(*d*) the wall details;

(*e*) architectural speciality in each case;

(*f*) axial spread;
(*g*) whether *sukanasa* is available or not;
(*h*) whether separate mandapas like the Nandi mandapa etc., exists;
(*i*) interior details, if any;
(*j*) nature of the sanctum;
(*k*) plinth type and details;
(*l*) the pillar order;
(*m*) the nature of the door frame;
(*n*) whether a gateway exists;

After this we should take note of:

(*i*) Iconographic details;
(*ii*) Cult;
(*iii*) the nature of the Linga or the worshipped image;
(*iv*) paintings, base-reliefs etc., which also have been created as embellishments; and
(*v*) the nature of the inscribed records.

Taking these one by one, we see that the *talachhanda* in the Pallava monolith gives us a range from that of an *alpa vimana* to a maximum storeyed division into four floors. These have two important stages where in the earlier one, each one of these *talas* or storeys carry the *hara* parapets with miniature chapel models, and in the later stage it became customary to depict the *vahana* or the cognizance animal or bird as the case may be, on the topmost *tala*. The *vimana* model itself is essentially of the *Dravida* type, viz., with octagonal *sikhara* in the earlier stages, although this phase shows the full variety of the various *vimana* types which includes the octagonal, the square, the rectangular and the apsidal forms, besides a native hut-shaped or *kutagara* model. The most outstanding arche-type, however, is that of the *Dravida vimana* in full complement of its constituent parts from the *adhisthana to sikhara.* In the second stage which is distinguished by the reign of Rajasimha (Narasimha Varman II), changes take place as indicated above in respect of the topmost *tala hara* and also in respect of the composition of the wall details. When we compare that with that of the Rashtrakutas, we see that in its earliest stage, viz., during the time of Danti Durga, the first Imperial Rashtrakuta monarch ruling from Ellora as his capital, a *mandapa* type comparable in general form with that of the *Kutagara* of the Draupati Ratha of Mamallapuram, but contrastive in some essential details, is seen. This detail is in respect of the roof in the Rashtrakuta example which has a slopy character and is raised with a clerestory, on the top of which some crest details are also found. When we move on to the next Rashtrakuta stage that of Krishna-I,—the creator of the Kailasa monolith—we see that he had opted for the *Dravida Jati Vimana* and had made it also into an *astaparivara* type in the light of which, however, is to be seen in Tamil Nadu only in the early Chola period. Similarly, the other roof top monolithic creations on the southern side of Kailasa, over the triple storeyed cave temple existing here, is showing a full complement of temple form with sub-shrines in the corners, a *prakara*, a gateway tower on each side etc. Moving to the next phase which at Ellora is of the ninth century A.D., and after, and for Jainism, we see in Chhota Kailasa a logical continuance of the architectural format of Krisna's Kailasa, but seen without sub-shrines as they are not customary for Jainism at that time; and in the next phase of the same stage, in the Chaumukh structure on the front courtyard of Indra Sabha cave, we see further developments important for Jainism in cult usage, along with elements like *prakara* and *gopuradvara* which continue to prevail. Comparing this with a third creative monolithic efforts of the Pandyan dynasty at Kalugumalai in Tamil Nadu, datable to the very turn of the ninth century A.D., we find that there again the *Dravida Jati Vimana* had been preferred whereas Chhtoa Kailasa and Indra Sabha Chaumukh shrine at Ellora, both show the *nagara vimana* type. It is very obvious, thus, that the Rashtrakuta creation not merely involved architectural designing and variety but also the polarisation of several religious and cult usages, besides the very sculptural art in stone itself, all of which should have spread further south already by the end of the eighth century largely due to Danti Durga's own dealings with the later Pallava kings, starting from Nandivarman II, his successor Dantivarman and followed by Nandivarman-III, the three outstanding kings of the later Pallava line.

In the case of the Pallava monoliths further both *sandhara* and *nirandhara* forms had been adopted and correspondingly the towers show both *anarpita* and *arpita* designs respectively. This feature would seem to show that its purpose is essentially to provide for circum-ambulatory not only at the ground floor level but also in the upper floor, for which these upper floors should also have had, as indeed they have at Mahabalipuram and Kanchi, shrines located in them and access to these had apparently been provided through portable or conveniently fixed ladders or hidden flights of steps in a structural model which, however, owing to exigencies of the rock available might not have been depicted always in the monolithic model. We see, for instance, that in the most outstanding creation at Mamallapuram, viz., Dharmaraja Ratha, while lateral flight of steps is seen carved behind the first *tala hara* to lead around the second *tala*, the corresponding arrangement to reach there could not be depicted because of the necessary rock mass not being available. In the case of the Rashtrakutas, however, as they were carving out of a whole hill range of the basaltic rock, such a contingency had never arisen and regular hidden flights of steps, wherever necessary, had been provided. Still, the Rashtrakutas themselves had only opted for the *nirandhara* type to preclude any hidden ambulatory passage at the ground floor level or any corresponding shrine set-up in the upper level. Thus, one might say that while the Pallava model being not only of a vanguard stage, but also essentially involving variety of religious usages current then in north Tamil Nadu for Saivism. Vaishnavism the worship of the Sakti and the Matris it had a necessity to show the arche-typal forms in temple construction suitable for a clear understanding by craftsmen for whom they were virtual field-manuals. When we go to Kalugumalai (which is later to the earliest Rashtrakuta monolithic creation at Ellora) we see that again *nirandhara* forms, as that the Rashtrakutas seem to have been preferred.

Coming to the wall details, we find that the Pallavas in their monoliths at Mahabalipuram utilising the standard pattern of division of the walls into central and lateral part by wall pilasters, either slightly projecting the *mukha bhadra* or having a straight linear outline for the *vinyasa sutra*, by which projections of any one part beyond the linear strike are avoided. In the case of the Rashtrakutas, while this is also followed, by and large, one may still see that they might have been influenced by the prevailing *ratha* usages appropriate for the *Rekha* or the curvilinear temples of the lower Deccan and the northern India much earlier than at Tamil Nadu where it is seen only from the tenth century A.D. and tend to combine this ratha-offset form also in their usages. For this, they have certainly their analogues in the early Western Chalukyan temples at Badami, Aihole and Pattadakkal on Karnataka zone already. Thus, the Rashtrakutas show a combination of usage, while the Pallavas in their *vimana* architecture, particularly for the walls depiction, adhere to the typical straight line within which projections and recessions have the *bhadra karna* and *salilantara* are provided, thereby showing that they are more conservative, pristine and primarily establish the basic grammar of *vimana* model. The walls, however, have certain ornamental characteristics common in the form of *torana* outline for the central part of the wall where niches would show special divinities, whereas the figures of divinities in other parts of the wall are not so provided with *torana* ornamentation. It would, of course, be possible to compare even the nature of this *torana* details which essentially depict a horizontal *makara* formation, both in Mahendra's cave temples as at Dalavanur and in the subsequent monoliths of Mamalla with the tail of the *makara* either lifted up or at the same level of the body. In the case of the Rashtrakutas also, during Danti Durga's time, this is more or less the case but in the next stage the floriated tail of the *makara* in the *torana* tends to droop considerably, though with a natural angle. It could be stated here that the corresponding usage in the Chalukyan *genre* (both Western and Eastern wings of that dynasty) also have a droop of the tail; but this closely follows an almost dead vertical drop line. At Kalugumalai, however, the usage of the *makara torana* had been optionally dropped and we do find that in most of the structural temples in Tamil Nadu from the late eighth century A.D. onwards this omission prevails although the cave temples of the Pandyas between 600-700 show a horizontally spread *makara* tail at a number of places.

In so far as the distribution of features on the wall part is concerned, an important feature is also initiated in the Pallava model, for the first time during the period of Rajasimha. This consists of utilising the *salilantara* recessed space (or in some cases the *bhadra* itself) for introducing either a *kapota panjara* or a cornice over the niche respectively. In the case of the former this space corresponds to the representation of the *panjara* in the *hara* parapet in between the *madhyasala* and the *karnakuta*. This is a very important development which acquire usage and currency extensively in the early Western Chalukyan region also almost simultaneously and is used further with great effect during the Rashtrakuta time. It is this feature that ultimately both under Rashtrakuta and under the Cholas, from the time of Parantaka I develops into a special motif known as the *kumbha panjara* and becomes a land-mark for fruitful further developments right down to the Vijayanagar period with profuse floral ornamentation. In the Chola times, however, this feature is called the *kumbha lata* and has highly flattened modulation and becomes well rounded almost like a flower base with an out filling bunch of blossom and creepers at the top only by the Vijayanagar time. However, the *kapota panjara* type which is seen at Mamallapuram and at Kanchipuram in Rajasimhas temples is a clear precursor to the Rashtrakuta utilisation, particularly at Ellora, and is seen continuing into their collateral tracts in the form of feudatory chieftaincies or independent contemporaries, as the case may be as, for example, in the Sindhas of Erambarige (modern Yelburga) who produced some very interesting temples as at Kakkurur and that of the Gangas of Talakad of the tenth century as in their temple at Narasamangala. It is with the introduction of the *kapota panjara* with the reciprocal character of the *hara* with reference to *pada*—the wall part assumes fullness. Another complementary design work on the wall is the development of niches surmounted by an *udgama* (pediment). These *udgamas* during the early Western Chalukyan phase tend always to be triangular in outline, whereas under the Rashtrakutas they tend to get into an elongated basal part and converging top. The whole basal part in such cases is decorated fully with *jalaka* patterns. This feature does not occur generally south of the Deccan and certainly under any other dynasty. The preference for this usage which is not only seen at Ellora in the Danti Durga mandapa, but also in temples in Karnataka, as at

Pattadakkal (Kasi Visvesvara temple) only under the Rashtrakutas, would have been a borrowal from central India and the Madhya Desa where under the Pratiharas of Kanauj, this was a very popular and consistent feature of the *udgama* type, as seen characteristically in the Teli-ka-mandir at Gwalior constructed by Pratihara Mihira Bhoja. As such, we do see that the Rashtrakutas had a certain degree of ambivalence, drawing elements both from the *vimana* architecture of the South and from the *Rekha* architecture of the north. This has been possible for them, as we know, because of their having several victorious campaigns across the river Narmada into the Ganga plain upto the Himalayan foot-hill, and across the Vindhyas and Satpuras and in the Kosala kingdom, towards the eastern end of the present day Madhya Pradesh. It was customary, however, that where a *kapota panjara* is shown, it is depicted, devoid of any profuse surface ornamentation.

Coming to the externals of the temple, like a *prakara bandha*, we find that this has not been indicated in any way in the Pallava creations at Mamallapuram prior to Rajasimha and do occur profusely during his regime, both here and at Kanchipuram, and in these circumstances they generally sport an embryonic *sala sikhara* for the *dvara* or entrance, and indeed belong to the *dvarasala* variety of the text. A corresponding Rashtrakuta usage is almost identical, with that of Rajasimha Pallava's, although one can note an interval of roughly two decades between these Pallava and Rashtrakuta usage. The *prakara* itself had seemingly been so much attractive to the Rashtrakutas that they persist in showing it even in monolithic media consistently, as in the four monolithic examples at Ellora, after Danti Durga's *mandapa* (where, however, we do not see this being an ancillary *mandapa* type). An interesting innovation, however, that Rashtrakuta Krisna introduces in his *dvara sala* at the Kailasa monolith is that of an overhanging balcony at the upper level just under the sala roof towards the front, with a *kakshasana* parapet. This feature is again under borrowal from the Gurjara territory, where the Rashtrakutas had a political stake having started a branch dynasty of their own there. This feature is called the *mattavarana* in the northern texts and is signally important in the capacity of the

Rashtrakuta craftsmen to combine both northern and southern architectural features within a general framework of their preferred *vimana* usage. This is all the more accentuated since the Rashtrakutas never seem to have made up their mind to erect a *rekha* type in their realm and were wedded to the *vimana* model right through.

Similarly, in the case of the feature *sukanasa* raised over the *antarala* and fused with the tower of the *vimana*, the Rashtrakutas tended to follow the prevailing western Chalukyan usage, while the Pallavas and indeed the succeeding Pandyas and Cholas had none of it. Here, once again, the Rashtrakutas demonstrated their selective adaptation of features by clinging to the Chalukyan types of *sukanasa* rather than that of the northern *rekha* type and thereby sensitively distinguishing between the *sukanasa* types of the two 'orders' as seen in the Chalukyan temples themselves and also confirmed alike their commitment to the zone of their domicility, viz., the lower Deccan as their predilection for *vimana* forms alone. This *sukanasa* of the Rashtrakutas as we know, is almost a *sala* type, placed end—on with a dormer window of the Chaitya type on the front inside, the *kudu* recession of which it was customary for the Chalukyas to carve an image of Tandava Siva and where correspondingly the Rashtrakutas, who had a hand in the spread of Mahesvara Saivism, located a carved figure of Lakulisa instead or Jain sub-shrines with *nidhi* forms of Yaksha outside, on the front *mukhapatti* base in Jain examples, as seen at Ellora.

Even in the *sikhara* forms, the Rashtrakuta examples are never to those Rajasimha Pallava in the octagonal and square forms and somewhat different from the forms adopted in the Chalukyas themselves. This was seemingly a selective setlhetic slant of the Rashtrakuta craftsmen and silpis.

Now, doming down to the *adhisthana* part we again see that the Rashtrakutas, while certainly continuing to use the *kapota bandha* type popular in the Chalukyan territory, had certainly displayed their great linking for the *pratibandha* type wherein a *tripatra kumuda* and a *pattika* features prominently in place of *vritta kumuda* and *kapota*, as in the former type.

An interesting feature that the Rashtrakutas had seemingly adopted, after their observations in the Pallava territory, is the creation of several ancillary minor monoliths in the courtyard of their main temple creations. We know that the Five Rathas at Mamallapuram are already notable for the minor creations of the bull, elephant and the lion, which, however, had been created there to fall in tune with the mounts of Siva and Durga and the design of the adjacent *gaja pristha vimana*, namely the Nakula-Sahadeva Ratha. All the same, the creation of such monolithic features elsewhere seen as at Ellora in the fore-court of Kailasa (and also in the Indra Sabha front), only under the Rashtrakutas, in the form of two large elephants, one on either side, and two large victory pillar models, one either side again, would certainly draw a parallel from the Pallava creation for their inspiration. This would underscore, however, the skills of craftsmen who, often part of the royal retinue during their campaign, were keeping their eyes open to outstanding creations in those regions and tended to emulate them in their home zone to vindicate their own corresponding calibre in such ancillary creations of great variety and pertinence.

The Rashtrakuta pillar order is itself a combination of that of the Chalukyas and of the lower south, under the Pallavas and Cholas. This is notwithstanding the fact that in an area like Ellora where have been created scores of pillar forms in their own cave and monolithic example besides those of the Chalukyans who preceded them here, and analogous to these Chalukyan as well as the other prevailing central Indian models alike, they could adhere to some unified features of the *vimana* order of pillars. This is reflected particularly in the utilisation of the *kumbha*, *padma*, *phalaka* and *virakanta*, as their components above the shaft parts that was consistently adopted in the monolithic models by the Rashtrakutas. Besides they were also the first to introduce a basal block called 'Oma' for the pillars to rest on, a feature which becomes diagnostic when compared either with that of the Chalukyas or with those of Pallavas and the Cholas and is often adopted by the succeeding Kalyani Chalukyas.

Getting into the interior of the temple, the *navaranga* type of main *mandapa* that they adopted is itself essentially a combination of 'Northern' and Chalukyan usages, for we do know that the Chalukyan front hall generally has a central clerestoreyed nave and sloping side aisles, whereas the conventional *navaranga* has a flat ceiling right through in the different compartments which tend to be rectangular in the central or cardinal parts of the periphery and square in the corner parts and the middle ones of the hall division. In such a ceiling, the Rashtrakutas at Ellora kept the *vimanas* almost flat and featureless and displayed mural paintings besides dikpala slabs etc. In the corresponding usage in lower South such features are totally absent. The projecting porch entrance on the three sides of this hall are again part of the Chalukyan usage and form also a corresponding northern usage in the form of *mukha chatushki* which are generally unknown in the Tamil Nadu region. In fact, the oft-repeated analogy between the Kailasa temple at Kanchipuram, the Virupaksha temple at Pattadakkal and the Kailasa at Ellora is strictly not admissible, owing to several essential differences among these three, while the comparative relationship between the features of the latter two, despite their subtle differences may not be gainsaid.

The exterior of the sanctum of the Kailasa monolith at Ellora showing features like divinities in niches of the *antarala* and a door frame with traditional *sakas*, *uttaranga* and *dvarapalas*, is only in tune with the general usage in that region, as in all their structural temples even, the Rashtrakutas generally followed whatever were the regional practices. It should, however, be added here that what they had shown in the monoliths at Ellora is also comparable with some of the corresponding examples in rock-cut cave temple art, as under the Pandyas who appear to have several similarities with the developed early Chalukyan cave art and the succeeding Rashtrakuta phase thereof, as seen in the complex of excavations at Tirupparankundram and some other places. Structural temples of the early Pallavas on the other hand, do not portray any such corresponding usage and appear to stick to a typical Pallava *genre* right through.

The interior of the sanctum in a Rashtrakuta structure or monolith generally located a Linga under Saivism with a circular *pitha*, first to be introduced in this manner by the Rashtrakutas before which square *pitha* alone had prevailed. The placement of the Linga is in the form of the *chala linga* type, with the *pitha* alone carved out of live rock with a socket hole in which the *linga* is properly consecrated as a separate part. This usage was common with the Chalukyas in their cave art as at Elephanta, Ellora etc., but the Pallavas never used the *linga* upto Rajasimha and the corresponding usage in the Pandyan cave art was to carve both the *linga* and the *pitha,* out of live-rock – a feature which the Pandyas depart from, only in the south-easterly part by their dominion and the continuous Venad as seen at the cave temples at Vira Sikhamani etc., where the *pitha* is made of several block of stones compositely forming the *pitha* scheme.

Coming to the distinctive features of cults under Rashtrakutas, it could be stated that, unlike the Pallavas who were wedded to the Trinity (Brahma, Vishnu and Siva), principles and the Somaskanda worship and have not initiated a regular *linga* worship until the time of the Rajasimha (Narasimhavarman II-700-725 A.D.) and even then of *Dhara linga* type which was typically without a *pitha*, the Rashtrakutas showed their preference for Mahesvara Saivism revealing in forms like Lingodbhava Aghora, Sankara and Anugraha forms of dancing Siva introduced by them for the first time, in great numbers and well before its advent to lower south. Some of these were prevalent in the Chalukyan stage also when a dominant figure of Pasupatisvara was current which gets overtaken by Mahesvara Saivism from about 700 A.D.

5

Description of the Monuments

(A) THE DANTIDURGA MANDAPA, IN FRONT OF DASAVATARA CAVE (XV)

THIS *mandapa*, situated in the courtyard in front of the double storeyed cave excavations going by the name 'Dasavatara' (cave XV), is unusual. Firstly its very lack of unity with the main cave excavation is outstanding; secondly, having come up nearly 50 rock-cut steps from the surrounding ground level, the first excavation presented before us, viz., this monolith, shows a false door, at its very entrance porch. (Plate II) This porch—a full unit in itself—is approached from the first landing by a short flight of steps leading to a second landing and from there by another flight of its steps flanked by a *gajamunda* balustrade, hardly finished. On the top of this flight of steps is found a plain parapet, oblong and low without *kakshasana* seat back and with two free-standing pillars at its front corners and two pilasters correspondingly at the rear also, of plain square-sectioned shaft right through, surmounted by a capital piece—a thin square block—over which the broad, but this *uttira* beam is placed running all along the four sides, followed by a *vajana*, a *valabhi* similar to the *vajana*, a simple offsetting, and the *kapota* on top. This *kapota* is, along with other members just described found, merging with the corresponding members of the main monolithic *mandapa* behind at their appropriate levels. The *kapota* is without undercutting, without external projection, with its quadrantal slope, well within the limit of the *valabhi* and with its front and underside chamferred. On this, again, is a plain parapeting of about 9 "given to the roof surface. The parapets of the *mandapa* seemingly of the front porch are intersecting at their outer corners projecting beyond the corner for about a foot in 'L' shaped arms. On the side walls of the porch below this parapet, the plinth mouldings are carved out in tune with the rest of the *mandapa* and they comprise an *upana*, a high *jagati*, placed a little wider than the succeeding mouldings, a *kantha* comprising a broad *kampa*, a pilastered recess, the pilasters themselves showing *triratha* pattern involving the shaft and their intersecting corbel arms and a niche recess inside each, with the *uttira* and *valabhi* represented over the corbels reaching the top most mouldings of the plinth, namely; the *kapota* embellished with *nasikas* and *madhyapattais* and *konapattais* at successive points and corners. The moulding corresponding to the *kapota*, however, has not been completed on the porch walls. In fact it would seem that this porch wall was one of the very last to be completed and so, even in the conception of the architect this entrance porch would not have any functional significance, but only form a false *mukha mandapa* Surmounted by an elaborate makara-Torana the back wall of which carries a *jali* window in the centre, (Plate III) corresponding to the similar *jali* windows on the three cardinal directions on the northern and southern walls; only the eastern wall carries a regular door frame giving access into the *mandapa*. This would mean that the *mandapa* was to be approached primarily from inside from the side cave excavations which indeed would signify that it was juxtaposed to the cave excavation and complementary to it and therefore, contemporary or, if necessary, subsequent to it. The pillars of this porch carry a *pitha* or *oma* comprising a *padma*, *kumuda*, and has a smaller *padma* of very subdued proportions not more than 9" together, and the capital blocks are in fact plain intersecting corbels cut at the corners corresponding to the lay-out of the *uttira* beams. The pillar together with its corbel above is apparently in tune with the corner cantoning pilasters of the *mandapa* and of the pillars of the double storeyed *mandapa* itself in rudimentary characteristics. Thus, there is no reason to believe that this front porch should have been subsequently added. If so, it is intriguing why the front porch at all should have been carved out, if it had to be closed by the *jali* window, particularly since similar porches are not to be found on the other three sides. It would seem, however, on second thoughts that the porch had a limited, specific purpose to serve namely, to shelter the 14-line inscription engraved in closely packed letters on the upper stretch above the *jali* window, from one end to the other. This inscription, of the time of Dantidurga, as we know, is vital to our understanding of Rashtrakuta genealogy which it covers in reasonably adequate terms, notwithstanding the fact that the record is incomplete to a degree. Thus, it would seem that this inscription was of great importance, even at the time when it was engraved thus meriting a shelter which should architecturally harmonise with the main *mandapa*, but would not unduly take away from its primary functional role. The inscription, apparently signifying the capital that 'Ellora' or 'Yelapura' formed for the Rashtrakutas of Dantidurga's time, marks the end of an era and the beginning of another—the downfall of the redoubtable Chalukyas of the Badami line, and the upsurge of one of the earliest dynasties of South India, namely, the Rattas or Rashtrakutas in one unified imperial lineage. Thus, Dantidurga was conscious of the occasion and the porch probably forms a justifiably fitting canopy to this valuble document.

At the same time, the fact remains that this *mandapa* has not been excavated primarily to be a mere appendage to the main cave excavation, but as a significant landmark in the art history of the times, notwithstanding its immediate purpose, perhaps of serving as the *Nandi-mandapa* for the shrine in the upper storey behind. For, we know that the *nandi* that is placed in the hall in the upper storey has no *lucus standi* and could very well have been in this mandapa, although it is not feasible to guess why a monolithic *nandi* could not have been carved out at the time of the *mandapa* was cut. This would show that the *mandapa* originally was not a Saiva excavation. It is, perhaps, reasonable to assume, consistent with the finished floor surface of the interior central platform of the *mandapa* that the monolithic *nandi* vested with Saivite powers should not be left without proper consecration which only a separate sculptured *nandi* alone might bestow, and herein might be guessed the relationship of a separate *nandi* for *nandi-mandapa* to the main cave complex.

One of the important facts to be noted in regard to Dantidurga's *mandapa* is that, unlike the carvings of the main cave complex proper which doubtless show a superimposition of Brahmanical faith over what had been started presumably for the continuing Buddhist need after the adjoining Tin-tal (Cave XIV), this *mandapa* was primarily exclusively and consciously carved out to serve the Brahmanical needs. This might mean that this *mandapa* came subsequently after the main cave complex in the background had been modified to the Brahmanical requirements. Before we sustain this, pehaps we might have to consider, if the main Dasavatara cave itself would not have consumed sufficient time for its reconditioning, and might not have stretched on to the time of the Rashtrakuta Krishna himself who succeeded Dantidurga, as probably suggested by the character of some of the sculptural panels found in the upper cave. Thus, it would seem that Dantidurga's *mandapa* while seemingly involving an anticipation of its need in relationship to the modified Dasavatara Saivite shrine, could well have been *a unit and entity by itself*, in so far as the architectural formulations and sculptural developments are concerned and this would have been one of the reasons why it did not *prima facie*, include a monolithic *nandi* in its patterning, and left the *mandapa* to serve any individualistic need connected with the temple. Thus, it might not indeed be unreasonable to consider this *mandapa* as a mere hall, probably the *bhoga mandapa* or the *Ranga mandapa*, as an auxiliary, but not an inconsequential addition to the main shrine; for, one thing is clear that it is not a shrine in itself and thus it had to be seen in relationship with the main shrine, but a simulation of shrine entity in itself has been created for Dantidurga's *mandapa*, and it is this characteristic that will be detailed further down on the basis of its own internal evidence.

At the time of its erection, namely, during the period of Dantidurga in the 6th-7th decades of the 8th century A.D., the temple form as adumbrated by the Chalukyas had evolved into a multiplicity of variant modes with some among these serving to integrate common elements of many of these modes. Thus, the provision of a 'northern' type of *sikhara* in what is clearly the typical Chalukyan pattern of a central nave and slopy sides was equally well applied to 'southern' type style of temples; thus differentiating what was a *local* impulse, namely, the slopy side and the central raised clerestory, from what is a stylistic *bias*, namely, the 'northern' or the 'southern' *sikhara* type. In the same way, Dantidurga who, apparently, was circumstantially wedded to rock-cut medium at Ellora, had to consider how best he could have created a model which would achieve the synthesis of his many architectural trends as have gone on by then, and at the same time would not involve the construction of a temple, in entirety, at this place. For, even Buddhists when they started the cave excavations here *could* very well have cut away all the rock in the courtyard before they reached for the cave behind, but had not done this, apparently to save avoidable wastages of time and energy and had left a massive block, intended to have scooped out open passages on either side and around skirting it, to reach the double cave excavation that was in their mind. After Dasavatara cave complex itself had been modified to suit the changed needs of Brahmanical clarity. Dantidurga's attention would have been drawn to this block which required to be dealt with and the idea that it should prominently display ultimately the inscription that he was to engrave extolling his dynastic lineage would also have arisen. This *mandapa* was inevitably born in these circumstances, but it is indeed remarkable that Dantidurga was able to introduce quite a good many of architectural and artistic elements on the surface patterning well as modelling of the *mandapa* that creditably reflects the state of art during his time, divested though these vestiges might be from any unified context.

It has already been mentioned that this Dantidurga *mandapa* was provided with a plinth forming an other cella border which rises like a *jagati*, a *kantha* above, followed by a *kapota* in fact forming a *manchabandha*. At the inner centre of its eastern face, this *mandapa* was provided with a flight of steps leading into its interior the approach steps themselves consisting of a very spacious *chandrasila* flanked by *gajamundas* very realistically rendered with the trunk part almost in the round and rolling over the ground in front and holding a foliage in their grip. (*Plate IV*) This *gajamunda* balustrade came up to the level of the top of *kapota* and on the four corners of the *mandapa* and the two equidistant middle points of the three wall spaces of the *mandapa* side, pilasters were carved, the former being of the cantoning type, which rise up to the roof level, as already described. It is on this triple wall section and the entrance door, and if possible on the exterior, that any innovation could be introduced. We shall now see that in incorporating all the known trends of the period, the architects achieved considerable success. The entrance door frame was provided with simple *trisakha* frame work of which the two inner *sakhas* were given a double *pitha* and the main *sakha* namely, pilastered *sakha* reproduces the simple square-section character of the 'southern' style temple pillar of the times. It was surmounted above at the lintel level in the *uttaranga*, by a *hara*, *chaturasra sikharas* of the *alpa vimana* type and *salas* alternating. This was different from the common practice of the Chalukyan temple wherever there was a combination of *nagara rekha prasada* relief and *dravida salas* and *kutas* on the *uttaranga*, but the character of the presentation of these units was, however, maintained close to the Chalukyan methods, namely, by introducing a clerestory like *kantha* above the *kapota* of these units over which the *vedi*, *griva* and *sikhara* rise correspondingly the uttaranga also shows an architrave, followed by a regular parapet in the case of the *chaturasra vimanas* placed on the ends, on the middle stretch. In the present case, it is clearly seen that while the *kutas* of the first *tala* are shown in the corners, the central part does not show the corresponding *sala*, but only a *nasika*. This is consistent with the method employed at Indra Sabha Chaumukh or Chotta Kailasa, and even in Kailasa. Thus, the intermingling of the *sala* of the simple type and the *sala*, with a central prominently projecting *nasika*, almost overwhelming its body structure, has been shown even in the miniature *uttaranga* models of Dantidurga *mandapa*. Flanking the door frame on the pilasters are shown *Ganga* and *Yamuna*, *Ganga* to the proper left and *Yamuna* to the proper right, as astride the *makara* and the *kurma* respectively. The animal cognizances are themselves rendered in a very realistic way, but the normal attendants carrying parasols had been done away with, but the parasols and the chauris themselves had been shown flanking the *kirita* and above the ground suggesting such attendants. The goddesses carry a lotus stalk in one of their arms, while the other arm is dangling free along the body. They are in *abhanga* with the outer legs straight and are decorated with *haras*, a *yajnopavita* which skirts across their breasts, *keyuras*, *kankanas*, a lower garments, weakly but adventitiously suggested as draped around the body, the hems of which are shown across the right ankle of *Yamuna*, the loose ends hanging between the legs, while on the left leg the hems are just above the knee; and thus the *kaccha* type is not shown. The *katibandha*, however, is hanging loose on either side apart from a *kativastra*, which is found in loops with festoons at intervals. Much of the face and head is lost due to wear and tear. It would seem that the *mukuta* is of the *karanda* type. The figure-sculpture shown inside the pilasters on this *uttaranga* units as well as in the recesses in between, had apparently been completed subsequently, since they tend to include erotic *bandhas* of *mithuna* pairs also in two of the instances, while the remaining ones show the seated figures of the type not common to Brahmanical usage. The wall spaces, while they are divided into three separate parts on the side walls, are shown as one the unified part on either side of the door frame on the eastern side, while a similar contingency as also on the western side because of the occurrence of the porch. Thus, it is interesting because while it divides the longitudinal access to the mandapa only in two parts with the door series as a central nave, the transverse access is divided into three parts with the *jali* pattern windows in the centre. The character of the wall spaces on the sections other than the *jali* windows, however, are broadly similar on all the faces, but introduce elements of architectural pattern which will be discussed now. This consists, in the main, of a central unit comprising a plinth and a pair of pilasters supporting an *udgama*. (Plate V) The plinth itself shows a typical Chalukyan moulding of a *padma*, a very narrow *kantha*, a *vritta kumuda*, surmounted by broader *kantha* and a *kapota* followed by a *prati*. The pilasters above this *prati* are of the same type as the wall pilasters including the intersecting corbel blocks on the top, and the *udgamas* which are rendered in three main nodes surmounted by the topmost trefoil *nasika* show a perfect clarity in the *jalaka* pattern in the superimposition of the *jalakas* and the central *nasikas*. The first three nodes above the *venukosa* are almost straight along with their side profiles, above which they become sharply triangular in the remaining parts. In some of these, the *kantha* separation between each of the nodes has been emphasised in greater or lesser degrees. But always along the outer corners such an *udgama* pattern as is delineated in the central part of the side sections over the niche is itself the nearest parallel in the sukanasa front age of the Kasi Visvesvara temple at Pattadakkal which by the comparative evidence of the temple on that side would be the latest built there and thus close to the line of Dantidurga. Inside the niche of the plaster is carved an attendant probably representing a *dvarapala* in *abhanga*, two-armed, one arm on the *kati*, and the left arm flexed high in *katakahasta*. The figure carries *jatamukuta*, whose side tresses are of a wavy character falling behind the ears, but not broadly as in the erstwhile Chalukyan cases. The ornamentations are mainly of a *kanthahara*, *katibandha*, *yajnopavita udarabandha*, and *kativastra* lower garments appear to have been restricted to the thigh like *ardhoruka*. Flanking this central pilastered niche are two identical sides and diminutive units each representing a plinth part, a pilastered part and a triangular or trefoil *udgama*. While the *udgama* and the pilaster are similar to the main niche in the centre, the elements below them show certain interesting features. In one of them, as repeated in many other instances on the side faces, the plinth mouldings comprise a *padma*, a high pilastered *kantha*, divided by three pilasters into two trefoil nodes followed by an *uttira*, a *valabhi*, and a highly drooping heavy *kapota*, succeeded by another narrow *kantha* and a heavy *pattika* with *patralata* band, over which on a regular *Oma* or *pitha* unlike the central larger niche pilasters stand. Correspondingly, the figures inside also stand on a *padma pitha*, similar in height to the *pitha* of the pillars. These are again attendants who carry various weapons and objects like flowers and *gada*, being idly kept on the side and the elbow resting on it, while the other arm is carrying a flower. This method of representing a weapon in one hand and an object like a flower in the other for a divinity or an attendant is a new mode and perhaps suggests two simultaneous trends set in motion by the Rashtrakutas, namely, power as well as art patronage. But it is the character of the plinth features mentioned above that would interest us. This would show that over the *kapota*, the *pattika* which in effect represents *vyalavari* of the plinth or *prastara* is introduced and in variant form, in place of the pilastered niches in the lower part of the plinth projecting beam work three in number are introduced. It would be only to recall that the *bhadra* parts of the plinth of many Chalukyan temples introduce below the *kapota* sometimes in the *kumuda* level, massive projecting beams whose ends are decorated. Thus, it would be seen that even in Dantidurga's time these architectural elements have been continued.

The main niches of the northern, southern and western faces flanking the grill windows show regular *dvarapalas* resting their hand on heavy maces. Such a position would indicate that each of the four directions was important and thus the *sarvatobhadra* shrine pattern was indirectly introduced into the scheme. Coming to the northern and southern sides alone it is additionally seen that the *dvarapalas* here are not placed in the main niches of the side wall sections, but on the pilasters adjoining the grill window framework. The grill window itself has been completed in its upper part fairly adequately on the southern side, while its lower part is well finished only on the northern side. On the northern side these grill windows show a regular *vedi* of the *manchabandha* type comprising a *padma*, a *prati*, multiple pilasters five in number, enclosing niches within, the pilasters themselves of the double pilaster type and the niches showing an inner counter-sunk part which carry *mithuna* figures in very intimate postures, but not unreasonably vulgar. Over these pilasters and their corbels rise the *uttira*, *valabhi* and the *kapota*, followed by a *prati*, upon which the main pilaster of the grill window rises in simple rectangular section and plain faces surmounted by a *torana*, which is of the *hamsa torana* type on the northern side and of the *makara torana* type on the southern and the latter is more elaborate. The hamsas, however, have been fairly gone through and even realistically shown as peeping out through slender necks in a curve and blocking the front out of a central receptacle. The upper neck of the birds has been crested with a continuous plume rendered picturesquely while at least six of them have been done in bold inward loops of conveniently seated pair of birds. This adoption of *hamsa torana* or can it be really considered as a *makara torana* where the tail-floriated tail as drooping down in the ultimate running in which case the plume also would fit better—alongside the *makara torana* of the conventional type had already been practised in Chalukyan temples, particularly of the middle and the eastern parts of Deccan. Such a variegation here, therefore, has more contemporary significance than has a stylistic adjunct and would further reinforce by the fact that at the time of excavation of this *ghanadvara* is reasonably near the time of the evolved western and eastern Chalukyan temples in the opening quarters of the eighth century A.D., as at Alampur etc. The *makara torana* on the southern side takes the form of a squatting *makara* with snout vertically up and curled and coiled like an elephant trunk on the top with the jaw wide open from which is also emerging *vyala* from the canines and the jaw spread forth. A garland like *torana* in double loop one on each side disappears into the corresponding double *makara* motif placed in the centre embellished by a *nasika* on the front. This inner *makara* also has a *vyala* coming out of its mouth and on the crest of the *nasika* a complete *simha lalata* of the *nasika* has been carved elegantly, while below the nasika the *dandika* support is shown as *kudmala* underlain by festoon in loops. The floriated tails of the outer *makaras* droop low and vertically almost down to 1/3rds the height of the grill window. It is interesting that this grill window should have a *manchabandha*, *vedi* and this *makara-torana* frame work. It would be recalled that *ghanadvaras* or false grill window openings of regular door size are a common motif set in the centre of the cardinal directions of the closed walls of the circuit around the inner shrine proper, and they would signify the presence of the shrine within whose cardinal niche would be in alignment with the *ghanadvaras*. It is this principle of an eastward facing shrine here which has its *ghanadvaras* on the three sides that has been suggested by these grill windows of the *dvara-torana mandapa*.

Coming to the figure carvings and starting from the eastern entrance door to the *mandapa* in clockwise direction, the first niche, of *Yamuna* which is partially damaged, shows a standing figure in *abhanga*, two-armed, one arm in *kati* and the other arm flexed high. It appears to have a *jatamukuta*. The main niche shows an attendant with *karanda* type of *jatamukuta*, left arm on *katibandha*, right arm holding a flower. The next smaller niche shows a *mithuna* couple with the female carrying her right arm around the neck over the right shoulder of the male, who is having his right arm in *kati* and left arm taken around the waist of the female and pulling her towards him. The female is having her legs cropped. The corner pilaster on the eastern face shows a very interesting and large-sized *mithuna*-couple, *(Plate VI)* the male in the rear and the female almost resting against his body, and being supported by him in a state of unconsciousness either due to intoxication, or in an intimate posture. Her right arm is dangling along the body, while the left arm is tucking at her *katibhandha* for support. Her left leg if bent behind the right which is, however, carried straight obliquely, the posture itself going to suggest that she is by no means intoxicated. The left arm of the male is gently taken behind the upper arm of the female and under the crook of her arm, holding her body by the upper part, while his right arm is gripping the right arm of the female at the elbow. The female wears *kundalas* of an elegant circular type, has a *yajnopavita* going between her breasts and a lower garment tied by a *katibandha*, in addition to *keyuras, kankanas* and *padasaras*. Foil to this love play is presented by a toddler-in-arms at the foot of the figure managed to rise up and grasping the feet of the male. The main pilaster on the south face shows a medium size female attendant without any outstanding characteristics excepting that her lower garment is tied in simple *vestita* type wrapped around the body, the lower hem shown in a mildly wavy pattern across the ankles, and stretching along the side, and the side hems similarly stretched alongside the figure. The upper part of the body is bare. The head is missing.

The *udgama* miniature-niche shows an attendant with *gada* and *padma* in two of his arms, the left arm is resting on the *gada*.

The main niche shows a *yogi* apparently, probably, with a *jatamukuta*, a nimbus behind, a tepering beard and moustaches, a yajnopavita, across the body and simple *ardhoruka* or more appropriately *nivi* or loin cloth tightly fastened and probably, tied behind. He is two-armed, standing in *abhanga* and his left arm is holding a *kundika* probably, while his right arm has perhaps an *akshamala*. The fact that there is a nimbus behind his head might suggest that he is a divinity, and, if so, the subdued presentation of the *urdhvamedhra* might suggest that the figure might stand for *Lakulisa*.

The next smaller niche shows a female attendant holding a flower in the right arm and the left arm resting on the *kativastra*, the drape of the lower body not in the kaccha fashion, but in the simple drape with the hem shown across the shin and knee. The next main pilaster shows a *dvarapala* with the *gada* to his right on which right arm is resting, the left arm on *kati.* The *dvarapala* to the other side of the grill window is almost similar and of corresponding posture. The next mininutive niche shows again an attendant resting his left arm on the *gada* and right hand on hip with a high tapering *jatamukuta.* The main niche shows again a standing figure in *samabhanga*, with a loin cloth around the thigh and waist, left arm holding a *kundika*, right arm in *katakahasta*, the head showing what appears to be a *jatamakuta* and the ornaments comprising *kanthi*, *yajnopavita*, *udarabandha*, *keyuras* and *kankanas*. There is no distinctive characteristics in the *kundika.* The next diminutive niche shows a female figure, the left arm on *kati*, right arm holding a flower. The drapery is similar to the other female figures on the other side of the grill with the only difference that there is an upper garment also taken around her shoulder and cross her arms and body, while the wavy zig-zag hem of antariya is carefully shown in between the two legs and body like an *uttariya.* The presence of this drapery would show that she is *not* an attendant. The end pilaster of the wall shows a *mithuna* couple, both almost in *samabhanga*, standing close, the left arm of the female dangling, the right arm taken around his shoulder, with the left arm of the male also correspondingly taken behind the arms and touching her elbow, while his right arm is flexed high, probably grasping the right arm of the woman, which is partially damaged. The complementary position of the two figures is brought out with minimum change in body stand. (*Plate VII*) The adjoining faces of the pilaster shows a female holding perhaps a water vessel in her right arm flexed high, while the left arm is touching the head of a *gana* attendant nearby. It is just possible that this is an actual representation of one of the river goddesses. The next diminutive niche shows an attendant and the larger niche represents a dvarapala with a heavy mace upon which the arm is resting. The last diminutive niche of this Sani is vacant. On the other side of the porch, the diminutive niche shows a female attendant, while the main niche shows again *dvarapala* but more elegantly stanced in *abhanga*, though a little squattish. The *jalaka* of the *udgama*, is most profuse in this case and at the top of the *udgama* is characterised by a pair of birds pecking at the *simha lalata*. The next miniature niche is empty. The corner pilaster shows a solitary female with left arm taken over her head in a captivated manner, while the right arm is flexed across the body and pressing against her left breast. This is apparently a representation of Surasundari or Vasudhara, the giver of the milk of plenty. The adjoining face shows a male, partially complete and badly damaged. His head, however, does not carry any *jatamukuta* but appears to be almost of a secular character. The next miniature niche shows a male attendant, right arm flexed high, holding a flower, left arm on *kati*. The next figure in the main niche is very interesting in that it introduces a regular divinity, namely, *Ardhanari*, inspite of the fact that the figure is in *samabhanga*. The characteristic elements on the *Ardhanari* form are mainly brought out by the presence of the decorated left arm, one breast being present, the *patrakundala* on the left ear, decorated hair-do on the left side in the form of a *karanda*, while the right side, the *mukuta* is of the *jatamukuta* type. The ears sport *nakra kundala* to the right, and *patrakundala* to the left. The right arm is flexed high holding a *naga*, while on the left shoulder and upper arm the *uttariya* is outlined. There is a *kanthi*, and *yajnopavita* taken through the centre of the chest. Both the legs show *padasara*.

The next miniature niche shows a figure of a *nayika* with the right leg flexed high backwards and taken across the thigh the right arm raised high and flexed and adjusting her hair-do, while the left arm is holding a mirror against her face. The adjoining main pilaster shows a *dvarapala* resting on his heavy mace. The *vedi* of the grill window occurring next here shows four *mithuna* pairs, the end ones being seated and the middle ones standing; one of them is also having an additional figure standing nearby as a mute witness to the scene. The main pilaster coming next shows *dvarapala* of an interesting stance with the body slightly thrown backwards in his position. The miniature *udgama* next shows a male attendant, right arm holding a flower and left arm in *kati*. The main niche shows a *nayika* with the legs in *padasvastika*, right arm dangling, left arm holding a mirror against her face, and the whole body gently lowered somewhat in the process, with the right leg gracefully having its foot tilted outwards. The next miniature shows a male attendant, left arm in *kati* and the right arm in *suchihasta.* The corner pilaster shows on the northern face a female attendant in slight *abhanga,* right arm in *kati,* left arm holding a flower. A part of the body is bare. The head is done in a *dhammilla* fashion. The adjoining eastern face of the pilaster shows a counterpart to the eastern face at the southern end and is one of the most amorous *mithuna* figures rendered in more than medium-size and showing an intoxicated *nayika,* completely beyond herself, holding her lover close but almost sliding down in the process. The left arm of the male is re-assuringly taken around her behind her back under her hair-do, while the right arm is gripping the nayika's own left arm taken around his waist. The left arm of the *Nayika* is tucking at the right elbow of the male. The male is almost in *samabhanga* standing self-assured and supporting this damsel in distress. Thus the representations of such interesting *nayikas* in a state of intoxication or love-play in the temple in such a prominent way would show that, secular sculptures like this have already been allowed in temple exterior wall, as was the case in the early Chalukyan period as well, and formed a part of the bracket figures, but in the absence of the bracket in this mandapa, the Rashtrakuta crafts men could not exclude these charming pictures of secular romance.

The miniature niche next shows a male attendant resting on the gada by the left arm, right arm holding a flower. The main niche shows an attendant, apparently a *dvarapala* in *tribhanga,* right arm on the *kativastra,* left flexed high in *katakahasta.* The lower garment is a drapery around the upper thigh and waist. The ornamentations include a *kanthi,* and *sutra yajnopavita, udarabandha, kankanas* and *katibandha,* apart from *kundalas;* the innermost diminutive niche a a male attendant with the *gada* by his side and lotus in the right hand.

The roof of the *mandapa* introduces the following interesting elements on the corners, at regular intervals : two on each face, are shown *nalas* cut into its parapet above cornice for draining storm water from the roof. These *nalas* when complete, as on the northern side, are taking the form of water-spouts or *gargoyles* and with *simhavaktra.* On the parapet on the four corners are placed couchant lions whose heads are turned inwards and whose faces are of the posture of emitting a roar, while at three points at regular intervals on each side are shown a central seated figure, (whose upper part of the body was lost, in all the cases) in *padmasana* pose flanked by two squatting *gana* one leg flexed laterally, the other leg flexed vertically with a capacious belly and probably representing the various *dikpalas* since they are two on each side. It may even be that of three figures on each side, which total to 12, eight of them would be *dikpalas* while the central figures on each side would be regular divinities. The roof of the *mandapa* has a centrally raised roof provided with a narrow clerestory half lay-out being of *triratha* pattern. This *triratha* pattern itself is interesting as it recalls the patterns at Chaumukh and Chhota Kailasa, and over the clerestory represented by a *kantha uttira* and *valabhi*, a *kapota* roof is provided. From this centrally raised roofing the surface is sloping towards the side walls. This is another important feature, which is a link with the past as it represents the characteristic slopy roofs of the Chalukyan period, as represented by Ladakhan and Chikkigudi at Aihole. It is thus very clear that, at least in this roof element, the Rashtrakuta craftsmen were close to certain prevailing Chalukyan proto-types inasmuch as Dantidurga himself was close, in time, with Chalukyan sway. The type of the raised roof part is flat and featureless, unlike the elements introduced on the roof of Chhota Kailasa and Kailasa. This again is a feature that separates Dantidurga's stage from the rest. It would thus be noted that the Dasavatara *mandapa* is almost a rare instance of one single, notable, monolithic composition of Dantidurga, synthesising a multiplicity of known nuances and idioms of the architectural and sculptural wealth to which the Rashtrakuta craftsmen were heir, and this would make this *mandapa* not a solitary aberrant specimen, but one that shows a clear parting of the ways and one that is compact with the outstanding elements of the age gone-by.

At the point of entrance into the front courtyard of Dantidurga's *mandapa*, on its western side, is found on the northern wall a cave excavation consisting of shrine and a squarish front *mandapa*. The shrine has a circular *linga pitha* surmounted by a cylindrical *linga*, with the *nala* to the proper left. Behind the *linga* on the back wall is shown the figure of Mahesha which is atypical by way of orientation and represents Vamadeva to the proper right and Aghora to the proper left. On the flanks of the door frame outside are shown *dvarapala* statues peculiarly by allowing their right leg and placing it on the head of a *gana* attendant below. Their hair-do also is found as falling in two heavy buns on either side.

On one of the corner pilasters of the hall a conch-blowing *gana* has seated on the top. The eastern and the western walls of the hall were desired to be decorated by divinities placed in niches of which the one on the western side has two niches, the inner having figures of Brahma and Visnu separated by a circular pilaster and surmounted by *torana* like loop. The figure of Visnu is holding a *gada* by the upper right arm, *chakra* by the upper left arm and *sankha* by the lower left arm and the lower right arm is in *varada hasta*. The figure of *Bhu* is shown to the right and *Garuda* to the left. On the right of *Garuda* is placed a *sankha*. The figure of Brahma is three-headed and four-armed, the arms carrying *akshamala*, *kundika*, *pustaka* and *sruk* and the face beardless. Here are shown what appears to be two frames one on each side. The other niche shows Parvati in *panchagni-tapas*, standing in *samabhanga*. She has a *kundika* in the left arm and *akshamala* in the right. Upper part of the body is bare. Four *ganas* are shown in the four corners. She is shown as standing upon a *godha* (*ignana*) and wears a cross-belt. The opposite wall carries only one partially completed niche showing a seated Ganesa with trunk turned to the left and resting on the left lower arm. The other arms are badly damaged. However, the *parasu* in the left upper arm is visible. The head is without a crown. The hall which is divided by a pilaster and a single corbel block from the projecting front porch is of a rectangular plain opening. It is very likely that this is very much later to Dasavatara *mandapa*.

(B) CHHOTA KAILASA

This imitates the Kailasa in the method of a free standing monolith with an inner shrine complete with *ardha mandapa*, *maha mandapa*, and *mukha mandapa* and a *dvara mandapa* separated from it within which around the main shrine the *prakara* runs, though not carved at the same level, owing to the incompleteness of the composition. The composition has been only brought down to the top level of the *adhisthana*, of the shrine proper unlike Kailasa which shows a very high *upapitha* of the whole *tala*. The main walls have not been completed (*Plate IX*) excepting for the projecting porch *mandapas* to the south and to the north, which show dwarf pillars on the parapets different from that of the corresponding *kankanas* in the Kailasa cave, and nearer to the southern style. On the roof above the *kapota* over the rafter frame work which is simply shown in blocks of projecting rafters carrying transverse beams above them is a *hara* of *kutas* and *salas* with *nasikas* coming in between, and above this the roof of the projecting *mandapa* is plain carrying only a *triratha* top parapet which forms the centre of the main *hara* of the *maha mandapa* roof just comprising *salas*, *kutas* and *nasikas*. (*Plate X*) Projecting porches have their own parapets which, however, do not project out in their end hara in *triratha* pattern. The centre of the roof of the *maha mandapa* has a square *sikhara* unit (*Plate XI*) mounted upon the *vyalavari*, *vedi* and *griva* limits, *triratha* projection on each side forming a *nasika*, with an upper step, upon which apparently the *kalasa* and *stupi* were placed originally. The main shrine shows on the ground *tala kutasikharas* at the corners of the *prastara*, and very bold *nasika* which is actually the end on projection of a *sala-sikhara*. (*Plate XII*) This *nasika* is rising higher than the *kutasikharas* of the first *tala* and is actually at the lowest part of a composite series of *nasikas* rising one above the other without any relationship to the *tala* levels on three of its sides. On the fourth side, however, immediately above the *ardha mandapa* and above the first *tala* ending with the *kutasikharas* at the corners, there is a transversely rectangular *pada* part with a central projection which has a front on of a very bold *nasika kudu*, the *kudu* showing a *stambha torana* giving access to an upper shrine chamber within the *ardha mandapa* roof. (*Plate XIII*) The *pada* part of this shrine chamber is surmounted at the corners by regular *kutasikhara*, while in the centre it has another bold *nasika* set a little behind the fronton above the *kapota* of this *pada*. Thus, while the composition is the same on the four sides, the front side has been elevated in its dimensions much more on the other sides. Inside of this upper shrine chamber and within a *mukha mandapa* and *maha mandapa* is a transverse rectangular chamber carrying the figure of a seated *Jina* with the *asana*-back supported by *vyala* pilasters and *makara* balustrades and carrying a *prabhavali* above them. Over the *prabhavali* is the *trichhatravali*. The figure is flanked by two *chamaradharinis*. This shrine is a variation to the Brahmanical temple pattern adapted to Jain usage and showing evolved architectural forms and idioms in the composition and superstructure, involving a composite unit of the typical southern style of receding tiers of *haras* and the provision of bold *nasikas* on the cardinal directions rising one above the other as in the northern style. It is nearer in style to the composition of the Chawmukh of the Indra Sabha. The composition is in its extant stature a *tritala vimana*, although the top of the three *talas* is abruptly ending in an incomplete character. The *maha mandapa* on the exterior wall shows, corresponding to the *nasikas* of the *harantara*, a pilastered composition in between the main pilasters which is of the *vritta sputita* type, carrying a *kapota* composition much below the main *kapota* and with its own *prastara* and *nasika kudu* above, the top of which is just below the *uttara*. The *potikas* of the main wall are of the *taranga* type with a scroll work median band. These *taranga potikas* have not been shown in Kailasa.

This monolithic excavation has been properly called Chhota Kailasa, owing to its broad comparative affinity with the Great Kailasa (Cave XVI), to which, however, by way of gross dimensions, it is lesser. Considering Kailasa, Indra Sabha front court with Chaumukh, and Chhota Kailasa, as also, to some extent, Dantidurga's mandapa in front of the doublestoreyed Dasavatara cave (XV), it would seem that each formed a specific stage in not only the mental disposition of the architects, but also the evolution of art trends. For instance, broadly speaking, Dantidurga's mandapa in front of Dasavatara cave excavation compares somewhat with the location of Chaumukh in front of a complex of cave excavation behind it; the Indra Sabha (Cave XXXII), in being a combination and juxtaposition of cave excavations of a major kind with monolithic units to the front; the Kailasa, and the Chhota Kailasa, on the other, form another comparable group wherein the inclination is only to carve out a single unitary monolithic composition out of the slope of the hill. Thus, seemingly Kailasa and Chhota Kailasa would be nearer in concept and execution, while Dantidurga's mandapa with cave XV would be comparable to the trend seen at Indra Sabha with its Chaumukh. On the contrary, the presence of the elephant and the *manastambha* at the latter brings it also nearer to the Kailasa composition, while the character of the Dantidurga's *mandapa* would preclude the direct comparison of it with the Chaumukh at Indra Sabha. As would be seen further down, the individual architectural features of Chhota Kailasa are nearer to that of Chaumukh than to the great Kailasa, and if Dantidurga's *mandapa* should, doubtless, be considered as the earliest of the monolithic series of the Rashtrakutas at Ellora, it might not be too far a field to consider Chhota Kailasa as the last. This, however, would imply understanding that the whole gamut of stages would have been well within the end of the ninth century A.D., after which excavations alike for cave temples as for monoliths practically go out of vogue, excepting for the nondescript hybrid series belonging to late to post tenth century A.D., as revived by the Yadhavas of the Devagiri (Daulatabed) which, in so far as the art of the cave shrines went, was secondary and inconsequential. Thus, we may plausibly take Indra Sabha-Chaumukh and Chhota Kailasa as having closely succeeded each other, but the distinction between the two, apart from what had been outlined above, is further highlighted by a very character of the units, namely, the complete temple in the case of Chhota Kailasa and what is seemingly an *affiliated* unit in the Chaumukh, but one should probably be ill-advised to take the Chaumukh unit itself as a complete temple, notwithstanding its auxiliary ritual nature and should consider both Chaumukh and Chhota Kailasa as, architecturally speaking, two variant models of temple composition extant at that period. The Chhota Kailasa, topographically as well, is comparatively nearer to the Chaumukh and is located in the upper slopes to the east—south-east of the latter, and even on this basis should be a cognate activity in rock-cut architecture. The reason, of course, primarily is that these two are of the Jain faith, while the other two monoliths are of the Brahmanical faith, and thus the isolation in physical location of the Jain group, relatively speaking, from the Brahmanical group further south, need not imply a quantitative isolation or separation in time from the Brahmanical counterparts at the hands of the Rashtrakuta patrons and artisans alike. The Chhota Kailasa had been selected at a place where the slope of the hill could accommodate a fully longitudinal strike of the temple, including the main *vimana*, its *Sabha mandapa*, open *Pradakshina patha* and a front unit representing either a *mukha mandapa* or a *gopuradvara*. In this, the front unit was sufficiently tall and still the main *vimana* could raise sufficiently high, almost corresponding to the slope of the hill. This front *mandapa* had not been completed externally to the extent its own interior had been finished, and this equally will hold good for the front porch of the interior of the *Sabha mandapa* itself as well as the superstructure of the main *vimana*. Two processes are to be surmised in this set-up; firstly, as called for in monolithic composition, the main *vimana* would have been begun from the top and would go downwards. At the same time, there was an urge to complete the interior ahead of the exterior in order that its ultimate consecration and use might not be unconscionably delayed. This has resulted, secondly, in the exterior even including the *pradakshina patha* having received only secondary attention and the superstructure of the main *vimana* and the interior having received primary attention. It would thus seem that in this two-fold simultaneous process set in motion, the ritual evidence of the temple for worship to be started was not impaired, notwithstanding the incomplete exterior of the temple. Apparently the finished character of the interior including the sanctum, and the provision for the placement of the *kalasas* on the exterior superstructure of the *vimana* were considered as sufficient for the inception of worship. This would be a matter of some significance, indeed, in respect of all such partially finished excavations of the Brahmanical as well as other kinds of this period as well as the other earlier periods.

As it is, Chhota Kailasa presents a rugged and incomplete exterior wherein stepped out blocks of rock mass had been left as different heights and stages around the main longitudinal lay-out of shrine unit, although the final disposition of the temple plan is patent.

Mukha Mandapa

Approaching the monolithic excavation from west—north-west, the *mukha mandapa* is seen as comprising a squarish front chamber of plain walls and ceiling, even whose facade has not been completely blocked out. (*Plate XIV*) It would seem, however, that in the ultimate picture, this front porch would have been of slightly lesser dimensions than its existing unit, since its southern part is less adequately preserved for a larger dimension than the northern. The door-frame through which entry would be made from this porch into the hall or vestibule of the *dvara mandapa* has not again been finished out of the massive inset given, and the analogy here in its completed character would again, have to be seen at the inner end of the *dvara mandapa*, overlooking the *pradakshina patha* where the wall and the pilaster or screen-projection has been finished to a much greater degree. This *dvara mandapa* was desired to be in two compartments divided by slight pilaster projections from the side walls in the middle of each; of which again the inner compartment is much better finished than the outer. This shows the innermost pilaster face overlooking the *pradakshina patha* bare and plain, while the recessed wall compartments as well as their own side eastern and western side faces were filled with figure sculpture. In a similar way, the median pilaster projection dividing the two compartments was also carved on its face with figure sculpture. These sculptures took the form of two polarised sets of carvings, the one to the south being invariably of seated *Jina* on a pedestal with the *simha lanchhana*; figure seated in *padmasana* pose with a balustrade showing attendants or *chauri-bearers*, the *trichhatravali* over the head of the *Jina* and with a group of *gana* attendants hovering in the air, above the *trichhatravali* on either side, playing upon drums, both vertically as well as horizontally placed, cymbals, as well as carrying garlands. These garland-bearing *ganas* are invariably placed in the figure in recess replaced by conch-blowing *ganas*. By the side of the main *chauri*-bearer attendants behind the seated *Jinas* and generally disposed along the corners where the two adjoining faces are also to be found paired *mithunas* in bold relief and of alluring postures as seen in the south-east corner of the southern recess of the inner compartment. The northern compartment, however, was desired to be confined to female figures of the Jain inconography and only the main recessed face of the inner compartment has been carved with one such representing seated *Devi* with *kiritamukuta* from the top of which is emerging a *padma*, upon which is seated a *Jina*. The *Devi* is shown with 12 hands of which practically all the hands are preserved on the inner side, while the outer western side are preserved only two of them, viz., the one on the lap and the one holding a sword of straight blade. The *devi* is shown with an oval nimbus behind her head, heavy *kundalas*, a *graiveyaka hara*, a *stanasutra* and *chhannavira*, skirting the bare breast and with a lower garment which has been badly worn-out. Her left hands are respectively, on the lap, holding *gada*, *chakra*, *sankha*, another *chakra* and *padma*. One of the upper right hands would seem to have held a *sakti*, an *ankusa*, from what is remaining on the top vestigeal parts. The figure apparently is Garuda whose *wings* are shown on either side of the shoulder is carved below the seat of *Devi* and represented as holding the set-up with his hands, while his legs are themselves flexed as if in the air. On either side of the *Devi* at the upper level, corresponding to *Devi* as well as the *Jina* seated over her crown are found attendants, one to the east and two on the outer (west) side of which the inner one to the west carries a lotus, the other two carry *chamaraṣ*. All these are female attendants, who are shown of the same dimensions as the male attendants of the *Jinas* on the opposite side, whose legs disappear behind the hands of the *Devi*. In the same manner as the legs of the male attendants on the opposite side disappear behind the balustrade forming the background of the *Jina*. On the side walls above these female attendants are shown two more sets of attendants one on the inner side, almost *alasanayika* reclining comfortably of the crook of her hand used as a pillow and with her hair-do cerefully kept above her fore-hand. She is also bare-bodied and decorated with a *kanthi*, *stanasutra*, *keyuras* and *kankana* apart from the lower garments, while the figure group on the outer side represents *mithuna*-attendants in a posture of embrace wherein the initiative has come from the female, who is shown on the inner side. The seemingly Brahmanical character of this figure is only superficial and is just possible that it actually represents *Chakresvari* of Jain iconography. The outer compartment is incomplete even in its surface finish as indeed is its own ceiling.

Entering the court-yard from this *dvara mandapa* by a short flight of steps, access is given to the *mukha mandapa* porch forming the integral part of the *Sabha mandapa* and corresponded by two more side porches on the cardinal directions north and south. This *mukha mandapa* porch is almost comparable to that of Kailasa and represents a parapet surmounted by a *kaksasana* and the setting within the angles of the parapet, two free-standing dwarf pillars corresponding to two pilasters at the inner end flanking the door frame of the *Sabha mandapa* and carrying on their intersecting corbels, the heavy cornice. It is to be noted that the inner pilasters do not have intersecting corbels and indeed have only one corbel arm frontward while the free-standing pillars, as already mentioned, have two outer corbel arms very much shorter and of the simple roll-type, while the two inner right angular corbels are well projected forward thin and broad of a simple curve, with a median band also plain. The dwarf pillars themselves show apparently their basal parts hidden within the parapet over which only the shaft rendered as also on the upper part in *triratha* fashion, and having a plain lower part a slightly constricted middle shaft, carrying a vertical *patralata* band in the centre of the broad *bhadra* of set surmounted by the *malasthana* showing two loops with pendentive strands, the loops themselves carrying *ganas* in posture of animation followed by a *padma bandha* which has a *ratnapattai* band in the middle and *padmakosa* above and below. Over this is found the ribbed *kalasa* with a very prominent externally rib at the neck and flaring neck part of square in section surmounted by the *tadi*, even heavier than the neck of the *kalasa*, but left plain, apparently incomplete, succeeded by *kumbha* with median horizontal band. Over the *kumbha* is the *virakanda* and on this occur the intersecting corbels mentioned above. Over the *kumbha* rises a bracket figure of roaring lion with fore-paw flexed up in air, supported from underside by a warrior with shield and sword, also facing front and dispositioned like a caryatid. This lion bracket recalls the corresponding lion motif in the bracket of the front portion of the *gopuradvara* of *Indra Sabha* and in the Chaumukh unit within. The lion bracket rises up to the rolled corbel and its horns are resting immediately under the *uttara.* Over the corbels run the broad thin *uttara* followed by the *vajanas*, which, however, do not follow the outline of the corbel projection as the *uttira* does, but form one broad spread projecting slightly beyond the limits of the outer corbel arms and their *uttira* parts and coming well under the *kogundai* of the cornice. This undersurface of the cornice is perfectly curved out and finished with the edge chamferred horizontally, but do not have transverse rafter parts, but only radiating ribbings, flat and broad. They would, thus schematically be a stage removed in time from those found at Chaumukh or Kailasa, where they are more realistically portrayed, following the wood architecture. The cornice practically running into the side walls adjoining the inner pilasters of this porch, forms, as it were, the canopy of full size figure sculpture shown between the pilasters of the porch and the first wall pilaster outside. The submerged part of these dwarf pillars is shown at the inner angle of the parapeted porch and shows below the continuing basal part of the shaft, the *pitha* of substantial dimensions also *triratha*, showing a lower *jagati*, and *padma* over which a *vritta kumuda* with median band followed by another *padma.* This base or *pitha* of the pillar as well as parapet is resting over a floor moulding, running all around, including a flight of steps forming the approach to the door way of the *mahamandapa.* The floor proper within this is at a slightly lower level. On the inner face of the porch below the ceiling over the *uttira*, a *valabhi* of the *padmavalabhi* type is represented, followed by a *kantha* and an upper *valabhi.* The ceiling shows in its central part located somewhat towards the front, a full-blown broad lotus-pendentive in two tiers, the *padmakesara* forming third bottom part. The main door frame has, as its basal composition a flight of steps including the lowest moon-stone and roll-ended balustrade and on these balustrades and carved against the pilasters are shown the *dvarapalas*, two-armed, with their outer legs flexed and heels slightly raised with a heavy massive *gada*, placed against this outer leg upside down on which one of the hands is resting at the fore-arm, while the other hand is held in *abhaya-mudra.* The body proportions are quite impressive, particularly, due to the lack of too much of ornamentation, comprising a *graiveyaka hara*, and heavy *yajnopavita*, *kankanas*, and *keyuras*. On the shoulders the *nakra-kundalas* rest and the hair-do is done up in *jatamukuta* with clasps at the lower side and middle upper levels. The lower garment is tied by two sets of *katibandha* and *kativastra* to the front and on the sides respectively. At a lower level, almost upto the roll of the balustrade rising up to the ankles of the *dvarapala* figures are shown standing *gana* attendants, followed on the northern side by a still more diminutive female attendant to this *gana*, holdidg a lotus in both her arms, one with stalk and the other without stalk.

The door frame is of the *trisakha* variety wilh the basal part of the jamb showing cut-in figures of attendants with *naga* hood of which the outermost on either side are male and the two inner are females. The *sakhas* above show at the innermost *ratnasakha* with a *Jina* as the *Lalatabimba* on its lintel unit, the next representing a net work of *vidyadharas* in various postures, bare in each case and also showing a seated *Jina* on its *lalata-bimba*, while the outermost *sakha* is the pilaster *sakha* showing the details as represented in the outer pillars, but without their roll pattern, with the corbel arms of longer stretch on the northern and southern sides and shorter on the front side, surmounted by the *kapotas*. The *kapotas* are mostly well-drooping out and undercut and are embellished by *nasikas* and *kona* and *madhya-pattais* and at regular intervals *uttaranga*. Over this occurs a series of three *salas* and two *kutas* both of them shown over a *vedi* and supported by two pilasters surmounted by a *griva* and *sikhara*. They are connected also by a *harantara*, whose recess at the base level shows a kind of varying arche with a *kudmala* on the top, probably representing the open wall of the cloister. Within the *salas* are placed seated *Jinaṣ* with nimbus behind their head, while inside the *kutas* are placed standing *Jinas*. Over this *hara* runs the upper *valabhi* of the ceiling with a thin *vajana* under it.

The interior of the *maha mandapa* or *Sabha mandapa* is of the *navaranga* pattern basically although each of the corner squares is itself comprised of four free standing pillars, four corresponding pilasters crowded together still leaving the axial and transverse parts prominently transversible. This central broad bay, both east-west as well as north-south gives access along the main axis to the *ardha mandapa* and cella and to the northern and southern porched *mandapas* respectively. The south side bays are much shorter and are divided on the floor by a total of 12 pillars and corresponding 12 pilasters, excluding the corner cantoning pilasters which are of the double pilaster variety. On the ceiling again these are divided into a central square in the centre of the *mandapa* and belongs along the main axis of the same width as the central square, smaller squares in the middle bays formed in each corner by four-free-standing pillars and 'L'-shaped continuous ceiling plan formed by the respective outermost bays between the free-standing pillars and the wall pilasters. The pillar scheme itself is of three varieties, respectively represented by the inner central *ankana* pillars the outermost corner free standing unit. The four free-standing pillars of the central *ankana* are similar to the free-standing pillar of the front porch, excepting that it is slightly more slender in its dimensions. The only difference, however, is that over the *virakanda*, which is also of *triratha* pattern, as in the outer porch pillar as well; the corbels are often of the *taranga* type, of equally distributed *tarangas* along the smooth curve, about seven in number, with a *patralata* median band and with floral decoration along the side faces. They are surmounted by a *vajana*, embellished like a *padmakosa*. The other free standing pillars of the second variety show over a *pitha*, similar to the first two, without the *triratha* pattern, and of prevailingly square-section, the basal part of the pillar, itself forming the lower *saduram* over which is a *ghatapallava* with the floral foliage overflowing at the corners on each face, above which the shaft becomes octagonal, carrying the *malasthana* and *ratnapattai*, the *kalasa* encased by *nasika* bands on its faces and has beaded necks, *tadi*, *kumbha*, *virakanda* also octagonal and the intersecting corbels above. These corbels are similar to the first mentioned pillar types. This third pillar type represented by the outermost corner pillars shows a squarish shaft over which occurs a high basal circular sectioned *kalasa*, *tadi*, heavy *kumbha*, *virakanda* followed by intersecting corbels. The pilaster variety is broadly similar to the pillar variety of the central *ankana* but shows a consistent square section right through without offsets from base to top and has on the shaft part below the *malasthana* central vertical band carrying *mithunas*. Its corbels are similar to the corbels of other two types. Along the corbels run the *uttira* are *valabhi* and the ceiling. The wall sections divided by the pilasters into four compartments at each angle from door to door are decorated by figure sculpture variously of seated Jina and the standing *Tirthankaras* respectively, the latter to be located on the wall section, close to the western door, to the north of it, on the wall section diametrically outside, on the *ardha mandapa* wall and on the wall section corresponding to the latter south side. Remaining are all of the seated *Jina* variety, which show two variant modes, namely, of a main seated *Jina* in the centre of large proportions with another seated *Jina* in the lower section and a third seated *Jina* surmounted on the *tricchhatravali* of the main central one. The other variant shows only two such *Jinas* in the middle and lower section, the upper sections represented by hovering *ganas* carrying garlands and other musical instruments respectively. One of the wall sections on the northern side of the eastern wall face of the *mandapa* is left unfinished, and plain. Those of the first variety are seven in number, confined to the north-weast, north-west and south-west corners, while the second variety is restricted to the remaining parts. The standing variety of *Trithankara* is interesting and shows in the two diametrical opposite examples, the carvings of Parsvanatha, with the figure Dharanindra, hooded above, with the chhatra held above the central hood, with the *yaksha* and *yakṣhi* attendants on either side, in addition to the *chauri*-bearer attendants and hovering *ganas* above. The inner example of this, does not show the attendants, but shows the coils of the *nagas* as speread on either side of the *Tirthankara* of grace and beautiful body up to the foot in a most characteristic way and are surmounted by attendants riding on buffalo and lion on either side of the upper level, over which are further *gana* attendants. The third variety on the south side does not show the hood or coils as any snake and is probably representing Bahubalin or Gommata. This is also surrounded by the *yaksha* and *yakshi* below and hovering *gana* attendants and paired *mithunas*, in addition to a surmounted seated *Jina* on the top.

The columniation between the *maha mandapa* and the *ardha mandapa* is effected by a *makara-torana* placed on the side pilasters, which are shown of the cantoning variety above angles of the *ardha mandapa* and which are partially supported by bracket figures, rising from lotus buds, attached to the *kalasa* of the pilasters. These bracket figures are female figures in standing posture in the form of *vrikshikas*. Over the *kumbha*, the actual *makara-torana* rises comprised of graphic *makara* heads with floriated tails, rising vertically high and looping inwards, with the riders on the snouts and with looped garlands emerging out of their mouth and forming the *taranga* ending at the centre in a drooping pendentive supported by sideward facing *makara* head and this is sporting the seated *Jina* placed in between the two *makaras*. It would be seen that this type of *makara-torana* was well prevalent during the Rashtrakuta times as seen in many instances of Rashtrakuta cave excavations, including Ganesh Lena, here at Ellora.

Within the *ardha mandapa* the narrow transverse bay is completely got by a flight of steps, including the lowest moon stone, showing *sankha* and *padma-nidhis* on the floor and having an elephant balustrade with a *gajamunda* frontally facing and carrying foliage in its twisted snout. The side walls show a standing *Tirthankara* on a *padma pitha* with female and male *saksas* standing below and probably representing Gommata, though not with the characteristic entwined creepers etc., in which case, they might just represent standing *Jina*. The lack of *trichhatravali* above suggests that either they had been unfinished in the upper block just leaving *in situ* or that they are to be taken as a *Tirthankara* and not as a *Jina*. The main back wall shows the *sakhas* of the door frame which are of the *panchasakha* variety with the *ratnapattai*, *vidyadhara sakha* as in the front door, pilastered-*sakha* as also in the front door, *patra-sakha* and *padma-sakha*, the outermost. The jambs carry cut-in figures of male and female attendants, the outermost females having hooded *naga* over their heads. The ceiling is left plain, the *uttaranga* is similar to that of the outer door, excepting that in the *kutas* also they carry seated *Jinas*. The underside of the cornice shows *kodungai* ribs, similar to the main outer cornice of the porch. The *lalata-bimba* is that of a *Jina*, probably Parsvanatha, with *naga*-hood above his head and with *maladhara gana* over it, as the centre piece of the *Vidyaāhara sakha*.

The sanctum is a rectangular chamber, whose outer wall sections are left bare, but the side-walls are fully completed in figure sculpture. Of these, the one in the back wall, which is the central piece and the main object of worship, shows a seated *Jina*, Vardhamana over a pedestal of *Triratha* variety and of *mancha-bandha*, showing lion frontally and laterally placed in the *bhadra* and *karna* recesses, between pilasters in each case and showing an elaborate nimbus behind the head over the balustrade of *makara* architrave supported by rearing *vyalas* on either side. There are two sranding *chauri*-bearer attendants on either side of the balustrade, while above the head of the *Jina* there is a *tricahhatra* rendered in a schematic fashion, suspended from a pendentive block of the ceiling. The *ganas* playing on conches and drums are shown at the top level. There are also male and female attendants to the *chauri* bearers followed by *vidyadhara* couple above hovering in the air on the side corners. On the southern wall there are two seated *Jina* figures placed on a low plinth representing a *padma-pitha* and continuous from end to end. The figures themselves juxtaposed without any point of deviation with their balustrade also shown continuous, with their *trichhatravali* above their heads, dividing the upper part of the wall into three sections, the middle section carried by the paired attendants, bearing *chauris*, behind the balustrade, while the upper portions show *ganas* in the air, placed like caryatids and sometimes carrying *chamaras* and found immediately over the *uttira* member. On the northern side, while the outer half shows a similar seated *Jina*, corresponding to those on the south, and differentiated only by another diminutive seated *Jina* placed over the *trichhatravali*, the inner half shows a seated female, almost exactly similar to the female divinity shown on the *dvara mandapa*, but here represented in eight-arms, having *khadga*, *trisula*, and *chakra* on the right arms and *gada*, and two *chakras* in the left arms, the remaining two arms respectively showing *varada* on the right and *abhaya* on the left, There is no figure of *Garuda* shown at the base and the upper part of the body of the divinity is bare, but for the *graiveyaka hara*, and *stanasutra* and the arms show *keyuras*, *kankanas*, the ears sport *patra*-and *nakra-kundalas* in their distended lobes and the head wears a *kirita mukuta*. There is a *makara torana* passes over this divinity with two female attendants standing above and with a seated *Jina* placed on the central loop of the *makara torana* on a *padma pitha*, himself under a *trichhatra* rising up to the *uttira*. There is an additional female attendant on the inner side standing. At the pedestal level of the main back wall on either side of the seated *Jina* the recess part carries paired figures representing either *ganas* or devotees, carrying a lotus in their left hand. The ceiling is otherwise plain.

Coming to the exterior, one may note at first the carving of a female divinity in the shaft part of the pilaster of the front porch, although this carving is carried out only on the southern pilaster, the northern not having been completed. This female carving though of a highly simplified character was apparently of a seated posture originally and similar to the one on the north wall of the sanctum and in the inner north bay of the *dvara-mandapa*. It is interesting to note that one of the *Vidyadhara mithunas* shown in the corners above this figure also is of the same amorous posture as now in the *dvara mandapa* example cited above. Just outside the pilaster nestling under the drooping cornice on either side has been shown very picturesque carved dancing figure in *chatura* pose in the case of the southern one and in *kunchita* or *parsvajanu* pose in the northern one. The figure shown ten-armed, has a *jatamukuta* and carries essentially *mudras* in the arms represented by the folded character of one or more of the fingers in their well known specific *yogic* types, the innermast hands are in *abhaya* and *dandahasta* symmetrically placed in the two fingers by reversing the *dandahasta* appropriately. There is a representation of a drummer placed at the foot and other attendants surrounding as different levels. The body of the figures carries a *graiveyaka hara*, *sutrayajnopavita*, *keyuras* and *kankanas*, *udara-bandha*, *kati-bandha*, and *kativastra*, the lower garment itself restricted to the upper thigh and looping across. There is nothing in these two figures to suggest that they are Jain figures, although equally well it can be claimed that there is nothing overwhelmingly of Brahmanical iconography in these. It is not known how these figures came to be carved in this stance, which, however, is so uncommon to Jain iconography, unless we are to take that the Chhota Kailasa originally was conceived as another Brahmaincal venture, but was later converted to Jain faith. There is indeed nothing inherently to contradict this possibility excepting the fact that in this eventuality the greater part of the architectural interior and exterior of the temple should have already been completed, when the important Jain enterprises proper had started at this end of Ellora hill, and thus would place Chhota Kailasa, slmost coeval with the Brahmanical group of the Rashtrakutas, especially, Kailasa in its final stages. This should mean that we may, however, place Chhota Kailasa under this reasoning around the end of the eighth century A.D., or soon thereafter. The only snag in the argument would be that there was no overwhelming reason why the locality for Chhota Kailasa of an initial Brahmanical faith should have been located towards this end of the Ellora hill, which as we see, is quite isolated from the Bramanical group, and was restricted only to the Jain enterprises. Be this as it may, it is feasible yet to read into the Chhota Kailasa a time-spread, stretching from the first quarter of the ninth century A.D., upto almost its third quarter.

The architectural features of the interior and of the exterior, however, are reasonably close to the Indra Sabha-Chaumukh which might, in essence, argue in favour of a relatively early place in the ninth century A.D., for the Chaumukh itself. The arrangement of the exterior wall in the four angles between the *vimana* and the three porches has a broad unity of composition best preserved in the south-west corner, although even here the plinth parts have been left unfinished, but from whatever left, it would seem that there was no intention of carving too high a plinth as in the case of Indra Sabha Chamukh, where it was a functional and physical necessity to highlight the shrine from the gateway and it would seem that the plinth mouldings should have been more than two feet in height, since the longest of the pilasters separating the wall sections are shown down to about 3 feet above the existing outer level and they are yet of unfinished character. These pilasters show at shaft part undifferentiated *kalasa*, *tadi*, *kumbha*, *padma*, the *padma* being sufficiently high, very thin *phalaka*, a *virakanda*, shown in *triratha* pattern, corresponding to intersecting corbels of the *taranga* type with a median *patra-lata* band, the outer limits of the corbel being much shorter. The wall sections have three such pilasters, the outermost represented as a cantoning pilaster and over their corbels run the *uttira*, *vajana* and a *valabhi*, the latter showing *bhutaganas*, as *malavahakas*, surmounted by another *vajana* and an almort vertical drooping *kapota*. It should be noted that this *kapota* does not in any way tend to over-shadow or partially shelter the *bhuta-valabhi* which is part of the vertical elevation well under the *kapota* in its visibility and might argue in an idiom which was more provisionally towards the close of the ninth century A.D., and later. The *kapota* itself is of a very subdued character without any under-cutting and it its proportions quite unlike the massive and expansive *kapota* of the porches. This *kapota* is embellished by *nasika kudu* and follows in its outline the projections and recessions of the wall. These projections are shown in the outer of the two sections at this south-west corner, while the recessed part carries in its main section a further pilastered *nasika panjara*, complete with all the elements of the pilaster, *uttira*, *kapota*, *prastara*, representing the *vyalavari*, *vedi*, *griva*, and *nasika kudu*, up to its *sakti-dhvaja* or *simha lalata* which is resting immediately under the sideward projecting corbel arms of the main pilasters of the wall. The *griva* is shown as supporting on the corners by rearing lions with tail lifted up and twisted. On the outer and the slightly projecting section of the wall the corner wall space towards its upper section, well relieved *Vidyadhara* couple in amorous postures, strongly recalling Kailasa figures, have been depicted. These corner pilasters of the cantoning type are in fact double pilasters. (*Plate XV*) Carried above the *kapota* is the *vyalavari* rafter composition directly resting on the *kapota*, unlike Indra-Sabha Chaumukh where it has been separated by an architrave in the form of a *kantha*, representing perhaps the clerestory: Here, the *vyalavari* composition recalls, however, the *vyalavari* part of the Chaumukh in showing a closely placed *lupa* and *jayanti* framework of small rafters whose ends, however, are shown here as quadrantally chamferred from all their four sides with a flat central section in the middle. (*Plate XVI*) It is interesting to note that we find similar rafter compositions in the early Chola or early Pandya temples of the ninth century A.D. and later in the Tamil country as at Tiruchchennampundi, Nemam, Sendalai, Kovilpatti etc., even stretching backwards in the cave phase of the Pandyas as at Pecchipparai cave. Over this close rafter frame work is found the broader and frontward projecting beams tied at the corners and in the *bhadra* part along the side ends owing to the *triratha* pattern. These have, however, not been finished in regular *vyalamukhas* or *makara* terminals but often as continuous lateral show of animals like lions and elephants. Over this upper frame work which follows the projection and the recession by carrying its main transverse beams in the recession, is found the *vedi* of the *kuta* and *sala* and *haras* of the parapeting of the roof. These, however, have not been found above the *griva* level. This *griva* is shown above the *vedi*, itself representing in the form of a *kantha* and *urdhvapadma*, and the *griva* itself shows paired pilasters in the centre.

Where completely preserved, as in the north-east corner of the *Sabha-mandapa* on the exterior the *kuta* and the *sala* are shown with their flat side faces and with the rolled edge, and their roll-edged central part of the *sala* is embellished by a *nasika* similar to the *nasikas* of the main *vimana*. But they have not been completed but only blocked out suitably for them. The *nasikas* of the *kutas* are comparatively less elaborate. From the interior the *kuta* itself is only 'L' shaped thin limb as seen from both the sides of the corner and attached to the *harantara*, which shows a pilastered *nasika* in the centre. Over the porched roof in order to highlight the existence of the *hara*, a *sala* is shown at a slightly higher level than on the side walls. The level of the *vyalavari* over the close rafter composition of this *sala* rising almost up to the top level of the *sala* of the side sections of the wall, flanking the porch, over which are respectively found the *vedi*, *griva* and the *sala* proper, the last of which, however, has not been preserved. On the porch itself over the *kapota* in so far as it could be seen the chamferred thin reaper ends having been shown, but only the *vyalavari* proper has been blocked out with its *bhadra* part and *makara* terminal parts. Over this occurs the *vedi* and the nrrow *griva* surmounted by rather subdued *kutas*, *salas* and *nasikas*. These *salas* are almost semi-circular in their side outline and even kept so apparently to bring out the *harantara* of the main *Sabha mandapa* roof parapet. Over this the roof of the porch is flat and is having its next upper step in the parapet of the main *mandapa*, whose roof within is also flat on its peripheral part, but shows three concentric rising steps leading to a central caping unit right in the centre of the *Sabha mandapa* roof, representing apparently a superstructural unit, if anything could be made out of its square basal *vyalavari*, *vedi* and *griva* and the partly preserved square-sectioned *nagara-shikara*. The members below its pilastered *griva* are badly worn-out. However, it is interesting that there are these three circular steps mentioned above. It is not known if these steps are their subdued and schematic analogues to a regular *Sabha mandapa* tower, as obtaining in the northern *prasada* types, since, however, the inner ceiling of the *Sabha mandapa* of Chhota Kailasa is of flat type consistent with the southern temple style, to which it belongs. This vestigeal *Sabha mandapa* tower characteristic is rather significant and might suggest the influence of the contemporary northern style temples impacting upon the southern style roofs in this region. As already mentioned, the wall section has primarily a straight *vinyasasutra* within the pilasters and reflected also only in the *kapota*. The main *vimana* appears to have been well harmonised with the *Sabha mandapa* by a deep recession in the *vyalavari* level over the *kapota* which also reflects the recession, though weakly, and this should be the portion represented by the *ardha mandapa*, which itself is narrow in the interior also. The main *vimana*, as in the case of Indra Sabha-Chaumukh, appears to be of *triratha* pattern with a well projecting *bhadra* and level *karna kutas*, the only difference being that the *bhadra* and the *karna* parts are almost equal, unlike those of the Chaumukh, where the former dominates the wall face. Although the *kapota* shows this continuous equidistant *triratha* pattern, the *vyalavari* itself tends to show a recession between the main *karna* part as signified by the two *nasikas* on the *kapota* and the main *bhadra* which is accommodated within these two recessions. This *vyalavari* closely follows the rafter composition as found in the *Sabha mandapa* roof and shows above the *vedi*, the *griva* with pilastered central *nasikas* and the corner blocks, apparently for figure sculptures of *ganas*, supporting *kutas* of which at least the one to the southeast shows the *kalasa* in tact up to top. In the *harantara* part over the *griva* the *kapota* parapet is continuous but for the *nasika* embellishment and on its *prati* on top the *pada* of the second floor is seen rising with double pilasters set well above in the corners and with the wall section at the angle very close to the Kailasa of the *kuta* of the ground *tala*, the rearing *vyala* bracket carved in the corner angle below the *kapota* of the *pada* of the second *tala* actually resting upon the *kalasa* top, as repeated on the next upper *tala* wall rising from the *kumbha* level of the pilasters. Between the paired pilasters there is a pilastered *makara-torana* within which are found seated divinities with or without attendants. These are a recurrent motif inside the pilaster compositions of the wall pillars etc., showing a pilastered *torana* within a pilaster, and would be useful as diagnostic trait of the stage. The projecting *bhadra* part has not at all been completed in the ground *tala* owing to the fact that the work could have been separated from the top and even the *nasikas* have been completed in a considerable degree only on the southern side up to the ground *tala*. These *nasikas* of the ground *tala* resting over the *vedi* of the main wall section which becomes their *griva* show a projecting wagon-roof with a mid-rib on the top and with the front face showing a barge-board of looped festoons rising to a *simhalalata* and *saktidhvaja* and looping at the base flanks into the foliage design emerging out of the *makara* heads. The *kudu* is not completed in the case of the ground *tala nasika*, nor is its *mukhapatti* typically cusped as in Indra Sabha. Over the back of this *sukanasa* is found a prominent *vedi* parapet (*Pl XVII*) with a *kantha* and an *urdhva padma* and a *prati*, over which the *sukanasa* of the next *tala* rises with the corners showing seated *yakshas* supporting the *nasika* with the centre having paired pilasters, with the recessions showing rosette design. This as also the *sukanasa* projection of the ground *tala* are in fact intersecting *nasika* design merged with the *sala* that would occur in the centre of the *hara* of each of these *talas*. This fact has been brought out only on the southern face of the eastern *sukanasa* or *mahanasika* of the second *tala* where the side face of the wall has been well-marked out with a cusped barge board, with a floriated basal motif emerged out of *makara* face and with *kudmala* like pendentives inside the multi-foil *kudu* representing the *dandika* pattern of structural support within. This would show that actually speaking these *mahanasikas* are the elaborations of the main *sala nasika* as sometimes shown to a lesser degree in temples of the 9-10th centuries in Tamil Nadu of the Ganga, Muttarayar, Pandya, Irukkuvel etc., with the only difference that the prominent central *nasikas* of the *sala* have been fully elaborated into regular frontward projecting *sukanasas* of equal dimensions as the *salas* and with the *mukhapatti* of an outstanding character. Thus, the consecutive *salas* of each of the *talas* carry a *vedi*, a *griva* and the *nasika*, while the main super-structural profile would carry a *vyalavari*, a *vedi*, a *griva* and the *hara* interposed by the *pada* of the *talas* in each case. (*Pl XVIII*) In this way the second *tala* in the main part shows comparatively less elaborate *vyalavari*, immediately over the *kapota* without the chamferred reaper ends, a comparatively low *vedi*, a *grihapindi* or a *prati* surmounted by the *griva* of the *kutas* and the *harantaras*. These *kutas* are smaller than the *kutas* of the ground *tala*. The third *pada* is also exactly similar to the lower ones in the pilastered division of the wall section excepting that the *bhadra* projection is also supported by a double pilaster combined with the inner pilaster of the wall and has figures within *torana* playing on musical instruments, both male and female within the pilasters. The *bhadra* part, where complete, as on the eastern side, shows over a *vedi* which, however, continues to be of the same dimensions as the *vedis* of the lower *talas*, the *griva* and the *mahanasika* projection, while the main *kapota* of the third *tala* carries above it a *vyalavari* composition showing, however, the chamferred ends as in the ground *tala prastara* and over it the regular *vyalavari* shown for the first time in complete form owing to the fact that work has started from the top, the animals represented in lateral postures in the form of lions, elephants etc. It is interesting to recall that in the Indra Sabha Chaumukh the representation of a realistic *vyalavari* with an animal pattern signified the topmost *tala* and here also it would seem so, since the *vyalavari* found on this top which is of a rugged and broken character would seem to signify the end of the *talacchanda* and only the *grihapindi*, *griva* and the *sikhara* would have rested on this. It is also interesting to observe here, that while the two upper *talas* are so organised as to show the *vyalavari* over the *kapota*, the basal storey has additional features of a schematic rafters representing the reapers and the *jayantis* running under the *vyalavari* and forming the basal frame work above the entire superstructure. This is a direct imitation of the wooden proto-type as in chariot manufacture and in temple models brick and wood and is not so employed at a later period, where this rafter course tends to get camouflaged as purely indistinctive ornamental motif.

It is difficult to surmise in the extent stage of spoliation of the top of the Chhota Kailasa as to the type of *sikhara* that would have rested upon it, but some points are worth noting here. Firstly, the lay-out of the superstructure, of the Chhota-Kailasa *vimana* seems to follow reasonably closely the lay-out of the Indra Sabha-Chaumukh. The *vyalavari* proper is shown at the topmost *tala* as shorter as well. Thus the *triratha* pattern of the *vimana* right from the base might have been more in harmony with the octagonal *sikhara* than with a square one. It is, however, to be seen that the roof of the *Sabha mandapa* would suggest that in favour of a square *sikhara* on it, this, of course, would not fore close an octagonal *sikhara* occurring on the main *vimana*, even if this represents only a *chaturasra sikhara* in its own *Sabha mandapa* roof, where it is an aberrant feature, seemingly patterned after *samvarana* roof scheme, capped by a large *kantha* and *kalasa* in the *rekha-nagara* style in upper India. On this basis, it might be taken as reasonable to hold that the *sikhara* of Chhota Kailasa would also be octagonal, but whatever little is left that would correspond to the *vedi* and the *grihapindi* level respectively over the *vyalavari* would have been cut along their angles to convert this square into an octagon. This, however, is a matter of detail, but since, normally the work having started from the top, this cutting of the corners would have been given early priority. It might, therefore, be possible to surmise that the retention of the square outline of the *vedi* and *grihapindi* might indeed imply *chaturasra sikhara*, but nothing much more than such a suggestion could be forwarded on the extant evidence, since even upon a square *vedi*, the *griva*, could be reduced to an octagon as a variant type.

The top of the *sikhara* had been badly damaged by a cleavage caused by a block lamination of the rock and has slid towards the front perhaps, as suggested by the slopy face of the lamination still extent on its top front. It is unfortunate that this should have happened, since otherwise, it would have preserved one of the most interesting superstructure of the *vimanas* of Rashtrakuta architecture known to us from Ellora. On the western side which is the main orientation, a regular *mahanasika* or *sukanasa* has been provided for the superstructure and this has been achieved by utilising the whole of the space available above the level of the *griva* of the ground *tala* and by raising a *vedi*, equivalent to the *kapota* or this *harantara* and carving a very large *nasika* on the front side backed up by a *pada* part, corresponding to the *pada* of the second *tala*, followed by the *kapota* of the second *tala* and surmounted by the next *nasika*, which, however, is of smaller dimensions that the large *nasikas* shown on the three cardinal directions of the *vimana*. Thus, it is, vero obvious that in the bettering of the eastern *sukanasa*, a deliberate desire to make it different from the other three and those constituted a regular *sukanasa* or barrel projection was seen. However, in making the rear side of this *sukanasa* a regular *pada* without *kapota* succeeded by a *nasika* at the next level in an equally deliberate purpose was implicit to make or provide for a chamber within to enshrine the divinities at this upper level of the roof. Thus the fronton or the *mukha patti* of the main *sukanasa* is alone outweighted towards the characteristic, while the interior is fashioned like a rim and not a barrel vault. The exterior of this *sukanasa mukhapatti* is flanked at its bottom level by two seated *yakshas* apparently the *nidhis—sankha* and *padma*—and the *kudu* of the *sukanasa* is itself made into a pilastered *makara-torana* with a Gajalakshmi on its *lalata*. Within this regular door frame a double *sankha* has been cut of copious dimensions giving access to the interior which itself comprises a narrow front part, a broader central and an interior end part, forming the sanctum proper. The two outer parts have not been signified by any architectural features of importance excepting that the middle one shows on its inner and outer angles corners pilasters surmounted by corbels. *uttira* and *vajana* all around and taken to lower level in a hub fashion in its median part owing apparently to the lack of regular mass on the roof at this place. The sanctum, however, is divided from the front parts by a wall pilaster described just above a double pilaster type and also by a free standing pillar adjacent to it snpporting Gajalakshmi on its *lalata*. While the pilaster is of plain oblong section, the free-standing pillar has on its *pitha* a lower *saduram*, an intermediary octagonal *kattu*, getting reduced to multifluted and part of the shaft, a circular *kalasa*, *tadi*, circular *kumbha*, circular *padma* and *phalaka*, upon which the *makara* flowing florial creepers are shown along the flanks and the floriated tails of the *makara* is drooping down the curving level of the *tadi*.

Within this in a rectangular chamber on a pedestal of *triratha* pattern with the continuous flanks running upto the wall is shown a seated *Jina* with head unfortunately lost, in front of a vertical balustraded seatback, supported by sideward facing reading *vyalas* with the architrave itself supporting a *makara torana* around the nimbus of the god. Two *chamara-dhari* attendants are seen standing just behind the balustrade with one of their legs alone visible outside, while above this the *tri-chhatravali* under foliage is hanging down like a pendentive, and originally would have been flanked by *ganas* playing on cymbals and *mridanga*, but only the instruments and hands alone being visible now. The attendants are rather squattish for their girth to show a clarity of presentation and ornamentation. The pedestal of the *Jina* is decorated by the full sideward facing lions with the twisted tails. Considering the depth up to which this has been carved, tt would look as if half the width of the main *vimana* proper would have been scooped out in the process. This upper shrine is the characteristic feature of the Jains, as found in structural temples as well, such as Meguti temple at Aihole, Chavundarayabasti at Sravanabelagola, and Melagudi at Hallur. The entirely secular character of these sculptures carved within the pilasters and in the *harantara* of the *padas* as also in the *nasika kudus* at successive levels in the *bhadra* parts is to be noted. These show musical figures playing on the harp, seated *mithunas* in postures of intimacy, and only occasionally *ganas* and thus (*Plate XXI*) indicate a transitional stage in Jain iconography with utter rigidity in ritual iconography has not been existed yet, although the interior multiplication of seated and standing *Jinas* in the *Sabha-mandapa* would suggest that the trend is already anticipated.

The corners of the *prakara* show large cubical chunks of regular leaf integral with the scarp of the hillock and with only bead alley for movement in a zigzag way provided around the main shrine. (*Pl. XXII*) While this would certainly be a natural arrangement in the process of excavating the main shrine for fixing of scaffolding etc., the fact remains that while a large part of the side walls corresponding to the *ardha mandapa*, the *maha mandapa* limits on the exterior show an almost sheer vertical removal of rock mass. The corners alone retain rock material to a regular cubical block and sufficient height, thus tending to support the presumption that these have been very likely intended for the diminutive shrine units on the corners, on the analogy of the *parivara* shrines of Kailasa and perhaps, better as on the analogy of the carved units of *panchayatana* monolithic unit found over the southern cliff roof of Kailasa the Great. It might even mean that they have a close temporal nearness in time and perhaps had identical *nagara-sikhara* in both the cases for the main *vimana* as well as for the corner diminutive units. On this reasoning it might even be possible to hold the central part of the cliff wall to the near of the *vimana* of the Chhota Kailasa and have been provided for a *sala gopuradvara* in high relief corresponding to the corner shrine units.

On either side of *prakara* cave temple excavations have been carved, apparently on the pattern of Indra Sabha, but not in so profuse and elaborate manner. Only the one to the south is finished, while on the northern side it had hardly been laid out. The southern cave temple annexe is approached by a flight of steps with *gudha mandapa*, balustrade, a parapet and seat-back with dwarf pillars and supporting *kapotas* doubly undercut and themselves supporting a *sala* on the parapet above, with *Jina* inside the *nasika-kudu* in the centre of the *sala* and with the *griva* of the *sala* decorated by rosette within pilasters and with *padma valabhi*. The *nasika kudu* itself is borne by two *ganas* at either end as are the *sala* themselves. There are three *kalasas* placed on the mid rib of the *sala*, while the end faces have been worked out like a regular *nasika* outside on the *harantara*. Continually conch-blowing *ganas* are placed above the smaller pilastered *nasikas*. The interior shows a chamber corresponding to the *maha mandapa*, whose walls are carved with standing and seated *Jinas* in multiple numbers on their back walls. Just outside free-standing pillars incompletely rendered show the figures of Matanga, and Siddhayika, Yaksha and Yakshi, of Vardhamana seated on the elephant and lion respectively as found else-where in a number of places in Indra Sabha. The free-standing pillar carries *makara torana* and gives access to the *ardha mandapa* which shows Parsvanatha and Gommata on the side walls and approached by door frame of *trisakha* variety and gives access to the shrine chamber, which itself is rectangular and shows a seated *Jina* on the backwall with *chauri-bearing* attendants. There is nothing special in the architectural lay-out of this temple to be considered as affiliated to the monolith that is being discussed.

The side porches of the *sabha mandapa* are almost similar to the front ones in their essential details, although not as imposing in their *dvarapala* and other features as the front ones.

The Chhota Kailasa thus combines the architectural elements, of Indra Sabha-Chaumukh as well as the Kailasa monolith, and further evolves a sculptural decor which would reinforce its being placed after these two creations.

THE JAINA 'CHAUMUKH' IN FRONT OF INDRA SABHA CAVE (XXXII)

Chaumukh (Cave No. XXXII) is a fine adaptation of the southern style for the *pancharatha* lay-out. (*Pl XXIII*) It has a high *adhisthana* (*Pl XXIV*) comprising *upana*, high, *jagati*, *padma*, a *kantha* a *tripatta kumuda*, another bolder *kantha*, *kapota*, and *prati*. The disposition of the pillars and pilasters of the shrine proper on it is just well within the *prati* on a minor *pitha*, itself comprising *padma* and *jagati*. This *pitha* has projecting porches on their cardinal directions and supported by a pair of free standing pillars on each side, while the main shrine is supported on four corner cantoning pilasters. While the pillars show an evolution similar to the Chalukya-Rashtrakuta idiom, the pilasters are nearer the unified southern idiom and are square-sectioned and the free standing pillars are circular sectioned in all their members (*Pl XXV*). Over the intersecting *potikas* of the pillar scheme run the *uttira* following the contours of the projections of the corbels followed by a *vajana* and a *kapota*, whose inner curvature shows the *kodungai* ribbings. The *kapota* itself is further supported by rearing *vyalas* with their feet placed upon the *kumbha* and had resting against the inside of the *kapota* in the case of the free-standing pillars and with their *padas* resting upon the *phalaka* and head resting against the corner *kodungai* of the *kapota* in the case of the cantoning pilasters. The superstructure shows *kantha* followed by *valabhi* and another *kapota*, forming the architrave above which rafter composition rises, with a series of basal frame work of projecting rafters followed by the end framework of projecting ends as well as transverse beams, the ends signified by *makara* terminals or other figure work. This is visible only on the *karnarathas*, (*Pl. XXVI*) while the central part is entirely depicting the bold *nasika* fronts in the form of a *sukanasa*, complete with the multi-foil barge board and *sakti dhvaja*. The way in which the *karnarathas* are shown as slightly projecting beyond the central or *bhadra* part and the way in which its own central part is showing a rectangular carved piece suggests that it was the *khandottara* type. Above this the *alingapatti* rises followed by the *griva* and the *hara* of *kutasikharas* in the corners, while the *harantara* shows *nasikas* surmounted upon pilastered recesses, one on each side, the *bhadra* part, however, though having the profile of a *salasikhara* is actually not surmounted by its own *kalasa* and all that, but by the mouldings which form the *adhisthana* of the next *sukanasa* and which rises vertically right up to the *mukha patti* and *simha lalata* above the *kapota* of the second *tala* up to the rafter composition, which forms the support to the *sikhara* (*Pl. XXVII*). Over this rafter composition on the second *tala*, the *grihapindi* head is placed and thereafter the central part is converted into an octagon, with its octagonal *kantha* octagonal *griva* and octagonal *griva* proper. The four corners of the *grihapindi* have *ganas* blowing conches, (*Pl. XXVIII*) a feature, which is met with some of the Rajasimha's structural temples in the Pallava country. The *sikhara*, however, is a little bulbous with the upper part flattened abruptly. The eight faces of the *sikhara* carry *nasika kudus* which are immediately surmounted upon a pair of free-standing pillars shown on the central part of each of the *griva* faces, complete in their pillar scheme. Unlike the *Chotta Kailasa*, the Chaumukh is a balanced composition which does not show a bolder *sukanasa* on the western direction, the reason apparently being that it is *sarvatobhadra*, and, therefore, has no specific orientation.

The monolithic structure in front of Indra Sabha (Cave XXXII) going by the name 'Chaumukh' owing to its ritual function in a Jain temple unit, has a well splayed outline in relation to the gate-way entrance leading into it and the further cave temples excavated on the rear. In addition, the two other monolithic features, namely, the now broken *manastambha* representing the pillar 'order' cognate to this excavation, and the elephant (*Plate XXIX*) in the round which are located on either side of the Chaumukh along its diagonal points in front court-yard between it and the gate. Also emphasised the unified character of these four units, namely, the Chaumukh the Gate-house, Flag-staff and the elephant. It is, thus obvious that notwithstanding the possibility of simultaneous excavations going on in the rear alongside the cutting of the monolith to the front a clear design in the mind of this monolithic model and the appertaining features mentioned above should have existed with the architects at the time the work was started, and the relationship of Chaumukh with what obtains in the rear should itself have been foreseen dependent on the physical character of the rock slope here; in other words, the Chaumukh for all practical purposes, was an independent entity by itself, although that it was to become an appurtenant feature to a larger complex to come in its rear and on the flanks was also a foregone conclusion. It is interesting to note that, well after Kailasa had been excavated, in the first half of the ninth century A.D., the excavators of the Chaumukh and the so-called Indra Sabha should have thought in terms of a monolithic creation only for the Chaumukh but not for the main unit behind it. The reason might be two-fold; firstly the importance already gained by the Chaumukh structure in Jain temples which called for a clear monolithic character for it in the courtyard of the temple. That this monolith should take the place of a perfect model of a *dvitala* temple of the Dravida style is itself of some consequence and pre-supposes that deep-rooted predilection of the Rashtrakuta architects in favour of the Dravida *vimana*, as adumbrated already at Kailasa and as further continued, somewhat later, in the Chhota Kailasa: the second reason would be that at the time when these excavations were going on, structural temples had been the norm so emphatically, and thus excavation of another large monolith to represent the main unit to the rear of the Chamukh was perhaps considered a shade too tedious and unnecessary. Simultaneously, the very excavation of the cave temple type here in storeyed form was essentially in multiple shrines of almost the same type, apparently intended to serve mainly as a balancing main backdrop for ritual iconography detailed, not to mention a proclivity to carry out painted scenes on the walls and ceilings for the Jain faith, complementary to the effort already manifest for the Brahmanical faith as in the Kailasa and Ganesh Lena groups. It is no less interesting thus that these logically led subsequently to an urge to carve out a monolithic temple exclusively of Jain character—as is found in the unfortunately incomplete Chhota Kailasa. Thus, the Chaumukh of the Indra Sabha is to be deemed as a significant predecessor to the Chhota Kailasa, and it is in this light as a monolithic that its creation was envisaged by the architects.

Physically speaking, the rock here taken up for excavation was much less expansive than at Kailasa and, therefore the side wings of the front court around Chaumukh are reasonably limited and are fully accommodated by the flag-staff and the elephant on either side. To that extent, they also highlight the *dvaragopura*, notwithstanding its unprepossessing size. Rigorous architectural simplicity, combined with sculptural richness, wherever called for, appears to have been the key note of the Indra Sabha complex and the sculptures are themselves of two categories, the larger ones mainly forming ritual images on the appropriate sections of the wall and in the sanctum, while the facade drapery, as it were of the main cave temple, tends to be on the side of diminutive carvings. As already mentioned, it is the monolithic carvings on the front part that would interest us directly here. It has been mentionad that the total width of the court in which the Chaumukh is set is reasonably restricted. As a matter of fact, it is approximately a square wherein the gate house is centrally located covering the middle one third with the bastion walls of equal proportions on either side. Originally there had been a desire to carve out the figures of *matanga* and *Siddhayika* on the extremities of the gate walls at the northern and southern ends, of which only the remnant of partially damaged Matanga figure seated on the elephant is vestigeally present, and would perhaps allow us to presume its counterparts at the northern end. The *gopuradvara* itself schematically represents a square chamber with height greater than its width and divided into three parts, namely, the front porch formed by the projecting cornice, the central vestibule borne on two pairs of pilasters to the front and to the rear and directly supporting the *sala gopura* above and the inner projection into the court-yard again sheltered under the cornice projection. No details of plinth or the under-cornice features are marked and the interior of the *gopuradvara* also is bare of any details, excepting for the door sill. The superstructure, however, is of considerable clarity, comprising as it does, a *vedi* above the cornice, constituted of a *kantha* and *pratikapota* above which the *griva* proper of the *sala* is shown in a rather squattish manner of about 9" demarcating, however, the *uttira* and the simple surved *valabhi* on it. It is itself of a plain character on the cornice but the *bhadra* projection presents a pilastered *pada* against the *griva* over which there is a parapeting in the form of a pilastered *kantha* occupying the level of the *uttira* and the *valabhi* of the side parts and immediately resting under the side face of the wall representing a *nasika* dormer. Here the seated *Jina* is found placed on a full-blown lotus resting over the pilastered kantha broadly whose uppermost moulding has a *kapota* and the sides of the *kudu* show a multifoil recess supported on the outer ends by a *dandika* framework taking the shape of *kudmalas* with the topmost part becoming a *trichhatravali* , appropriate to *Jina*. The crescentic barge board or *mukhapatti* around it is sharply cusped in its lower edges, but with *vyala* scroll work on the sides outside it, and crested by a *Simha-lalata*. The *mukhapatti* is also encased in a *puspakosa*. The *kantha* in the *griva* of the *sala* where fully preserved, shows at its angles seated *yaksha* and *Yakshi*, one each at the corners placed in such a way as to support the *sala* on their shoulders. The *sala* proper is well-flanged out and of a smooth curvature in its body and in the cardinal points of the centre to the front and on the rear it shows a projecting *sukanasa* comprised of a central pilastered *kuta-mandapa* encased within the *nasika* in the multifoils of the *kudu* and with the outer edges of the *nasika* borne by the figures seated with hands in *anjali* pose. The inner ends of the *sala* back carry *kodikkarukku* (*patralata*) designs engraved on them, while the crest shows two lions laterally placed one either end, seated with face and neck turned to the front and one of the forepaws (*inner*) raised and with the mouth gaping open. The centre of the crest of the *sala* would have carried a *kalasa* only set on it, as is preserved on the *sala* rock. The front side of the *gopuradvara* has a projecting plinth feature in the form apparently of a balustrade showing on *upana*, in its extant level the top of a *kapota* apparently holding the *kantha* under it, above which a straight face representing a parapet is shown. It is just possible that the upper part would have been carved with elephants. The projecting cornice forming the front porch of the *gopuradvara* is supported just within and in the centre of the corner pilasters at the corbel level by rampant lions with forepaws bent forward and with an outrider squatting under its body, with his hands supporting the lion.

The door frame within this has not been completed but is broadly of a *trisakha* variety, the central *sakha* being of a recessed kind.

From the interior of the court access to the Chamukh shrine proper has been given by a fight of six steps on the western and eastern sides, but not on the other two directions, thereby seemingly enforcing the *parikrama* of the image slab within.

The monolithic pillar shaft to the north of the Chamukh has a plinth which is similar to the Chaumukh in its being essentially of the *triratha* type, the corner portions much narrower than the *bhadra*. The mouldings show an *upana*, a *jagati*, with a better, a *padma*, a *kantha*, a fairly heavy *vritta-kumuda* followed by another *padma*, and a heavy *prati*, upon which the base of the shaft proper is continued again in *triratha* form, the *bhadra* showing prominent pilasters which themselves would have represented in miniature the monolithic shaft. Within the pilasters are shown individual figures one in each carrying objects like flower-buds with the lower stalk and showing, by the other arm the *vismayamudra*. The figures are themselves placed within a *makara-torana*, the *makara* having their mouths gaping upwards from which *toranas* rise, leading to the termsnal *makaras* facing each other at the top. Below the *makaras* the pilasters show the same details as the main pilasters of the *bhadra*, namely, square-sectioned shaft part, an undifferentiated *kalasa*, *tadi*, *kumbha*, *padma*, *phalaka* and *virakanda*. Above this the main monolithic shaft had been badly mutilated and had fallen in three parts, as preserved in the courtyard. This fall took place due to natural phenomena, about a century ago. The reconstruction of the full shaft from this base would show that a part (basal part) just described rose the main shaft represented by an octagonal *pattai* surmounted by a *padma bandha* and followed by a sixteen-sided shaft, circular *malasthana*, and telescoped *kalasa*, showing very weak ribs and of two equal parts, one fixed into the other, ending with the neck of the *kalasa*, drooping in and flaring out in a beaded rim above this, started the next piece with the ribbed *tadi* in double unit, multiple ribbed *kumbha* with equatorial *ratnapattai* band, a circular recession left plain, a flaring and ribbed *padma*, expanding as wide as *kumbha* and with the tips of the ribs worked out as the outturned petal ends. On this *padma* had rested a *phalaka* square in section decorated by a band showing a series of rosettes within squares. On the *phalaka* over a *padmapitha* formed of the *urdhvapadma* petals was carved the *padmasana* postured feet of the *yakshas*. The body and the remaining part of the shaft itself being found in the lowest disunited piece. The way this piece has detached itself from the lower in such a smooth horizontal plane would seem to suggest that it was never intended as a monolithic part, but at the same time the absence of any dowels or binding-mode like iron nail holes etc., would show it was just a natural lamination that has resulted in this cleavage.

These *Yakshas* are four in number in the four cardinal directions apparently and have a heavy body, pronounced belly, a well decorated *kirita*, *kundalas*, *graiveyakahara*, *yajnopavita udarabandha*, *keyuras* etc. Their locks of hair are spread on the sides in the form of luxuriant, but well coiffeured coils, and face particularly in its prominent and somewhat bulged eyes, heavy lips and pouting chin would seem to mark out typical Rashtrakuta character. Much of the four-arms of all the figures had been lost, although it would be possible to presume that they would have been resting on their elbows in *yogasana* pose, since they are not to be sound attached to any part of the body upto the belly. These four figures are themselves having their backs to a central shaft part which rising in the form of an upturned petal end on the tip of which would have existed the topmost piece, but had been again lost completely leaving only the irregular upper surface. It would be seen that the reconstructed totality of this pillar order, though divergent from the Kailasa monolithic pillars and apparently representing 'carry-forward' of the seemingly Chalukyan features like *kalasa, kumbha* etc., of ribbed and circular forms, is primarily to be taken in chronological succession to the time of Kailasa,and not very far removed from it. It is in this context that it has to be viewed and compared with the Chaumukh unit itself. It is also to be noted the elephant figure which occurred at Kailasa also occurs as a monolith here at the inner and of the front court, although the elephants had been a favourite motif under the Rashtrakutas and even shown in countless places in the Indra Sabha complex itself. The very manner of representation of the monolithic elephant in the front court, however, would keep this monolithic excavation as close to Kailasa, as one can make it. This elephant is placed with an elliptical pedestal which in itself is an interesting shape formed of a bold *upana,* a high *jagati,* a *padma* and a *prati* and shows the animal in a rather staid posture of tranquility, with all the four legs placed almost vertically, of which fore-legs have been separated in the rock, but the hind legs had been carved out as one block with the intervening part thinned out, apparently in an incomplete character. A perfect balance in its body dimensions and pleasing homogeny and realism in its head has been considerably highlighted by the inturned proboscis drooping right down to the floor and holding in its terminal a floral foliage. It would seem that the north side flanks of the court had been cut in, in the process of accommodating the rear part of the elephant. While the elephant had been almost finished from base to top, the flanking walls shows mere rock scoops. This would tend to suggest that the Chaumukh with *manastambha* and the elephant forms a primary focus of attention and the rear cave temple of the side flanks followed in gradual stages.

The Chaumukh itself had been raised to appropriate height in its plinth in order to give not merely an elegance proportionate to its wall and superstructure, but also to make full utilisation of the rock mass available upto the natural gradient of it at the top. At the same time, the character of the plinth mouldings, the way in which the *jagati* is considerably tall and plain in common well with the *jagati* of the elephant and the basal part of the *manastambha* and this again would suggest the unity of conception and execution of these three.

The plinth of the Chaumukh is as mentioned of *triratha* character, with the *bhadra* part very broad and was intended to accommodate the *sarvatobhadra* form of the main shrine above, with four doors with porched front projections on the four cardinal directions, and with the *kapota* alone carrying the *triratha* outline. Above the plinth the structure thus has a very compact shape and had been arranged in such a way that its plinth, as tall as its wall and superstructure, is approximately double its height in two *talas*. The plinth mouldings above the high *jagati* show a narrow *padma*, a narrow *kantha*, with a *kampa* above and below, a tripatta *kumuda* with *pattais* rather feeble and subdued, followed by more prominent *kantha*, whose recesses show pilastered separations carrying rosettes and the *uttira* and *valabhi* members above surmounted by a rather drooping *kapota* with flat underside and with *nasikas* embellishing its front faces. Over the *kapota* is a *prati*. It is on this *prati* that the shrine chamber proper is resting. The bottom most part of the shrine chamber proper, forming its, base, as it were, is represented by a *padma* and a high *prati*, providing for projections wherever the freestanding front porch pillars of the *sarvatobhadra* shrine are to occur and the pillars themselves are placed in such a way that their lower pedestal corners are projecting out of the corners of the basal mouldings. These immediately recall to our mind the device characteristically depicted in Lankesvara Cave in the outer pillars of the inner *maha mandapa* and would seem to form part of a community of wood-architectural ideas drawn by the Rashtrakuta craftsmen. The pillars again have their own *Oma* or *pitha* represented by *upana*, *padma*, a *vritta kumuda*, and a superimposed narrower *padma* over which the shaft part rises and this shaft has a square section, but oblong lower *saduram*, a brief octagonal *kattu* extending for a longer stretch into a multi-faceted central part and mainly standing for the *malasthana* and *padma-bandha* over which telescoped rises the small narrower and smooth circular-sectioned plain *kalasa*, *tadi*, *kumbha*, *padma*, and an octagonal *phalaka*, followed by a recession and intersecting corbels of simple curved with a median plain band with their own *vajanas* above. These corbels support the *uttira* which themselves are of the intersecting type, the frontward projections supporting the *karna* parts under their *kodungai* beyond which the *kapota* or the main cornice droops out. The *kodungai* has a transverse rafter resting partly on the *uttira* tied by frontward ribs and fixed at the joinery by nails represented by *kudmalas*. These *kodungai* rafters are additionally supported by bracket figures of rearing lions, springing from the *kumbha* and carved back to back with the *padma*, *phalaka* and *potika*. The free-standing pillars leaving a little walking space between the main shrine and the outer plinth have been added by the simple pilastered character of the main shrine, the corner pilasters being of the cantoning type, while the central pilasters are of a very plain simple type. The corner pilasters show features akin to the other free-standing pillars only from the *kalasa* level with the lower part of the shaft severely plain and even above the prevailing cross-section is square instead of circular as in the free-standing pillars. This divergence is of significance since the cantoning pilasters form part of the square shrine and are consistently square in outline, and they elaborate all the details up to the *padma*, *phalaka*, *virakanda*, *potika*, *vajana* and *uttira* and its own *vajana* of which the members above the *phalaka* are recessed and almost applied against the wall, whereas the lower members are projecting farther. This has been intended to relieve the additional rearing lions that have been placed in these corner pilasters at the very corner of the cornice supporting the *kodungai* rafters under their neck and diagonally springing out from the *phalaka*. Within the free-standing pillars the ceiling above the *uttira* is left plain in the shape of an *ardha mandapa*.

Inside the chamber the side walls are kept fairly plain only the door frames showing a simple recession set within the thickness of the walls proper. The ceiling carries only the *valabhi*, an element all around with the central part showing a *vitana* of full-blown lotus, with the *padmakesara* in the centre, immediately under which is the monolithic carving of the main object of worship in Chaumukh, namely the four important Tirthankaras, Mahavira, Adinatha, Vrishabhanatha, and Neminatha. They are all shown on low pedestal formed by an *upana*, and a high *jagati*, and an upper pedestal of a similar character, but with broad *bhadra* projections in the form of a *vedi* in which laterally placed lions with forepaws raised and tails twisted are carved with the wall placed along its edges in the centre within the pilasters. This is consistent with the Jain art motif common under the pedestal. The upper moulding of the pedestal is a *kapota* in the *bhadra* part and on this under a simple *padma pitha* are shown the Jina figures in *padmasana* which the two arms on their laps, palm on palm and with pilastered framework against their back carrying a *makara torana* architrave, two *Yaksha* attendants and *chauri*-bearers, with a circular nimbus behind their heads, *tricchatravali* above it and two more *gana* attendants hovering in the air, in the corners, one of them with a garland while the other is blowing a conch. In other places they are playing on drums etc. The niche which forms the four faces of this central image unit is itself supported on two plain lateral pilasters and a *kapota* on top, forming the beam in the centre of which a *nasika* has been worked out. Above this, apparently the superstructure should have ended in the form of a *kuta shikhara* but had unfortunately been damaged and shows only corrugated broken upper surface.

The superstructure of the Chamukh is laid upon its substantial and prominent cornice outline whose surface has been perfectly smoothened out with sharp corner edges fastened by *konapattai* bands with the central part also picked out in similar foliage ornamentation. Above this a pattern has been worked out which broadly speaking harmonises two elements, namely, the storyed superstructure rising in two *talas* ending in a *vedi*, *griva* and *sikhara*, and a projecting *sukanasa* found on all the four cardinal directions and one set each for each of the *talas*. In order that the full dimensions and modulations of the *sukanasa* could be well brought out, its own basal mouldings have been restricted to the minimum with the result that they form their own scheme of rising tiers up to the topmost *vyalavari*. The main body of the superstructure, however, follows a more well-proportionate scheme, namely, that of a fairly bold *kantha* above, the *kapota* itself comprising a *prati*, a *kantha* part, an *uttira* a *valabhi* and an overlooking *kapota* together forbing the clerestory of the interior elevation of the structure. On this smaller kapota is placed the intersecting rafter course which itself is of an interesting pattern, namely, that it forms a series of *lupas* and *jayantis* of smaller rafters at close range forming the bedding plans above which the more substantial transverse rafters and projecting beam ends occur. These beam ends are represented in the form either of rosettes pattern or with figure work in the centre *mithunas*, while the lateral parts are carved with floral designs. These are shown one on each side of the *sukanasa* . The *sukanasa* part itself is shown as by a transverse rafter and apparently its own structure in the form of an apparel vault is represented by the *dandika* pattern shown on this *kudu*. The terminals of the rafter projections show *makaras*, both at the *bhadra* terminals as well as the *karna* terminals. These are fastened by another broad frame work rafters tied only at the corners over which on a *vedi* with a *triratha* pattern of *kantha*, *prati-kapota* and a *prati*, the *griva* and the *kutasikhara* of the *kuta* unit occur. The *harantara* which is shown well recessed in order to bring out the prominence of the *kuta* elements shows *nasikas* with lotus bud within and supported on the paired pilasters, complete with the *uttira* beam on them. Such pilastered *nasikas* occur on the faces of the *kutas* also. The *kutas* have almost vertical drooping profile and are surmounted by *padma* and the *kalasa*, the *kalasa* missing now. As far as the *sukanasas* are concerned in the first *tala* of the superstructure, they have a basal pedestal comprising a *kantha*, *prati-kapota* and *prati*, above which is a narrow *griva* with seated *yakshas* with leg flexed inwards and backwards and with arms in different postures bearing on their shoulders, the corners of the floral ornamentation of the flanks of the *nasikas*, while the *nasika kudu* proper is borne upon two free-standing diminutive pillars shown in their various elements in a schematic way upto the *kapota*, over which the *kudu* shows standing *Jina* within a multi-foiled *dandika* arrangement, *dandikas* turned into *kudmalas*. Around these the barge board is of sharply crescentic and cusped lower part and with a prominent and tall *simha-lalata* and shovel finial. The apparel body, *sukanasa* if projecting from the level of the clerestory part of the main body of the superstructure and is fixed in its position upto the level of the *harantara* by a *bhadra* projection of rafter ends with upturned and curved terminals supporting the transverse joists and tied in the corners by schematic *makara* faces. On these, the rafter course by pilastered *kantha*, and a *prati-kapota* itself resting upon the elements of *uttira*, *valabhi* above the *kantha*, the *griva* of the *sukanasa* of the upper *tala* is placed. This also has the same features as those of the lower *sukanasa* in its *griva* and in its *nasika* exception that its own *nasika* proper is much more subdued than the lower one, both in its height as well as in its frontal projection.

The *pada* of the second *tala* proper is represented by highly abbreviated cantoning pilasters, mainly showing above the *kapota* of the *harantara*, the *tadi*, *kumbha*, *padma*, *phalaka* and interesting corbels, the shaft part, apparently having been harmonised from within, as in the wood-architectural pattern and murged at the corners of the structure. Additional pilasters of the same type occur across the close of the corners and these pilasters are double-pilasters forming equal parts of the well as the *sukanasa* of the *bhadra* projection here. Over the corbels of these, the pilasters are intersecting *uttiras* with their front projection and transverse joists followed by their *vajanas* and plain curved *valabhi* and the drooping *kapota* of the second *tala*. This *kapota* has been provided with *konapattai* in the corners, but has been incompletely finished and shows the characteristic *vyalavari* rafter course, above it, and is varied from rafter course of the first *tala*, in depicting laterally placed lions and elephants and in showing *makara* terminals, well relieved and finished, both in the corner and in the *bhadra* parts. Over the rafter course the actual *grihapindi* slab occurs, above which the square is reduced to an octagon with multiple pilasters, the corner pilasters along with *nasikas* of the octagon showing a double spread and followed by a *prati-kapota* or *urdhva padma* the characteristic upper part of the *vedi*. Above this, there is a more recessed octagonal moulding, which supports the octagonal *griva* and the *sikhara* through a series of free-standing miniature pillared porched *nasikas* on each of the faces of the octagon. The pillars are almost similar to the pillars of the ground floor in their broad character and the *griva* showing all the details of the wall, the *uttria* and the *valabhi*. The *sikhara* proper is almost vertically drooping with a very feeble principal flange and with the angles of the facets fastened by *konapattai* floral decoration. The top of the *sikhara* has been almost flattened out with a very narraw central coarsed part to accommodate the *kalasa*, which is missing. On the corners of the *grihapindi* slabs above the vyalavari corresponding to the corners of the *griva* of the *sukanasa*, conch-blowing *ganas* have been placed. These *ganas* somewhat recall similar ones to be found in the Pallava structural temples at the time of Rajasimha and later, but are found here mainly in the place of the usual bulls or *garuda* of the Brahmanical temples, since in the present case it is a Jain monument.

The character of the whole superstructure is somewhat different from that of the Kailasa monolith, primarily owing to the fact that we are dealing here with four *sukanasas* in view of the *sarvatobhadra* form of the shrine below and in view of the *salas* having been completely replaced by the *sukanasas*. Even so, the variety of patterning of the *sukanasa* series and the main shrine superstructure, the differentiation of the *vyalavari* of the two *talas*, representation of the clerestory element immediately above the main cornice, all these are a stage somewhat more followed than that of Kailasa and partly represented already a triple-storeyed structure of the south of Kailasa. The *sukanasas*-themselves are of the more typical northern form of Chalukyan style and are well harmonised on that section with what is typical and southern model. The fact that the structure had been raised only to two *talas*, in spite of the distance of time between Kailasa and Chaumukh, while the Kailasa itself has been of a *tritala* structure, would show that a *dvitala* model had been preferred in general whether for a structural temple or a monolith as has been corroborated by the Chhota Kailasa itself and the many structural examples of this period.

The individual features which would be ascribable to the earlier stage of Rashtrakuta efforts, between the time of Dantidurga and up to the time of Indra are too many to be ignored, and thus it would be appropriate to date Chaumukh as essentially pertaining to the latter half of the 9th century A.D., while the main cave temple complex to its rear could have been accomplished in the century that followed in its own slow pace inter-related to structural activities going on elsewhere. It is necessary, however, to stipulate here that the whole effort should have been well confined within the age of Rashtrakuta supremacy, and thus by no means, later than the mid tenth century A.D., in its final stages. The Chaumukh itself, however, as already stated, should have closely followed the Kailasa complex and, in its turn, should have been closely followed by Chhota Kailasa.

THE 'KAILASA' MONOLITHIC AND ROCK CUT COMPLEX

Facade

The front aspect of Kailasa cave indicates an essential *pancharatha* lay-out in which a central entrance is the *bhadra* part showing on the pilasters Ganga and Yamuna. These pilasters are raised over a parapet, and entrance is thus in the form of an *agra mandapa*. Immediately outside this porch are found a pair of *nagas* and *naginis* of full stature more or less serving the purpose of *dvarapalas*. These *naga-nagini* sculptures are continued on the adjacent right angular panels without a corner pilaster immediately to the north and south of the entrance, whereas from this stage onwards the wall space is divided into pilastered niche spaces of which the inner corner offset has two pilasters and the outermost *karna* part has four pilasters dividing the wall into three spaces. These wall spaces contain figures of *dikpalas* (to which is included the figure of Karttikeya) and run as follows from north to south.

Karttikeya, Agni and Vayu are in the *karna* part, Varuna in the *pratiratha* to the north and Indra in the *prati-ratha* further, continued by Yama and a very badly damaged and worn out (*Pl. XXX-XXXI*) wall section probably intended to carry *Nirriti* and Kubera on the southern side. While the northern section shows the sculptures mainly in the upper part, the southern section shows them almost from top to bottom indicating that the flanks had been carved in two stages. The northern section is completely present from basement to the *kapota* and the *vyalavari*, whereas the southern section is in a badly preserved condition in its upper members. The complete northern section shows an elephant frieze immediately below the *pattika* of the plinth with a *prati* above upon which the wall rises, the pilasters showing plain square-sectioned shaft with an undifferentiated *kalasa* followed by *tadi*,, square-sectioned flattish *kumbha*, *padma*, and *phlalaka* with a very narrow space between it and the laterally projecting corbel arms which are of simple curved character with undecorated *vajanas* above them surmounted by very heavy *uttira* and *valabhi* some which carries the *atlantis* motifs of *malavahakas*, over which the narrow projecting and vertically drooping heavy *kapota* rests. On the *kapota* in the lateral parts is again an elephant frieze standing in the place of an *alingapatti* above which in the *karna* and *pratiratha* parts the second *tala* part starts straight away in the form of pilastered wall spaces surmounted by the next series of *valabhi*, *kapota* etc., while the central *bhadra* entrance part alone manages to show over its main *kapota* (unfinished) a *vyalavari* and a seat-back *kakshasana* being the top member of the parapet whose uppermost course is *vyalavari* and thus suggesting a projecting *mattavarana*. The rest of the *agra mandapa*, however, has been left incompletely excavated in so far its ceiling and superstructure are concerned.

Beyond this *pancharatha* lay out of the axial temple unit to the south and north, is a recessed panel after which the side walls come forward well beyond the limit of the entrance porch itself and turn further north and south apparently intended to enclose the subordinate shrines within them. These also have been divided into wall spaces by pilasters and carry tall statured figures from bottom to top of which an *urdhvatandava* Siva and a Lingodbhava (wherein the lenticular recess of the *linga* is shown thrice in the *linga* shaft) on the northern side, and the figure of *varaha* and Trivikrama and Narasimha on the southern side would need special mention. This side section did not rise above the limit of the *prastara* of the first *tala*, which itself comprises human frieze surmounted by a series of adjacently placed *nasika kudus* with a trefoil barge board within, forming the crenellated battlements of the temple *prakara*. The *dandika* point of the *kudu* carries a *ghanta* or bell, as an ornamental feature.

Before we enter the *agra mandapa*, the detailed carving forming part of the outer wallings beyond the main central block might as well be considered. Starting from the northern end the first niche is practically incomplete, the second shows Siva in *urdhva-tandava*, apparently eight-armed of which not much of the details are present (*Pl.XXXII*) excepting for one of the left arms holding the fire bowl. It is obvious that in its original set it must have been the most arresting and even parts of the head and some hands perfectly smooth and in finish. The head is thrown back somewhat and wears a heavy *jatamukuta* with well prepared curls of hair dangling behind and one of the top left hands is graciously opening out a lock of hair by two of the fingers as in the Gangadhara pose.

while another of the left hands is raised high towards the corner and is supporting something above as in the *Gajantaka*. In fact that it is a combination of many iconic forms like Gangadhara, Gajantaka and *Urdhva-tandava* is further strengthened by one of the lowest left hands holding the tail of the elephant's skin apparently. The face is lit by a beatific smile, notwithstanding the badly damaged nose pnd low cheek. The most interesting part of the stance, however, is how one of the upper right hands is holding in a gingerly fashion the heel of the lifted up left leg apparently in order to keep the foot absolutely vertically. There is, thus a considerable innovation in the figure as not usually seen elsewhere.

The next is the figure of standing Brahma, three-headed with the heads shown not in a side spread but in three cardinal directions, continuous of one another. His left hand is on the *kati-vastra*, while his right hand has not yet been finished. In fact, part of the lower body of this figure has not been finished but only blocked out. The figure is in *Samabhanga* and among its ornamentation the broad *udarabandha* and the *yajnopavita* might be mentioned running in *nivita* fashion. The *jatamakuta* is somewhat tapering. There are two *vidyadharas* hovering in the air, in the upper corners; at the turning of this wall here, beyond Brahma panel, the first of the three figures facing south is that of Lingodbhava which is unique in many respects, (*Pl. XXXIII*). Firstly, it shows the *linga* itself as a very tall cylinder. Climbing half the way from base to top, the top just merging with the *uttira* above. This *linga* shaft has been divided into three parts deliberately, each part having oral or lenticular slit opening and showing an emergent standing figure within in simple form, Correspondingly three stages of the attendant figure work of Brahma and Visnu respectively are also shown, the lowest being the standing forms of these two in *anjali* pose on either side in a reasonably life size, followed by a figure in flight of the same gods, four-armed and capped by one more representation each of these two gods at the very top level. It is possible that this three-fold division was intended to cover *prithvi*, *akasa* and *antariksha*, across which the pillar like shaft of fire stood from end to end. It is such a concept that perhaps was responsible even for the creation of special architectural compositions and as we find in the Eastern Chalukyan region *pancharamas* like Amararama, Draksharama, Bhimarama, Chebrolu and Palakollu; wherein the main shrine is raised in two storey high with the *linga* shaft itself rising through both the storeys and essentially worshipped in the upper storey.

The next figure is in *samabhanga*, four-armed with *jatamukuta* of the tapering type, two lower arms in *kati* and *abhaya*, perhaps, two upper arms holding *ankusa* in the right arm and locks of hair by the pataka-mudra in the left. The rear part behind the head is practically gone but from what could be made out of the fact the tresses of hair spread on either side radially combine with the figure of Ganga shown just to the right of the crown and the *pataka-hasta* on the left upper hand might show that this is in fact a Gangadhara figure as a standing figure adjacent to the left at the bottom. The figure is in *samabhanga*. The *yajnopavita* is rising over the right elbow at the crook and is disappearing behind. The continuation of the Chalukyan mode the the presence of the head of the bull to the proper right of the god as cut out of the pilaster would suggest that it is Vrishabantika Siva.

The corner panel was apparently intended, despite its highly mutilated character, now to represent Ardhanari, as could be shown by the *abhanga* and utterly feminine outline of the left side of the body, including the tilt of the head towards the left. Although much of the tips of hands and almost whole of the head and the legs are lost, the squared up shoulder of Siva and the smoothly curved shoulder and breasts of Uma and the *lola-hasta* resting partially on the well formed hips at least remain to tell the story.

The next panel in the recess and the turning of the wall now facing west is completely gone, and similarly the further turning of the wall with a very narrow niche section facing north is also practically eroded, although it would seem that it was the representation of a dvarapala.

The main figure already mentioned as representing the *dikpalas*, Karttikeya and others would seem to have their direction of movement towards the temple as suggested by the motion of the animals. No specific detail of these might be necessary, but it may be stated that Karttikeya is having *Sakti* and *Kukkuta* in his two hands and is shown with only one head, and without *chhannavira* as is usually shown in later sculptures.

Of the corresponding outer niches on the *prakara* walls of the southern side, first is that of Bhuvaraha, facing to his proper right, eight-armed, a part of the upper most right arm where Bhudevi would be seated, unfortunately broken. But the way in which the crowned head is tilted completely backwards and the manner of the *yajnopavita* would show that they are in close continuity of Chalukyan tradition.

The next at the turning of the wall now facing north would be that of Gajendra-varada Visnu, seated on Garuda, four-armed, the two lower arms in *kati*: the left upper arm apparently is holding *sankha* and is badly destroyed and the right upper arm is holding aloft the *chakra* in *prayoga* aspect, ready for discharge.

The next panel is that of Trivikrama with the raised leg reaching above the left shoulder, with his eight arms flailing in the air with appropriate weapons held, but most of them badly damaged, with Mahabali holding the *kundika* for solemnizing his promise shown to the proper left below.

The last corner figure is that of Siva in the ecstacy of dance, (*Pl. XXXIV*) apparently in *lalita* mode, not unlike that shown in Lankesvara cave, with the left hands becoming *danda-hasta* and one of the top right hands holding the *damaru*, much of his hands, face and legs are lost.

Turning round the corner the next panel facing west is that of Hiranya being destroyed by Nrisimha, (*Pl. XXXV*) who has kept the demon on his lap and is tearing the entrails. The only graphic and arresting head of Nrisimha is fairly well preserved, while the rest of his arms and Hiranya's own figure are badly damaged excepting for the *simha-keyuras* carved in the left upper arms of Nrisimha.

The next panel is that of dancing Siva gyrating in *pristhasvastika* form during the dance, with the head turned almost 180° around and the hands properly twisted around. The head is thrown back. The lower part of the sculpture appears to have been left unfinished, but the witnesses to his stance have been somewhat completed, as for example, Parvati is seated to his proper right in *ardhaparyankasana* and fully taking in the imposing spectacle.

The next panel had only been partially worked out and with that we come to the end of the wall section. This side section did not rise above the limit of the *prastara* of the first *tala*, which itself comprises human frieze surmounted by a series of adjacently placed *nasika kudus* with a trefoil barge board within, forming the crenallated battlements of the temple *prakara*.

The Dvara Mandapa

The *dvaramandapa* shows front pilaster, upon which on the front face are carried Ganga and *Yamuna* with an inner corner pilaster space within which is carved in the form of a small niche of half the total dimensions, carrying the figures of two sages seated in *ardhaparyankasana* on a low stool, two-handed, left hand carrying *pustaka* and the other hand raised and flexed, apparently in a posture of exposition *vyakhyamudra*, taking into consideration the fact that the shoulder behind is well finished. They are otherwise identical in the *jata* type dress and appearance and might be representing the schools of silpa like *Visvakarma* and *Maya* or by the same token might represent the *Brihaspatis* of the *Devas* and the *danava* guru *usana*. The pilasters above the *kumbha* immediately show corbel arms followed by the *uttira* and its *vajana*, which is not, however, found on the eastern side above the inner door frame. Immediately beyond the main *uttira* north-south, the *kapota* is internally representing a quadrantal mould instead of a curvature. The door frame itself is plain with only an abbreviated *trisakha* overdoor, the sides forming the pilaster screen, the lower part of which is again out into a pair of slit niches carrying *Ganga* and *Yamuna*.

Immediately within the *agra mandapa* porch the central passage is flanked by two jambs one on either side of two units each having an inner chamber, and has an outer corridor with a facade of two free standing pillars and two pilasters on each side. The raised parapet is borne on *gajamundas*, resting immediately under the pillars, and pilasters. On the ceiling there are four cross-beams resting upon their own *potikas* and *vajanas* which in their turn are resting under the *uttira* and the double *vajana* of the main *tala* below this has enabled the upper *tala* to be reared upon this *mandapa* actually in line with the orientation of the main shrine-complex of Kailasa. The pillars of the side-chamber facade have a *bhadra pitha* formed by an *upana*, *padma*, *kantha* and *tripattakumuda* above which followed by another *adhopadma*, the lowest part of the shaft rises which has been left plain above which the main shaft has an *urdhvapadmadala* with a corner scroll work and central *patralata* band ending up at the *mandi* level which has been left plain but has a slight offset forward. Above this are shown the multi-fluted terminals of the shaft followed by a *padma bandha* and succeeded by the typical *ghatapallava* surmounted by *ardhapadma* medallions on the four sides and a top band of a series of rosettes surrounded by bead work. It is upon these that the double corbel arms rest. The inner door frame of this *agra mandapa* is of the same dimensions as the outer door frame and has a single bold offset. The main screen pilasters either side are carved with two *nidhis* held by Kubera, the one to the right holding the *sankha nidhi* and the left holding *padma nidhi*; the figure of Kubera himself in each case is seated upon a *pitha* borne upon four rearing lions with the front paws raised of which only two are shown in perspective. Above Kubera are shown flying *Vidyadhara* couples.

The inner porch of the *agra mandapa* made into a corridor or *prakara* comprises nearly two parapets upon which are resting a major corner pilaster of the cantoning pilaster type and an inner pilaster within it. On the inner face of the screen wall flanking the door-opening and facing east are shown two *dvarapalas* cut into the rectangular niches four-armed with one of the legs placed upon the mace and one of the hands resting upon their grip ends. The broad wall space on either side has been fully covered by two panels depicting Ganesa and Mahishamardini Durga. These panels are supported in the case of Durga upon very detailed *adhisthana*, *pada* and *prastara* ending up in a *sala-sikhara*, while in the case of Ganesa no *adhisthana* is shown excepting an *urdhvapadma* dala course upon which the main pilastered niche composition from pillar to *sikhara* is shown as in the other, but is slightly more stunted, in the case of the niche space proper, than the other. The Durga side shows upon a plain high *upapitha*-like course, *upana*, *padma*, *kantha*, with a *kampa* on either side and divided into a series of pilasters, a *knmuda* with a median scroll work band followed by another *kantha*, which in the recess between the pilasters shows rosette knobs actually standing for nail heads, followed by *uttira*, *vajana*, and vertical *kapota* decorated with a series of *nasika kudus* and *konapattais*, which represent the corner fastening plates of metals. Upon them at the *potika* level rests a plain *uttira* followed by its *vajana* and the *kapota*. On the *kapota* rises the rafter frame work composition of the *prastara* in *triratha* lay-out with the *bhadra* part comprising a series of *bharaputras* supporting the *kampa* above and standing for the forward projecting rafter ends, while the transverse ends are shown both in the *bhadra* parts as well as in the *karna* parts with *makara* terminals. In the case of the *karna* part, the forward projecting rafter ends which ties the frame work is also shown as a *makara*. Above this comes the *kantha* again divided into pilasters followed by a *prati-kapota* course over which the *griva* of the whole composition is indicated, with the *bhadra* stretch characterised by a niche frame work flanked by rearing *vyalas*. An alongated *sala sikhara* comes above this with the central *nasika* complete with its *simha lalata* and with two *kalasas* one on either side of the centre. The sala *sikhara* is borne at the two extremities by the *Vidyadharas*. There are similarly two *Vidyadharas* shown at the level of the *uttiras* of the first *tala* and there are two armed warriors shown further below standing at the base level of the pillars immediately outside the pilasters.

The opposite panel of Ganesa differs mainly in *bharaputras* having been replaced by *vyalamukhas* in the *karna* parts in the *griva* being higher than Durga side and in a *hamsavalabhi* shown above the griva and the *nasika kudu* itself of the *sala sikhara* showing an inner pilaster in a side barge in *kudu* proper and there being three *kalasas* on the crest of the *sala* roof in addition there are *vidyadhara* couples supporting *sala sikhara* and at the lowest level there are two *chamara-dharinis* in the place of armed warriors of the Mahishamardini panel. The Ganesa figure is rather damaged in his two lower arms, but the upper arms carry *parasu*, and *padma*, with the left leg flexed vertically and the right leg flexed laterally under the belly. Durga is shown as standing upon the *Mahisha* which is represented both with the animal head as well as the human body emerging out of the neck in addition to the other figures shown one on each side fighting with Durga. It is just possible that this is a synoptic version, all the three *asura* figures perhaps being one and the same. The figure is damaged in respect of its *ayudhas* but shows *sula* embedded on the neck of the human form of the demon. On the outer face of the inner pilasters of this proch are shown *dvarapalas* facing inwards with one of the legs and hands either resting on the *gada* or taken around it. In the case of the proper left side *dvarapala* his upper right hand shows *pataka* indicating that it was holding something. The *kundalas* are both *patra* and *nakra kundalas*, and the figures have the *trinetra* also. They are four armed *dvarapalas*. They are succeeded by a similar pair of *dvarapalas* on the inner face of the *prakara* passage wall, whose main central panel shows Gajalakshmi. These (*Pl. XXXVI*) *dvarapalas* have the same posture more or less, excepting that one of them is wearing a grin. The Gajalakshmi panel is rendered (*Pl. XXXVII*) differently than at Dasavatara cave, the elephants being disposed of in the lower zones of the panel in two pairs, one above the other in each case. While the upper ones are shown as discharging water simultaneously on the head of *Shri*, the lower ones are just filling the pots from the lotus tank shown below in a highly conventionalised fashion by crowded series of half and full blown lotuses and lotus leaves. Above the upper elephants are shown two pairs of *Vidyadharas* one on each side in addition to a male and female attendants, the female attendant playing on a lyre and the male attendant in *vismaya-hasta*. They are apparently celestial figures, perhaps *gandharvas*. The seated Lakshmi is rather rigid in her composition with both the shoulders, face and thighs rendered in highly flattened modelling. The Gajalakshmi panel is framed by double pilasters, the outer of which is larger carrying the *dvarapalas*. The *pitha* of these pilasters shows a multi-fluted *kumuda*.

The Monolithic Pillars and Elephants

The *prakara* leads, as one traverses in the clockwise direction, into two front courts in front of the main shrine proper on either side, which have been utilised for the erection of the two *stambhas* indicating in macro-cosmic fashion the nature of the order of the pillars. These show a weak *triratha*, plan for the *pitha* which has an *upana*, high *jagati*, a *kantha*, a *kumuda*, another *kantha* with two courses representing the *kampa* and *valabhi*, followed by a *kapota* upon which there is a rafter frame work composition, whose forward projecting rafters are indicated by laterally shown lions in pairs in the case of the end parts, and in individuals in the *bhadra* parts, while the transverse terminals, where complete, show *makara* head. Upon this frame work is rising the shaft which has a plain lower part of square section occupied by a *Padma-bandha*.

Over this comes the slightly recessed central section with pilastered niches in its central part slightly projecting forward, flush with the lowest section of the pillar. These pilasters are rendered in the form of *makara toranas* and carry the figures of divinities within. Above these is the *malasthana* with a series of festoons emerging out of the *vyalamukhas* followed by a number of bands and pilastered recesses and ending with *urdhvapadmadala*. From this the *kalasa* above starts sloping inwards with a bold *nasika*, carrying lotus medallion knob in its *kudu* and ending with another looped garland arrangement emerging out of *vyalamukhas*. Over this the frame of the *kalasa* ends and in a series of horizontal course gradually expanding are shown the *tadi*, followed by bold recesses and succeeding *kumbha* with median *patralata* band, upon which the *padma* rises with the corners drooping forward and supporting a *phalaka* which has been camouflaged by the decoration of *malavahaka* motif. Thus, in effect, these *stambhas* are the detailed representations of pillar forms at Kailasa cave employed to occupy the vacant open court and by their slenderness furnish a measuring rod to the stature of the Kaiḷasa temple itself. A similar role is played by two elephants facing inwards at a slightly lower level in the *prakara* court one on each side which have been carved out of the rock here.

At the lower level of the court are shown to monolithic elephants facing into the temple, south and north and reared upon a rectangular platform. The platform has the mouldings of a *padma*, a *kantha*, a *vritta kumuda* and another *kantha* and *kapota* in the case of the northern one and more simplified *jagati, kantha, kapota*, in the case of of the southern one. The elephants are in absolutely still pose and are not characterised by any animated features or attendant details. Apparently, the purpose of showing these elephants on the lower court a little to the rear of the flanks is to indicate in full form the popular motif of the Rashtrakuta, namely, the elephants and to place them at the very entrance of their temple.

Inner face of the front prakara scheme

Corresponding to the *pancharatha* pattern of the *dvaramandapa*, as we find on the outside, the inside also shows a similar offset dividing the walls into a series of sections by tall pilasters of which the corner ones would be of the cantoning type. Taking the northern side first, the wall space immediately adjoining the northern *dvarapala* of the *prakara* passage shows Durga fighting with Mahishasura in the whole of the panel. The upper part is taken by celestial divinities who are not only parties to the transaction, but also witnesses to the spectacle. Thus, the figure of the *dikpalas* like Indra, Yama, Agni, Nirriti, Varuna, Vayu and the *Vidyadharas* in pairs below are shown. The main scene depicts Durga seated on the lion in an easier *ardha paryankasana* pose as if the whole thing is a sport and discharging arrows from her bow held in the left hand. The bend of the bow is suggesting that it has been stretched full in the discharge of the arrow. The remaining of her eight arms carry different weapons like *Sula, khadga, khetaka* etc.. The lion which is charging laterally trampling upon the litter of dead and dying warriors, and is mauling another, who is frontally attacking it with sword and shield. Over the head of Durga are shown *chhatra* and two *chamaras* in relief on the wall without the attendants, however, would hold it. The Mahisha demon in himself shown in alinda pose slightly bent forward in human form with human face but two *mahisha* horns, his left hand holding a shield and right hand lifting a mace fully and bending it and sweeping it backwards prior to attacking. It is interesting that this full scene does not show either the *mahisha* demon with his buffalo face or has been actually destroyed by Durga. It is, thus, to be taken that it is the only graphic perspective of battle scene as conjectured by an artist. It recalls as its parallel a small cameo carved on one of the pillars in Vikramaditya and in its turn it is clear that it took its inspiration from the classic Durga-Mahishamardini battle shown in Mahabalipuram in Mahishamardini cave.

The adjacent wall section facing east shows Krishna as Govardhanadhari lifting Govardhana hill and protecting the cattle and the *vrjis* from the anger of Indra who sent down torrential rains. While the figure of Krishna two armed, lifting the hill with one of his arms by the palm and resting his left arm upon a slightly raised and flexed left leg, is larger, the attendant figures, namely, shepherds and the cattle are shown in highly diminutive forms in groups.

The next panel shows a God and Goddess, or a *mithuna* couple, as the case may be. The figures are shown two armed, they are both in *abhanga* and the male is holding the female by the hip from behind and having his right hand on the *kati*, while the female is similarly clasping the male around his back at the upper chest level and is having her left hand as *lolahasta*. There are *Vidyadhara* couple hovering in the air. If this is taken up as a divine figure as might be suggested by the fact that the head of the male wears a *jatamukuta*, this could be a form of Chandrasekhara, which is reinforced by the fact that the female is shown with her upper part of the body bare, as in the case of Uma. Along the turn of the wall the niche facing north shows a male attendant in *abhanga*, while the corresponding turning again of the adjacent now facing east, shows a female, again in *abhanga* with left leg planted vertically and right leg slightly bent, and right arm holding a flower.

The adjacent main wall panel further to the north shows Kama and Rati standing side by side with the *Ikshukhanda* in between on top of which the *makara* banner is depicted; Kama being called *makaraketana*. Since *ikshukhanda* itself forms his bow, a corresponding arrow is held on the right hand. Both the figures are in complementary *abhanga*.

The next panel shows Garudarudha Visnu, apparently as Gajendra-varada, riding on Garuda in human form with wings shown on the sides. The interesting feature of the figure is Visnu having *tunira* or quiver on both his shoulders. This is the last panel beyond which the inner side of the *prakara* wall shows a full excavated cave temple having a facade carrying the flight of steps in the centre with parapets on either side provided with seat-backs and two free-standing dwarf pillars and two pilasters. The pillars are of the type of massive square sectioned base, surmounted by ribbed *kalasa*, *tadi*, *kumbha* a recess and broad *taranga* corbels, following the residual Chalukyan pattern. Within this facade there are two holes the outer being broader and the inner slightly narrower divided by two free-standing pillars incomplete and two corresponding pilasters at raised level within which on the back wall two cells have been partially excavated probably providing for the third also, but left incomplete. It is adjoining and at right angles to this and facing south, that the river Goddess temple has been excavated which we shall come to after covering the southern wall flank of the open court.

Immediately adjoining the south side *dvarapala* of the passage at its inner end, the wall section corresponding to the Durga-Mahisha battle on the northern side is continuing to cover also the adjacent east-facing wall space—depicts Siva as Tripurantaka. The figure of Siva Himself as standing on the chariot, driven by Brahma and Bhrigu by prancing horses, is shown on the western wall, while the northern wall section is accommodating the casualties in the battle in the lower part and the triple cities or *tripuras*, in the form that the demons took by virtue of their boons, are shown in the forms of pavilions, packed with men and women. Over them are also shown hovering *Vidyadharas* at top level. Siva is standing with his legs apart, with his body taut in the process of bending the bow and discharging arrows from the left shoulder from the left ear level. It is very likely that it is this arresting scene depicted here and which has been repeated at a number of places in the Rashtrakuta and Chalukyan temples that should have formed the inspiration for the famous painting of Tripurantaka in the Great temple at Tanjore.

The next wall space flanking this to the south shows a figure in ascetic form with four hands, the upper right hand holding a *gada*, the lower right a cobra, the upper left on the *kati* and the lower left holding what appears to be a *kundika* or flask. The hair-do is done in heavy curls of *jata* flowing and one twisted turban like row resting on his head and the ears sport *kundalas.* Owing the four hands, this will represent a form of Siva and if the *danda* is any criterion, it should be Lakulisa, as also partially suggested by the *urdhvamedha,* but the *kundika* is not expedient. The cobra, however, falls in its place, although this is a rather unconventional representation, if it is to be of Lakulisa. The character of the ascetic's head-gear is, however, in tune with the *jatabhara* of the Dakshinamurti figure. The *yajnopavita* is shown as running over the elbow. There are two *Vidyadharas* hovering in the air above. It would appear that this figure is having his legs crossed. If it is not the *kundika,* but a head cut from a body that is held in the left hand, then this could represent a form of Bhairava as well. The adjoinining figure at the turn of the wall is partially complete and would appear to represent an attendant.

The next figure is the form of standing Visnu, left upper arm holding a *chakra* and the right a *sankha,* left lower arm on the *kati* and the right holding a *gada.* The figure is in *abhanga.* The following figure is that of a dancing Siva, in *pristhasvastika* pose in the movement of gyration with the head turned back, four-armed. The last wall section which comes next apparently shows a rightward facing Andhakari figure, holding a *sula* by the left hand and thrusting it upwards seemingly into the body of the Andhaka demon who is, however, missing. Part of the figures below is also partly broken. Adjoining this, corresponding to the other unfinished temple, there is a similar cave excavation, also unfinished, and less empirical in its form. But a part of its front wall is taken for carving a panel of sculptures which seems to show Siva and Parvati, Umasahita form seated on a bench in *ardhaparyankasana* in the case of Uma and partially *utkutikasana* for Siva. The head of the bull is shown at the appropriate right extremity. The left arm of Siva is placed upon the bench. Alongside are shown the *gana* in rolicking sport, while at the front end of the wall to the north, there are two figures, one male and another female, the female cross-legged and in a mode of indecision, while the male is with his legs placed forward and arms in fained protestation, seemingly forcing the female to make the next move. This posture would indicate that the incident intended to be depicted here is that of Uma and the garrulous Brahmachari—which form Siva took to test her and then to win her. The fact that the upper body in bare in the case of the female fits in, that it might be Uma.

The river Goddess shrine excavated at the north-west corner of the Kailasa courtyard is a very interesting excavation. As it stands, it rises to two storeys high, above which there appears to have been a definite indication of the superstructure arising in the form of a *sukanasa* or as the frontal aspect of an apsidal temple. In fact, the *simha-lalata* of this *sukanasa* is carved towards the very top of the ridged wall available here and in its completed aspect, it would certainly have carried the appearance not very much unlike that of the front view of the apsidal like Sahadeva ratha, notwithstanding the storeyed and facade entrance character of the temple. The pillars of the facade, of which the ground floor ones are well finished, show a *pitha* of *padma*, *kumuda* and another *padma* or ribbed shaft above of multiple ridge in three stages, the central stage being recessed and the terminal stages being slightly thicker and apparently representing the *mandi* or *malasthana*, followed by the high fluted *kalasa*, *tadi*, flaring *kumbha*, *padma*, undercut square *virakanda*, and laterally projecting corbel arms of simple curve, themselves resting under the *uttira* and the *vajana*, from which the *kapota* is projecting forward. Over the *kapota*, the *vedis* stand erect for the upper floor, the vedi comprising of a vertical wall section which forms a *manchabandha* with pilasters separating the *kantha* and showing *mithunas* seated and with another deep *kantha* above, the *kapota* picked out in rosette design and having only four pilasters, two on each side immediately below the pillars that come higher up. The topmost member is that of a seat-back, decorated on the external face with *purnaghatas* between pilasters. The upper storey has its pillars rendered in an octagonal outline, but unfinished. This way of rendering the pillars had been known in Ajanta and in the Cave 27 at Ellora and is generally to be taken as an influence rather than an index of chronological point wherever it is seen, as for instance, even at the upper large cave of the Akkanna-Madanna group at vijayawada. The ground floor is itself having a plinth in the form of a *mancha-bandha* with wall sections separated by pilasters and showing divinities, all badly worn out, followed by the heavy *prati*, upon which the free-standing pillars and two end pilasters stand. The interior has only a rectangular chamber with corner cantoning pilasters at the inner angles of the back wall and the main wall section carrying two more pilasters in the middle, corresponding to the facade pillars, the wall space thus divided into three parts showing the figures of three river Goddesses with *Ganga* in the middle, *Yamuna* to the proper left and perhaps Sarasvati at the proper right, the former two on their cognizances, viz., crocodile and *kurma*. They are ally two-armed, all of which are holding floral rolls, except for *Ganga* who is *samabhanga* in the middle. The lateral figures are complementary and symmetrical together. They are themselves carved within a *makaratorana* comprising a prevailing circular-sectioned pilaster showing all the elements of a pillar surmounted by *makara-torana* proper which rises in high loop out of the mouth of the *makara* up to the bottom of the *uttira* where the double *makara* bracket holds it in position. While the cognizance of *Ganga* and *Yamuna*, viz., *makara* and *kurma* are explicit, not so is the case with the figure which by traditional association is being taken as Saraswati. The specific way in which the Sarasvati concept is seemingly brought out is the fact that the number of *hamsas* are decorated as rising over the floral stalk on the right side of the figure, since *hamsas* from the cognizance of Brahma, whose consort Sarasvati is. It is obvious that Sarasvati figure is meant. At the same time, *hamsa* is the unique evidence known from literature elsewhere, but not substantiated by sculpture, of the fact that it is Goddess Sarasvati that later on transformed into Vakdevi Sarasvati, thereby suggesting that the original association of river Sarasvati (Drishadvati) in the Brahmavarta area which is inhabited by the Vedic Aryanas, when they entered India. This is the hypothesis of reparian association of clearly Vedic culture in India.

This, apart from the carving of the unit in its fullness in the form of an apsidal entity, is well shown by an attempt to cut out an apsidal chamber within the facade room of the upper storey; which perhaps might have signified a possible original intention of the sculptors to carve it out in the monolithic apsidal shrine model. It is to be noted that the other opposite end also, the unfinished cave excavation (*Pl. XXXVIII*) represents a vault in its central nave at a higher level, not unlike that of the vaulted ceiling arrangement of apsidal Buddhistic Chaitya. Since, however, The north side apsidal unit utilises full rise of the cliff scarp, and delineates the major elements of the facade of apsidal temple structure, we should note that this model was quite familiar to architects. This would additionally lend some associative importance to two elephants which are placed at either end of the court-yard, close to the apsidal cave shrines to give inspiration to such an animal model, for the temple model, having already been so available at Mahabalipuram, where again close to the Sahdeva ratha of Gajapristha kirti has been carved the monolithic elephant. The unit, in the same way, is monolith. If it were so, it would mean that the Pallava centres, Mahabalipuram etc., were active and inspiring places of comparative study for the Rashtrakuta architects and sculptors also who carved Kailasa.

The Main Unit

It has already been mentioned that the *main* Kailasa temple unit—by which is meant the axial block ending with the *mukha mandapa* porch of the *sabha mandapa* has been raised upon a solid ground floor, forming a massive plinth. This scheme, however, does not apply to the *nandi-mandapa* and much less, to the *dvara-mandapa* which is already described. In fact, it is seen that these three units, viz., the main temple proper, the *nandi-mandapa* and *dvara-mandapa* are reared on three different levels which were controlled entirely and ultimately by the prevailing slope of the rock available, from the highest to the lowest point; and thus we find that the outer court upon which the elephant was standing forming the lowest, the next upon which the *nandi-mandapa* and the pillar models are standing the next, and the main temple on the high plinth the thrid. Correspondingly, the roof projection spanning the *dvaramandapa* with the *nandi-mandapa*, and the next shrine roof projection spanning the *nandi-mandapa* and the *mukha mandapa* porch of the main shrine, are themselves at dissimilar levels, in relation to the ground *tala kapota* of the *nandi-mandapa* itself, and in a similar way the intersecting *sala sikhara* of the *dvara-mandapa*, the flat roof of the *nandi-mandapa*, and the parapeted *hara* of the main temple ending with the *sikhara* of the *vimana* are in successive ascending levels. It is this deliberate depiction of the full compliment of the longitudinal temple lay-out, consciously harmonised without appearing to contrive or artificial, that is the main charm of Kailasa monolith. This effect has been caused primarily by the introduction of the truly architectural elements in their appropriate places, each linked with the next, instead of merely depending upon surface ornamentation and art motifs to fill these link-members. The balconied and double storeyed *dvara mandapa* capped by an intersecting *salasikhara* provided with four bold *nasikas* in the four cardinal directions, is of a scheme entirely different from that adopted for the *nandi-mandapa*. This *nandi-mandapa* consists of a plinth, a *pada*, followed by a *kapota* over which the *pada* of the second *tala* rises, followed by its own *kapota*, *vyalavari*, *vedi*, *kantha* and its *kapota*, capped by a final *vyalavari* frieze, the idea being that together with the topmost unit represented between two *vyalavari* courses, the *mandapa* has actually been raised in three *talas*, the third being attennuated. Of these, the plinth comprises an *upana*, a *jagati*, a high and bold *kantha* without any pilaster division, followed by a thin *kapota* and *prati*. On this *prati*, there are four corner free-standing pillars very carefully separated from the main wall, which is closely adjoining it. Between these four pillars in the corners, the main body of the wall is itself divided by the series of pilasters ingeneously camouflaged in figure work to remove their monotony, and provided with independent niche panels surmounted by *nasika panjaras* showing a regular *alpa vimana* between each of the tall thin pilasters of the main wall. There are four such pilasters and the wall sections thus separated show also in the broader central section a niche along the *mandapa* relief, surmounted by a *uttaranga* of *kutas*, *salas* and *panjaras*. The base of the wall has a *vyalavari* course wherein the laterally carved elements in pairs or in singles and human figures are shown and only schematic *makara* terminals in broad *triratha* pattern are indicated. The free-standing corner pillars show for their base a rectangular basal block succeeded by *padma* plinth, *kumuda*, and thinner *padma*, a shaft section comprising of a cubical base part, a *padmakosa*, a middle shaft part decorated by *patralata* bands in the middle of their faces, succeeded by *malasthana*, *padmabandha*, *kalasa*, *tadi*, *kumbha*, *padma* and *phalaka*, on the top of which seated figures in the form of *ganas* or caryatids with legs flexed vertically and stemmed firmly on the *phalaka* are supporting the massive *kapota* which, though not as heavy as *kapota* of the *dvara-mandapa* roof, are about half their thickness. These *kapotas* are very acutely drooping without their outer edges, and are only decorated with *konapattai* and *madhyapttai* decorations, within the pilasters of which there are four members mentioned already rendered in the form of *dandika*-like brackets at their base in three continuous sections with mild outward concavity and horizontally ribbed basal and top parts. These obviously represent transversely projecting rafter ends joined by vertical members. On these the main beam projection which again would be transversely running north-south is shown in the form of a *kalasa* decorated with *padmakosha*, and on this *kalasa* beam projection *gajamundas* are shown surmounted by *vyalas* and carried through finally by shaft members whose exterior has been converted into figure work, in 3/4th relief, of semi-divine *vidyadharas* and others with bodies bent in flexed and rising up to the bottom of the *kalasa* of the pilaster, and surmounted by their own *tadi*, *kumbha*, *padma* and *phalaka*, upon which the *kapota* itself is resting, (*Pl. XXXIX*). The niches in between show in the main wall section, the figure of dancing Siva in *urdhva-janu* pose, eight armed, with *nandi* shown one side playing on the drum and Parvati seated on the otherwise other side, looking up in wonder. One of the left arms is taken across the body and almost raised upon the raised right knee in *danda-hasta*, while the lower right leg is following the direction of the left thigh in a careful symmetrical posture, corresponding to the well thrown back head. This figure has been formulated between the two pilasters, themselves raised upon a parapet of floral decorations and are flanked on two sides by paired *Vidyadharas*, hovering one above the other, reaching up to the level of the *uttaranga*. Over the *hara* of *uttaranga* also *Vidyadharas* in couple are shown. Since this *hara* is accommodated within the lateral corbel arms of the double pilaster unit which adjoins the main forward projecting pilasters described earlier, on these corbels the *uttira* beam runs followed by a *vajana*, and *malavahaka bhutavalabhi* under the *kapota*. It is to be noted that, while the horizontal projection of the *kapota* underside is considerably plain, this tends to shelter and partially hide the *valabhi* zone. The corresponding *valabhi* of the *dvara mandapa* forms a regular beam-like course under the very narrow underside of the *kapota* and is thus well exposed. It is this *dvara gopura* of *valabhi* type that is followed in Chhota Kailasa.

The smaller niches on the side wall spaces show standing figures of Harihara to the proper left and Gangadhara to the proper right. The Harihara figure which is in *samabhanga* has on the right side two arms holding *trisula* and in *kati*, while the two left arms hold *sankha* and *gada*. The crown is of the *jatamukuta* type to the proper right and *kirita* type to the proper left. The *yajnopavita* is again running over the elbow. The Gangadhara is also in *samabhanga*, eight-armed, one of the left upper arms removing a tress of hair from his head, and an expedient figure, probably that of Bhagiratha, is shown in diminutive form to the main left. The superstructure above the niche in both these cases shows a *kapota*, a *vyalavari*, a *vedi* well recessed back and a *nasika* top, itself surmounted on a pilastered *griva*.

On the corresponding southern side of this *nandi-mandapa*, the central niche shows Hiranya and Narasimha in sanguinary battle. Hiranya trying to overwhelm the enemy by bearing down on Narasimha in an all-out attack, but Narasimha well staving off the attack, the posture of Hiranya with right leg planted forward, left acutely twisted backwards, trying to grip the waist of the god, who in his turn with his six arms has firmly held the left hand of Hiranya above shoulder and head, and right hand holding a spear below his waist. This is by way of contrast of a conventional representation of Narasimha type and suggests a new spirit pervading the Rashtrakuta craftsmen, enabling them to rise to new and untrodden heights of art endeavour. In a similar way, the subjects of the side niches which are *mithuna* couples in highly endearing and intimate postures of love-play, also do not conform to any conventional category. The upper *tala* of this *nandi-mandapa* is provided above the *kapota* variously and the main wall section wherein corresponding elements of free-standing corner pillars, bold wall pilasters adjoining the intersecting corbel arms and niche frame work with *nasika panjaras* above on the side wall sections, are all depicted, and the only new element is that a single section shows a door opening flanked by a pilastered *makara torana.* The bold wall pilasters projecting forward also show a variant motif in that, in place of the *Vidyadharas* rising high shown in full body-stance, they represent caryatid-like figures holding garlands in their hands. In fact, one such figure is shown on the south side in the ground floor pilaster as well. The main difference is in the pillar form as represented in the corners wherein the tops are much thinner than in the lower floor and show at the bottom level an over-flowing petal in the corners. The wall sections show the same *uttira*, *malavahaka*, *bhuta-valabhi* and have well projected *kapota* whose underside carries a transverse rafter and radiating *kodungai* ribbings, each fastened with the other by nail-heads at successive intervals. The *kapota*, is slightly thinner than the lower ground floor *kapota*, and on this, as already described, is the attennuated third *tala* suggested by *vyalavari*, *vedi*, *kantha* and another *kapota* and a succeeding *vyalavari* course forming the top roof of the *nandi-mandapa.* The niches on the side wall sections of the upper floor show again single or double amorous figures, while the *makara torana* itself is rather of the same outline as the door frame, the *torana* proper running almost horizontally though in loops, floriated tail of the *makara* drooping vertically up to the *kalasa* levels on either side.

The second cross-passage, followed by its own roof, has been between the *nandi mandapa* and the *mukha mandapa* porch of the main temple occurs beyond, and is approached in its main gangway by a short flight of steps from either side and provides a setting for two important panels of Sivayogi and Gajantaka Siva sculptures of full size, which occupy the whole of the wall sections to the east and to the west of the passage. These are flanked by double pilasters of a massive type having a *pitha* of *padma*, *kumuda* and shorter *padma*, the *kumuda* being of multiple rib, a shaft having a basal block of *patralata* design and *padmakosa* top surmounted by *nasika kudus* and continuing vertical *pattais* of scroll work, while the top of this square sectioned shaft shows the *malasthana* with looped festoons holding *ganas* in the loops, *padmabandha*, *kalasa* with the *ganas*, supporting the overflowing foliage arising out of the upper member of the double *kalasa*, capped by a roll *padma*, and *malasthana* frieze and corbels, over which very thin flat *uttira* beams run.

The roof of this passage shows a *vedi* above the thin *kapota* divided by pilasters, followed by a bigger *kapota* and succeeded by a seat-back at a point where it joins the main unit. This unit, itself representing the projecting plinth of the *mukha mandapa* porch of the *sabha mandapa*, shows flying *Vidyadhara* figure one on each side holding the corner up. Above this shown a regular *gajamunda* balustrade with the seat back above separating, on the inner side, two free-standing pillars and two pilasters at the corresponding eastern end forming (*Pl. XL*) the frame work of the *mukha mandapa* porch. These pillars are of a simple square-sectioned type with undifferentiated, but massive *kalasa*, square-sectioned *tadi*, *kumbha*, surmounted by corbels, over which thin flat beams occur and are capped by projecting and heavy *kapotas* with *kodungai* ribbings and transverse rafter frame work running on the inside of the cornice, while the well projecting cornice has in its exterior profuse and well-relieved *konapattai* and *madhya pattai* floral devices. This cornice is running into the back wall where it is not returning (*Pl. XLI*) but tied from within, since it is an appendage to the main *Sabha mandapa*. The *uttira* beams below this cornice actually are juxtaposed to the beam scheme of the *Sabha mandapa*, and thus together with the side porches in the north and south, they form attachments to the main *sabha mandapa*. The only difference, however, is that whereas this *mukha mandapa* porch is a well distinguished member of the axial lay-out and thus does not partake all the plinth mouldings of the main temple unit, the south side porches in the north and south are integral and organic continuations of the plinth scheme, which is well seen by the running of mouldings right from the bottom of the outer court up to the very level upon which the balustraded (*Pl XLII*) *kakshasanas* on the north and south are raised for the porch projection. Over the cornice of the porches there is a *vayalavari*, a slightly recessed *vedi* a high *kantha* followed by an *uttira* beam, a *malavahaka bhutavalabhi* and the top *kapota* itself followed by the topmost *vayalavari*. On the corners of this topmost course are placed strident lions. These appear to be found only on the eastern side but not on the southern and northern sides. The roof of these projecting porches is otherwise flat on top.

The main Kailasa unit takes the form of a *triratha* lay-out in its *sabha mandapa* harmonised with *triratha* lay-out (*Pl. XLIII*) for the temple and its sub-shrines at the plinth level. It would be seen that there are seven sub-shrines around the upper open *prakara* of the main *vimana* of which five are fully free-standing monolithic models in themselves while the remaining two are actually integral part of the corner compositions of the *maha mandapa* or *sabha mandapa*. These corner compositions thus are represented in all the four corners, although only at their inner corners they had been converted shrines. Nonetheless, in order to achieve homogeneity these two corner shrines and correspondingly two more door projections towards the western ends have been raised for double storey height, surmounted by the *kutas* (*Pl. XLIV*) of the *hara* over the *sabha mandapa* roof, while the main external wall of the sabha mandapa is shown as rising in one single wall space of one *tala* over the massive and solid *bhumitala* forming the plinth proper. These corner shrines thus have necessarily to be square-sectioned in shape supported by four cantoning pilasters enclosed by wall spaces in between and surmounted by a *vayalavari* and *vedi* and upper set of four cantoning pilasters (*Pl. XLV*) seemingly rendered as an open *mandapa*, surmounted in their turn by a *prastara*, *griva* and *kutasikhara*. This double-storeyed composition is of equal height—a thing which is normally not extant in regular double-storeyed structural models. The outer walls of these corner shrines of the *sabha mandapa* are decorated with sculptured niches, showing *Kalantaka* form of Siva on the western face of the north western corner projection, Vrishabhantika Siva on the northern face, of the same corner part, Gajendra-varada-Visnu on the northern face of the reared shrine at the north eastern corner, Ganesa on the eastern face of the same shrine; Hiranya-samhara-Narasimha on the southern face of the south eastern corner shrine, Lakulisa Siva on the southern face of the south-western corner shrine and Brahma on the western face of the same corner shrine.

In order to accommodate these corner shrines of the *sabha mandapa* and to relieve them from the remaining parts, the *sabha mandapa* itself has been rendered into three projecting parts with two recessions along the same *vinyasa-sutra*, except for the ground *tala* of the corner shrines, whose upper *tala* merges with the main wall sections, (*Pl. XLVI*). The central or *bhadra* part is very wide, while the *karna* part is equal to the recession and one fourth central part. Surmounted over the *kapota* of the upper and the main *tala* of Kailasa *sabha mandapa* is found the *prastara* and the *hara* comprising the *kuta* in the corners, the *sala* scheme of three telescoped *salas* in the middle and the end parts of each *bhadra*, the central *sala* rising much higher than the lateral ones by the representation of a regular *pada* over the *vyalavari* of the roof of the *prastara* and surmounting another set of *prastara* and *sala* over this. This is apparently intended to serve two purposes. Firstly, it would make the *haras* visible particularly in their cardinal points from the ground level. This would actually be its spectacular character. Its functional character, however, is that in the cardinal points these *salas* actually represent *dvarasalas* and thus they are to be one storey higher and distinguished from other *salas* of the *hara*. It would be seen that the analogy of these *dvarasalas* is well (*Pl. XLXII*) preserved in the temple wich has formed one of the models for Kailasa, namely, the Virupaksha temple at Pattadakkal. While the *harantaras* are running into the *sala* side faces, the main *dvara sala* being lifted up higher has a well decorated *nasika* face at either side within which *vimana* models are executed in the *kudu*. The wall sections either within the corner parts where shrines are located are relieved of the shoft plainness by 3/4th relief carvings of *mithunas*, *vidyadharas* and other endearing erotic couples at different levels, usually at the lower and the upper levels. It is also to be seen that the tall pilasters of the main walls show in their corbels a true *taranga* corbel with median band, with the *uttira*, following the contour of the corbel where-ever it is intersecting.

The Staircase Approach

In order to provide access to the upper and main *tala* of Kailasa, a device was invented by king Krishna's architects which not only tended to camouflaged a flight of steps, leading from either side to the open court at the *mukha mandapa* porch level, but also to provide for individual elements embellishing this enclosure, closing the flight of steps as well as for relief friezes of the most notable and sacred puranic sources for art and iconography namely, epics of Ramayana and Mahabharata, (*Pl. XLVIII*). Accordingly an 'L' shaped walling which covered the flight of steps leading to the *mukha mandapa* porch was carved on the southern and northern faces with rows of friezes of diminutive character, rendered in a synoptic way, the entire story of Ramayana and Mahabharata and Krishna myths, while the western faces of this enclosure were given the usual treatment of plinth wall and *hara* and a regular *dvara sala* was also set at the very entrance point. This *dvarasala* was raised, though of a single storey in a tall scheme by introducing an architrave or clerestory forming *kantha* and *kapota* over which the *vyalavari*, *vedi*, *griva* and the *sala* with well projected median *nasikas* were placed. It would be seen that this feature for providing a pilaster, and *kapota*, *top kantha* over the *prastara* of the ground *tala* upon each of the successive *talas* had been an important device adopted in Kailasa monolith as well as in the other Rashtrakuta monolith at Ellora; even incidentally shown in the Dantidurga *mandapa* roof and such device is taken as an inspiration mainly by Ganga craftsmen in the southern country followed also by the Pandyas, Irukkuvels etc., but does not usually form part of the prevailing Pallava or Chola art in the Tamil country.

The entrance flight of steps leading to the upper floor was itself provided with a special plinth of its own, with an elephant and attendant on either flank for the balustraded steps and, as already mentioned, the western wall face was carved with sculptures rising over a plinth consisting of a high *upana*, a *vajana*, a *kantha*, *kapota* and *prati*, over which pilasters, corbels, *uttira*, triple members, radiating *vajana* and *valabhi* occur followed by a *kapota*, *vyalavari* in weak relief and *vedi*, *griva* and continuous of a very vide *sala* and two *kutas* with *panjaras* in between. These *salas* have three *nasikas* and three *kalasas* on their body.

On the northern side wall face the figure carved is that of a *dvarapala* resulting on his mace at the northern end with the upper arms holding *damaru* and in *vismaya mudra* and the lower left arm in *kati*. The middle panel is that of Ravana shaking Kailasa in a crowded scene wherein Ravana is shown in larger size than Siva and Parvati to suit the perspective, and tree-like 20-arms of Ravana spread out to lift Kailasa and the scenes of trepidation in the upper register excepting for Parvati and Siva. The inner panel also shows a *dvarapala* with a hair-do different in the form of a bun, recalling those of Bhairavakonda and some of the Pallava examples, who has his right arm on the *kati* and left arm placed upon the thigh of the raised left leg, itself placed on the hatchet of the mace. On the southern side the central figure is that of Brahma in *padmasana* over a *padma-pitha*, four-armed, the lower right arm in *varada*, upper right arm holding *sruk*, unfortunately damaged, the upper left arm flexed high holding a *kundika*, and the lower left arm holding a *pustaka* also damaged. Brahma is shown in moustache and beard, with tapering *jatamukuta*. The only decorations are a *kanthahara*, *yajnopavita*, *keyuras* and *kankanas*. Flanking Brahma and in smaller niches (not reproduced on the northern side) but formed here by spacing of the pilasters suitably are shown two female attendants, standing at the inner shrine. At the northern end of this wall face the niche shows a standing Visnu in *samabhanga* on *padma pitha*, right lower arm resting on *gada*, right upper arm holding *chakra*, left upper holding *sankha*, left lower in *kataka*. The corresponding figure on the southern end is that of Siva seated on his bull with the lower right arm flexed high in *abhaya*, upper right arm holding *khatvanga*, the lower left arm on the lap, and upper left arm holding the *sula*.

Dvara Mandapa Upper Storey

The interior of the upper floor of the *dvara-mandapa* below the *salasikhara* is longitudinally of three compartments, approximately of equal dimensions, in the case of the latter two, while the outer-most is relatively smaller in the case of the former; the outer and the inner, however, the corner angles show double pilasters and an additional feature is that while the outermost *mandapa* shows only side pilasters at the outer ends and the seat backs and balcony, the inner compartment not only shows the seat back *kakshasana* on a higher parapet, but also a more drooping and massive *kapota* as already described earlier in such a way that there is hardly a distance of little more than a foot between the lower edge of the *kapota* and the upper end of the seat back. The central compartment provides access to lateral compartments at lower levels through flights of steps which ultimately lead to the open rampart walls. These lateral compartments again having double pilasters apparently of the cantoning type above corners in addition to two more pilasters along the middle part of the wall. The access to the rampart is made through regular door opening of *makara-torana* type which are themselves flanked by the wall pilasters of the middle section of the exterior upper floor of the *dvara mandapa* as already noted. Leading from the *dvara-mandapa* into the *nandi-mandapa* the span ends with a flight of steps flanked by two niches within pilasters up to the corbel level, all their elements inside which the figures of Kubera and Ganeṣa, the traditional guardians of the doorway, proper of the main unit of temples have been properly stationed. The flight of steps itself reaches the upper landing, the level of the top of these niches described, upon which the wall section as already mentioned in addition to the pilastered *makara-torana* door-frame in the centre has *nasika panjara* niche frames of pilasters inside which sculptures are found within the western wall representing *mithun* to the north, standing Siva with *naga* and *parasu* in the upper arms, and *abhaya* and *kati* in the lower arms, riding upon the figure of Apasmara shown in the pedestal to the south. In the central crest of the *makara-torana* of the door frame forming its *lalata*, as it were, full double *makara* clasp is shown the figure of a boyish person riding on the elephant, apparently a representation of Kumara or Karttikeya. While the wall sections otherwise are of the same type as described for the northern and southern faces, the only important feature to be noted would be the provision of a curved bracket like *dandika* rising from the level of the *phalaka* of the pilasters and resting immediately under the *kodungai* ribbings of the *kapota*. These *kodungai* ribbings are laid horizontally in this case. These curved brackets themselves show elements of the pillars, like *kalasa*, *tadi*, *kumbha*, *padma* and *phalaka*, the *kalasa* part curving back, laid into the wall over the main wall pilasters. The wall niches and the wall pilasters are almost of the same degree of relief projection from the wall surface whereas their own *nasikas* on the top and the *makara torana* of the central door frame are somewhat subdued and this together makes a pleasant effect of interesting side light on the caryatid figures shown as supporting from the free-standing corner pillars is that some of them show *udaremukhas*. It is also interesting to note that the *gajavyalas* or *matanga-nakras* which are shown as rampant along with their outriders and top-riders over standing *gajamundas* on the pilasters are the precursors to the ubiquitous *vyala* figures in the recesses on northern *prasadas* although these motifs are much less common in the southern temples of the mediaeval period, in any comparable degree.

Nandi-Mandapa

The *nandi.mandapa* is a square chamber, whose interior shows a level sarface, in the centre of which the loose *nandi* is placed, whose head is damaged, while the corners show double cantoning pilasters shown completely from *pitha* up to the *phalaka* in prevailing square section the *kumuda* of the *pitha* shall be representing a multi-fluted character. The corbels shown over the *phalakas* are closely restricted to the wall and over them run the *uttira*, and their own *vajanas* in double courses, followed by the *valabhi* and the ceiling. The ceiling appears to have been decorated in painted designs, divided into compartments at a slightly later period. While most of the compartments of the ceiling paintings would have shown original interesting painted figures or groups as could be made out here and there, vaguely, nothing, practically remains at present, because of the highly stunted character of the surface due to dirt.

The eastern face of the *nandi-mandapa* wall is almost similar to the western excepting that because of the higher level of its plinth, there are no niche figures with corresponding to Ganesa and Kubera on the western end. The floor has been projecting the *nandi-mandapa* and the *mukha-mandapa* porch of the main temple is very much higher on the western side and correspondingly its side parapets are also relatively shorter. The niches on the eastern walls of the *nandi-mandapa* are damaged in their interior, although on the southern one it could be faintly seen that the figure would have represented a standing Siva, (*Pl. XLIX*).

The front appearance of the *mukha mandapa* porch of the main temple unit is made very impressive on account of three elements; firstly, the *vedi* parapet and the seat back above it is raised reasonably high almost to a man's height together with the lower member showing *purnaghatas.* Within this, rising on the sides are massive dwarf pillars of a square-section with their lower part, the *malasthana,* an undifferentiated *kalasa,* a multi-ribbed *tadi,* a well cut *kumbha,* a very narrow *virakanda* are followed by 'L' shaped right-angular corbel arms of a smooth simple curvature and succeeded by thin, but broad *uttira* members which run only on the three sides, but do not return on the fourth side, where the door frame is located, but run into the wall over the corresponding wall pilasters. Over these *uttiras* there is a brief *valabhi* and a high *kantha* again in the form of an architrave over which the ceiling is reached. Shading this is the massive *kapota* whose inside has been lonely provided with criss-crossing *kodungai* ribbings fastened by sumptuous transverse and longitudinal reeper pieces and this well undercut *kapota* has on its smoothened exterior a deeply picked out decoration of *madhya* and *kona-pattais* of elaborate floral devices in bunches, the *madhya-bandha* particularly in the hanging and the centre is merging on the *vyalamukha* shown on the top of the *kapota* edge and above it are shown a series of seated *ganas,* numbering nearly 8, in the centre of which is a leader. These *gana* figures are apparently harmonised with the main figure sculpture of dancing Siva shown on the superstructural wall above the *kapota,* this superstructure rising over a *vyalavari* wherein the forward projecting rafters are shown as a regular full size *vyalas* with grinning mouth, while the transverse rafters shown with *makara* terminals have above them a *vedi* of almost equal height. Both the *vyalavari* as well as the *vedi* and the wall sections rising above show a kind of a *pancharatha* pattern, wherein the *bhadra* is very broad, the *pratiratha* is very narrow and the *karna* is equally broad. On this *vedi* rises the *pada* part which in the *bhadra,* as already mentioned, shows another *vedi* with pilasters above the *bhutavalabhi* above followed by a *kapota,* within which inside the pilasters directly carried on the *nasikas* of the *kapota* and themselves carrying in many feamle figures, probaply representing *nayikas,* sculpture of dancing Siva is carved out. This sculpture is unfortunately badly damaged but for a few of his arms visible carrying *trisula*, *kapala* etc.. and only the part of the northern *nayika* figure is also preserved, but what little is preserved of standing body shows proportion and a degree of unconventional freshness in the drapery and modulations. The *nasikas*, as already mentioned of both the central part as well as the end parts are already rendered like the *pancharatha* lay-out, the middle ones are projected well forward with a deeply cut *kudu*, well projected by the base. Inside the niche section within pilasters of these *nasika panjaras* figures of standing *nayikas* have been engraved, rather feebly. Over this superstructure which forms the third *tala* of the porch unit there is a further *vyalavari* capped, as already mentioned, by rampant *vyalas* placed in the corners with one of their paws raised.

Mukha Mandapa Porch

This frontage, as one approaches from the *nandimandapa*, is impressive by any standard on its exterior and the interior is further high-lighted by the *dvarapalas* who are placed against the side pilasters of the back wall, almost facing each other. It is on this inner pilaster point that the flight of steps leading from the lower court turns into the porch and thus the side parapet wall would have been cut short to provide for the ingress leaving the back pilasters shown fully whereas in the case of the front free-standing pillars, their base is partially hidden under the parapeting and the seat backs, although shown from the *pitha* upwards in the inner corners. It is these outer pillars alone again that show a representation of two rearing lions rising from the level of the corbel at the corners and supporting the roof on their heads. This *mandapa* should have been completely painted in the original condition, a large portion of which though in patchcs, still exists on the underside of the *uttira* beams on the architrave *kantha* and on the ceiling, in addition to comparatively cruder painted designs executed perhaps in successive periods on the pillars and their members. These earlier paints mentioned had displayed a mastery over the brush and colour and eye for minute details. Of these, the figure of elephant group around the central medallion at the north-west corner, the figures of divinities within bands in the north-east corner representing Karttikeya and others would need special mention. The centre of the ceiling shows large-sized lotus medallion in three concentric tiers of petal rows ending with *padmakesara* or the ovary flat in shape. The *dvarapalas* are of considerable stature rising from the second step of the balustraded door steps up to the limit of the *kumbha* and have slender bodies, massive *gadas* or four-armed have a multiplicity of body ornamentation in which particular mention may be made of a long garland of gingling bells and another loop of bells from the hip around the waist. These would particularly represent the conventional ornamentation of certain categories of ascetics of the Pasupata group known as Srinkhalikas to whom some variations of (Saiva) Gods in Tamil Nadu like Sangalikkaruppan should be traced. The head-gear which is slightly tapering is elaborate in its details. The door frame within the *dvarapala* location is of *panchasakha* variety, the innermost being a *ratnasakha*, followed by Ganga and Yamuna figures in bold relief at the angles in its second *sakha* and surmounted by a series of *Vidyadhara* couples in different postures of intimacy, all along upwards and succeeded by a series of *bharaputras* across the lintel; the third is the pilastered *sakha* and the last one was the *padmasakha*.

The interior of the *sabha mandapa* has broad axial base across cardinal directions. while the remaining base on either side all around are much narrower. These have resulted in a peculiar cloister of four free-standing pillars which together with the corresponding pilasters of the wall double up to 8 and an additional double pilaster of the cantoning type of the corners. Thus, the central *ankanas* is of broad square, while the lateral *ankanas* of the axial and transverse bays along the cardinal directions are rectangular of the same length as the central *ankana*, but of very narrow width. The *ankanas* from a cloister of four free-standing pillars and are a small square on their ceiling. While the corner parts on their ceiling take the 'L' shape continuous ceiling roof. It would be noted that this is almost exactly followed in Chhota Kailasa as well. The pillars are all primarily of two varieties represented by those of the innermost *ankanas* and the surrounding *ankanas* of free-standing types, while the pilasters are similar to the pillars of the innermost central *ankana*. These represent over their massive *pitha* a basel shaft, above of low cuboid shape, surmounted by *padmakosa*, over which the shaft proper of the same thickness rises, embellished by lotus medallions inside the *nasikas* in the centre, surmounted by *patralata* bands, followed by regular *malasthana*, and *padmabandha*, characterised by *ganas* inside the loops of the former and figure sculpture of men and animals, in different religious and secular scenes in the latter. Over this *padma-bandha*, is again a *nasika* on the four sides of the really undifferentiated *kalasa*, which is followed by its own *tadi*, and *kumbha*, a narrow square *virakanda*, and a long and reasonably broad and smoothly curved corbel with median band, over which an *uttira* and *vajana* occur, supporting the ceiling. In the lateral bays the corbels are practically meeting each other because of their nearness. The other pillar type shows the *pitha* of the same form as the first type and even the shaft part also excepting for variations in ornamentations. Over the *mandi* part it shows along a very elaborate and massive *ghata-pallava* wherein the *kalasa* is ribbed and provided with a band offrame work towards its upper part, followed by a *kumbha*, from which the foliage is over-flowing and extending up to the frame work band mentioned above which is supported from the bottom of the *kalasa* level by rampant *vyalas* striding over the elephants. The top of the *kumbha* shows a *padma-bandha* and what would appear to be a capital piece decorated by looped festoons in its upper part and floral motifs in its lower part.

The wall sections of the ceilings are bare of sculpture, excepting for the central *ankana* where the ceiling shows a *tandava* Siva, Siva dancing upon *Apasmara* with *nandi* and Parvati shown seated and standing on either side respectively. The figure is in *lalita* pose with one of the left hands is taken across the body as *danda-hasta*, and one of the right hands raised high with the fingers drooping as *gajahasta*, and one each of the right and left hands in *kati*; one of the hands resting upon the shoulders of Parvati, standing nearby and the other remaining hands holding a *naga* in *abhaya* and *varada-hastas*. The dance is thus actually of the *katisama* type. The *Apasmara* is shown as lying on his side. The carved figure is in bold relief, on a main central base which itself is out down a little. Ventilation and light, apart from the cardinal door frames, are provided by a series of *gavaksha* windows of the rectangular shape in adjacent wall sections of the four corners excepting at the inner where the door frames leading to the *prakara* substitute one of the pairs of such *gavakshas*. The side porches also show door frames of *panchasakha* variety with Ganga and Yamuna group and other similar details as the main door except in slightly more simplified manner, and also *dvarapalas* which in this case are placed upon a frieze of *ganas*, themselves carved on the parapetted seat back level, in the case of the northern wall, while on the southern side they are made to stand on a thin pedestal over the parapet. Vestiges of painted ceiling design of considerable beauty occur on the southern porch. One of the *dvarapalas* on the southern side is also almost cut-out in the round only a part of his right knee and right arms touching the pilaster, while the remaining part of the body tilted sidewards well off the pilaster is almost in the round. It is interesting to note that we have such *dvarapalas* completely taken off the wall, represented in one of the cave temples in Kerala viz., Trikkur, where obviously a guild inspiration could be seen.

It was mentioned while describing the exterior *sabha mandapa* unit that the corner double-storeyed *kuta vimanas* are actually of the false type in the north-west and south-west corners, but form regular shrines of applied variety only at the inner ends, supplying the two shrine units required to make the temple complex *asta-parivara*, since one of the five free-standing monolithic sub-shrines have actually been carved around the main shrine. The fact that the *sabha mandapa* corner walls represented by double pilasters, do not, in any way affect the true or false character of the shrines is very interesting and would very favourably bring out the innovatory skill of the architects in camouflaging elements as much as in displaying them. It would thus be seen the outer corner false shrine unit is visible from the exterior rear of the slopy character, while the inner corner ones are of the hollow and truly structural type. An interesting feature of the central or axial bay, however, is that in the innermost bay just adjoining the *ardha mandapa*, there had been the depiction on its three sides excluding the outer of the *malavahaka* atlantes frieze as a *valabhi* with painted ceilings within. This does not obtain in any section even of the central nave and thus perhaps suggests that in the superstructural scheme, the *sukanasa* is actually raised additionally appon this innermost bay as well, beyond the *ardha mandapa* itself. The central figure on the ceiling of the *ardha mandapa* is interesting in that it portrays a female on *padmapitha*, standing in *samabhanga*, with a *kundika* held in the left arm and the right arm in *kati*. The hair-do is a *jatamukuta* and the bare upper body would suggest that this is Uma or Parvati. There are two attendant figures on either side, apparently representing Brahma and Vishnu. Seated on the wall in the four corners are found *Vidyadhara* couples or single figures hovering in the air. There is a tree motif over the head of Uma. The *ardha mandapa* iiself is separated from the *sabha mandapa* by a wall pilaster, almost serving as the screen by its oblong cross-section and its projection beyond the normal thickness of the pilaster over the *kumbha* portion, there is a narrow bracket resting against the corbel up to the *uttira*. The north *uttira* is also showing the *atlantes* or *malavahaka* or *bhatavalabhi* which has not returned on the other three sides. There is an additional pilaster on the side walls towards the inner end, but just away from the backwall, which also has a bracket figure but this time in *mithuna* couple on the top. The pilasters are of the same type as the pillars of the innermost *ankana*. The back wall shows a separate corner pilaster, itself projecting from the corner, right up to the door frame like the screen and apparently forming part of the sanctum wall. Against this pilaster facing forward are shown very large size figures of Ganga and Yamuna, right over their respective animals and with a parasol raised over their heads. The figures in complementary *abhanga*, with their inner hips raised and with the other leg placed slightly forward, right arm resting on the hip and the inner arm in *vismaya mudra*. The door frame which is in *panchasakaha* is almost exactly similar to the door frame outside the *sabha mandapa* in all its corners except that over the kapota the *uttaranga* is also shown in the form of the *haras*, *kutas*, *salas* and *panjaras*.

Roof of Nandi-Mandapa

The top roof of the *nandi-mandapa* is shown embellished with a low central platform over a broad and thinner platform, the latter of which are placed four *ganas* facing in pairs west and east. In the central narrow platform has been placed in regular frieze in deep relief of *ganas* supporting a *padmadala* over which the *kalasa* has been placed. It is thus in the manner of a mere top embellishment in order to highlight the roof that this has been mainly employed. On the *sabha mandapa* porches, however, the roof itself has been made to slope from the centre and a large multiple course *padmadala* in four rows of receding tiers ending with a *padmakesara* has been carved. This, as it would seem, expresses a desire to integrate elements which are foreign to the southern type of temple with this monolithic model, even though more clarity of a pure southern *vimana* has been maintained in the general lay-out, and even buildings. Thus this lotus medallion *dalas* in receding courses on the *sabha mandapa* portion have also to be compared with the much larger similar lotus medallion *dalas* placed (*Pl L*) in the central part of the *sabha mandapa* roof itself in three bold steps, with the innermost *padma kesara*, however, being substituted by a typical *alpa vimana* of the *chaturasra* type, representing a *vyalavari*, a *vedi* a *grihapindi*, *griva* and a *sikhara* in regular *phancharatha* pattern. It is such a *chaturasra* superstructural model that has also existed in the Chhota Kailasa, though partly damaged. The representation of standing and animated group of four lions with one of their paws raised around this central *chaturasra sikhara*, as if constituting the guardians of the temples proper is another innovation that Krishna's architects introduced. Similar lions had been placed on the roof of this *mandapa* to maintain the axial lion. These two features of the *padmadala* courses and the lion on the crest are essential features of northern temples and would represent there the roof scheme or the tower of subsidiary *mandapas* and they have no place in the southern *vimana*, where the *mandapas* excepting the main *vimana* have flat roofs.

Sukanasa of Main Vimana

The *sukanasa* of Kailasa Vimana is an interesting exercise in architecture by itself. It is one of the most perfectly harmonised elements, nonetheless, an example that could not be said to have been after Chhota Kailasa. The actual roof of the sukanasa starts from the second *tala* just over the *hara* of the first *tala* on an architrave or clerestory like intermediate stage. Over this the wall of the *sukanasa* is also an organic continuation of the wall of the second *tala* and show indeed over the *kapota* and the *vyalavari*, *vedi*, *griva* and fronton *sala sikhara*. It is to be noted that the *sukanasa* rises only up to the top of the middle bend of the third *tala* from the base of the second *tala*. This has apparently been intended to prevent the *sukanasa* from overwhelming the talachhanda of the main *vimana* and also since this is the norm that is followed in the temples of the Deccan where the *sukanasa* element is applied even to the southern type as in the Virupaksha temple at Pattadakkal. The perfect *sala* of this *alpa vimana* type of *sukanasa* has a very elaborate frontage which, however, continues to show the third *tala* lay-out up to the *griva* level but only from the *griva* it represents the *nasika kudu* with very carefully picked out *mukhapatti*, *dandikas* carrying figure work and a centrally seated Siva in *dhyanamudra*. There cannot be a better choice of Siva as Yogi in contemplative calm for the *kudu* of the *sukanasa*. This again is a daring departure from the conventional representation of *Tandava* Siva in this *kudu* in the Chalukyan temples. Similarly also the representation of the *sukanasa* itself has a temple longitudinally with its own inner part constituting the shrine and outer slightly narrower constituting *ardha-mandapa* and the *triratha* frontage of the *sukanasa* lower *pada* comprising a fitting *mukha mandapa* projection also of this again are elements showing the skill in harmonising temple units. The *valabhi* of the *sukanasa* is of the *hamsa valabhi* type and the corners of the *rathas* show springing from the *phalaka* level *vyalas* in rearing posture. What is additionally interesting feature at the base of the *pada* in front of the *sukanasa* is the provision for a couchant bull laterally placed north-south, with face turned slightly east-west and very unfortunately damaged. This is most peculiar and at the same time a device for providing a most honoured place for the bull in the hierarchical scheme of Kailasa. It is all the more appropriate when Siva as *yogi* is placed on the *nasika kudu* above and his mount is placed below. It is, however, significant that this has not been an erratic feature, since we get an exactly similar representation, though in structural temple in the smaller of the two Shore temples of the time of Rajasimha at Mahabalipuram although the Pallava example does not have a *sukanasa* and the bull is thus placed on the *ardha mandapa* roof, as it were. It would perhaps he not a coincidence to suggest that Rajasimha's handiwork was deliberately imitated by Krishna's craftsmen at Kailasa in Ellora. The primary features of the *sukanasa* there is its semi-circular character unlike the normal horse-shoe shape. This is, of course, controlled by the *sala* behind but also the same there was no desire to raise the *mukha patti* and *saktidhvaja* unduly high and their own skylines itself in relation to the main *vimana* behind.

The side faces of the circular *pada* are shown in the form of pilastered divisions in which there is one *kapota panjara* under the *nasika* on either side of the centre of the inner part of the *pada*, while the central or the *bhadra* part of this inner section shows a regular double pilaster one on each side with *vyalas* rearing from the *phalka* level and with all the elements of the pillar shown including the *hamsa valabhi*. Inside these *kapota panjaras* and the central pilastered niches are shown figures of mother and child in the former and what appears to be *nayika* in the middle. This provision of a central projection and a lower wall projection in the from of a *kapota panjara* is itself in tune with the progress implicit in Chalukyan architecture already and this only has been effectively utilised in the temple mode at Kailasa here both in the main *vimana* as well as in the *sukanasa*. On the right of the circular *sala* is again placed the motif of the lion, this time trampling upon an elephant just shown in relief, although the confined elephant could not be visible from the front, but only from the sides. There is only one *kalasa* that is placed in the centre of the mid-rib.

Subsidiary Cave Excavations Along the Open Court

The subsidiary cave excavations on the flanks of the courts of Kailasa do not have any order or regularity. They were perhaps intended mainly to provide an outlet for the various ideas that were working in the minds of the artisans and patrons in their day.

The River Goddess Shrine

On the northern side of Kailasa open court, as it stands now, has been flanked by cloister passage of six bays stretch adjoining the river goddess shrine and giving access to the Lankesvara excavated temple in the upper floor. The corresponding ground floor of the Lankesvara also is part of the cloister passage which continues practically around the three sides of the temple unit reaches the triple storeyed cave excavation on the south side in front of the panel of Ravana-shaking-Kailasa, wherefrom the ridge wall is further taken up by such individual cave excavations like the so called *yajnasala*, further to the west in the upper floor, Surya temple on the ground floor and ending with a partially completed front portion of the barrel vaulted cave already mentioned. In this scheme it would appear that many of these individual cave excavations including the river Goddess shrine itself would pertain to different periods both contemporary and succeeding Kailasa, for, it is obvious that the main unit of Kailasa itself would have taken considerable time. It is, however, also shown in the study of cave temples, that the Lankesvara excavation would conveniently precede Kailasa, while the corresponding south side triple storeyed shrines would in a similar way well succeed Kailasa. Thus, it would appear that insofar as the cloister walks of uninterrupted character from the middle of the northern side to the middle of the southern side are concerned, this sould be taken as coeval with Kailasa, while the remaining part between the river Goddess shrine and the ground floor of Lankesvara had already been existing, when Lankesvara was excavated, since this is the only access to Lankesvara.

Insofar as the main Kailasa monolith is concerned, we have already dealt with the *dvara mandapa* in double storeyed series, from its exterior and interior aspects. It has been shown that the upper floor of the *dvara mandapa* shows a more plain wall section, divided by pilasters surmounted by the *kapota* and *vyalavari*, while the main axial part shows projecting balcony arrangement to the west. It is also the case on the inner side as well where the massive *kapota*-nearly 5' high—that would have over-shadowed the balcony projection is fortunately preserved for us, though only partly completed, as suggested by the *konapattai* floral plate fastening decoration shown in the north-east corner. This *dvara mandapa* is connected with the main unit by the roof of the corridor passage between the two open courts along the axial line, which spans the upper storey of the *dvara mandapa* with the *nandi-mandapa* and gives direct access through the *nandi-mandapa* to the *mukha mandapa* porch and *sabha mandapa* onto the sanctumsanctorum.

The vault of the central nave had been carried beyond the facade pillars in the excavation, on the south-west corner facing north, which is an aberration, if a *chaitya*-dormer face was intended to be cut-out ultimately. The excavation itself has not proceeded beyond the front facade *mandapa* comprising two free-standing pillars and three side pilasters and correspondingly a set of four pilasters on the back wall of which the corner ones have been found to be double pilaster type. The barrel vault has been kept rather flattened-top with the axial rafter shown from one end to the other, the radial rafters just being cut-out; the fastenings of these two series indicated by a series of bud-like projections. Since no direct flight of steps was provided for this and since it is connected to the adjoining cave temple type, this was probably an after thought.

The cave temple which is further to the east is of the simplest type with a well projected cornice beyond the facade pillars formed, as it were, the porch, an inner hole and an interior shrine carrying a rock-cut *linga* platform, circular in shape, was the only evidence to the *linga* projected well up to the wall having a cylindrical *linga* in the centre. Its pillars are all of similar order, well-known to the Rashtra-kuta times. This excavation is facing north.

Tke third miscellaneous excavation is just beyond the *yajnasala* carrying *Saptamatri* sculptures at the upper level and is found at the very ground level facing west and provided only with an open entrance *mandapa* carried only on two double pilasters in the sides within which the inner shrine proper is approached through the wall screen comprised of double pilasters in the corners, namely, the door-keepers, probably Ganga-Yamuna and an inner engaged pillar which is provided with *makara torana* on its top forming a 'W' shaped loop, whose *lalata-bimba* appears to be that of a seated figure of *Surya*. The pillar type is somewhat of the early from with a *ghatapallava*, basal square shaft of octagonal type, complete with *malasthana* and *padmabandha*, followed by a *kalasa, tadi. kumbha, padma* and *phalaka* over which the seated caryatid *ganas* support the capital blocks above, themselves decorated with looped festoons and immediately coming under the *valabhi* zone, the capital itself continued elsewhere in the *mandapa* as the *uttira*. Carvings of the river goddess, door-keepers, are of striking balance of daintiness and compare favourably with carvings in the Kailasa temple itself.

The interior is a rectangular hall against the wall of which is a pedestal of the *mancha-bandha* type, ending with a *kapota* on top, rectangular in shape and of *triratha* pattern is carved with provision for a socket on the top over which the figure would have been fixed. The figure is surrounded by two attendants, a male and a female on each side, female on the inner side and the male on the outer. The female is carrying flower in the hands, while the male in one case is carrying spear, while in the other *pujasamagri*. The central image of worship is missing, but it is just possible that it might be *Surya*, although the shrine is facing west. The character of the headgear of both the attendants calls for more remarks, since it comprises a conical upper part, mechanically continued to cover the neck beyond the ears, apparently forming a kind of an armour of protection. The image niche itself is flanked by pilasters surmounted by *makara-torana*.

The Vimana and the sub-Shrine

The main Kailasa *vimana*, set amidst a group of five subsidiary monolithic shrines in addition to the two more sub-shrines integrated with the corner of the *sabha mandapa*, is a balanced composition wherein the corner subsidiary monoliths on the north-east and south-east rise exactly up to the first *tala hara* top of the main *vimana* while the three subsidiary monoliths carved on the three cardinal directions of the court of the main *vimana* come only up to the *kapota* of the first *tala* of the main *vimana*. Again it is seen that of the five, the two former mentioned are also of the octagonal type of *sikhara*, while the three latter are of the *sala sikhara*. It has already been mentioned that the corner integrated *vimanas* of the *sabha mandapa* carry *kutas* or *caturasra sikharas* on their top as is quite necessary. The roof of the *sabha-mandapa* also carries in its centre a *samachaturasra sikhara* above set on a *vedi* and *griva*. Thus, the temple provides a range of representations well confined to the *chaturasra, ayatasra. astara* for the most but does not show of the *vritta* or circular from in any place. This is not to be taken as a deliberate omission, but rather as an intelligible application of the then extant practices which had not yet apparently introduced *vritta-sikhara* for shrines.

We would remember that in all the original uses known by this time whether the Chalukyan or the Pallava or the Pandya, the circular form had been employed only very rarely. In the Chalukyan region the circular form is practically not utilised excepting as in the Mallikarjuna temple at Pattadakkal which is seemingly closer to the Kailasa monolith in age, and all the prevailing mode after an early octagonal form is of usage that of a square. The Pallave does not introduce the cicrular *sikhara* until the closing years of the reign of Nandivarman II, whose Muktesvara called by the name of 'Dharma-mahadevisvaram' (by one of his queen's name) has the circular *sikhara*. Probably, this temple had not been constructed before the closing century A.D. On the Pandyan side, the famous monolith decades of the eighth at Kalugumalai to be dated perhaps around the eighth century A.D., if not slightly earlier, again opts for the octagonal *sikhara* and almost all the temples in the South Pandyan country have octagonal *sikhara* while in the north Pandyan area, square is more fovoured. Circular *sikhara* is very rare in the Pandyan country generally. Even in the early Chola temples it is primarily in some of Aditya's temple in the very last quarter of the ninth century A.D., that circular form had been introduced. The Muttaraiyars had already distinguished themselves by one of the earliest notable circular *vimana* itself with circular *sikhara* as at Vijayalayacholisvaram that could be dated just prior to the middle of the ninth century A.D. The Irukkuvels of Kodumbalur had consistently perferred the square shape for the *sikhara* until the close of the ninth century A.D. after which under Chola aegis, the circular form is dominant or found side by side with the square shape octagonal *sikhara* is very rare in the Chola country.

Thus, at the time when Kailasa was carved out, there was not even an anticipatory accommodation or suitability of the circular form for the *sikhora* of the southern *vimana*. It is in this context that those

Krishna's architects preferred to use almost all other shapes in their monoliths, major and minor at Kailasa.

Another interesting feature of the Kailasa *vimanas* with its *parivara* group is that the square and rectangular balance have been used more from the point of view of symmetry than any other ritual requirements. As already noted, the sub-shrines–monoliths on the three cardinal points are of rectangular shape, while the remaining two sub-shrines are square. Since these sub-shrines were intended for the *parivara devatas* respectively illustrated as Surya, Durga, Ganesa. Karttikeya, Jyestha, Chandesa and Saptamatris, it would be readily apparent that excepting for the Saptamatris, all the rest would appropriately be requiring a square shrine. the governing factor being that for individual deities only square shrine is proper, while for multiple deities rectangular shrines are a necessity. It should be noted, however, here that by the multiple deities what is meant is deities in groups each of whom are individualistic in their own right and not merely comprising the main divinity and their consort or consorts, Even the very possibility of the consorts being shown alike with the main deity does not gain currency in structural temples till very late and by that time the consorts had claimed independent shrines additionally, whether broadly of Saivite or Vaishnavite character in the form of Amman or Sri shrines. Unfortunately these was no early context that for an individual deity a rectangular shrine was carved. But here in the Kailasa group this has seemingly been introduced. From the internal evidence it is only the southern and cardinal sub-shrine that has inside a continuous pedestal along the back walls for Saptamatris apparently, and in all other cases there is only one pedestal, but it should be noted that in the rectangular shrines rectangular pedestals had been employed. Besides, in the cave temple period for all divinities, even single rectangular pedestals were common, in preference to square pedestals. The earliest such could be quoted at the Vaishnava cave of Badami, squarely dated by about 570 A.D., and instances may be multiplied. The usage had been complicated because of the practice of cutting the pedestal against the back wall and providing a socket for the placement of the divinity where separately shown. This practice itself is prevailing consistently in most of the Eastern Chalukyan cave temples and even at Ellora in temples of the transitional period from the late Western Chalukyan stage to the early Rashtrakuta as at Ravan-ki-Khai (cave XIV), Darsvatara (Cave XV) (in the cardinal sub-shrines of the *mandapa*). Thus, it was perhaps appropriate that rectangular pedestals were employed for individual deities as well and in consideration of this primary practice, it is likely that craftsmen for the Kailasa group carved out rectangular or *ayatasra vimanas* more than one in number for the sub-shrines with rectangular pedestals inside. Considerations of of symmetry no doubt prevailed also since otherwise, only Saptamatri shrine would be rectangular and all other square. This would have introduced an element of disunity in the very plinth lay-out of Kailasa, since, as would be seen, the projections of the massive walled plinth of Kailasa themselves show rectangular offsets between the eastern corners and the western *mahamandapa*, while the very *karna* parts on the eastern corners are essentially square. Thus, in order to harmonise the plinth scheme on the one hand and exploit the permissible rectangular pedestal usage for individual deities on the other, carving of multiple rectangular sub-shrine had been adopted.

The stature of the sub-shrines wherein the two corner ones are of *tritala* scheme and the three cardinal ones of the *ekatala* (*Pl. LIII*) scheme again was perhaps deliberate, since the subsidiary shrines were operating under certain limitations (*Pl. LIV*) imposed by the rituals by now expanding in operation. By these, the subsidiary shrine has necessarily to be of a storeyed stature less than that of the main shrine. It is not merely a matter of shrine alone, but of constituent or comparable elements. Thus, since the main Kailasa *vimana* is of the *chaiustala* type, no subsidiary shrine can also be of *chatustala* character. Thus the *tritala* stature of the corner shrines was well informed. As regards the rectangular shrines, it has been a general practice, particularly in early stages, not to raise *ayatasra vimanas* to more than *dvitala* height, at best. In fact, *ekatala ayatasra vimanas* were the norm. The tallest (by way of *talachhanda*) *ayatasra vimana* with *salasikhara* as exemplified in Ganesh Dath and Bhimaratha respectively well conform to this stipulation. Thus, the *ekatala vimana* character of the rectangular cardinal sub-shrines is olso well founded. It may actually be noted that in Kailasa while carving the *maha mandapa,* Krishna's architects had introduced in their very work whole concepts of dvitala, *chaturasra vimanas* as in the corner elements or *karnakutas*, and *ayatasra dvitala vimanas* as in the *bhadra sala* over the projecting porches, wherein the lowest *tala* is an open balcony type, but a second tala to it had been well provided and integrated with the *sala* forming the organic part of the *hara*, this style having been raised in order to accentuate this *dvitala* stature. This, considered from all angles, the craftsmen working on their major assigment, namely, Kailasa monolithic complex, were confining themselves scrupulously to the existing norms and usages, and at the same time introducing innovations which were not violating the canonical injunctions.

The main *vimana* and the subsidiary *vimanas* show another incidental features of signsficance. The last *tala* of the main *vimana* shows on the *grihapindi* monolithic *nandi* carved out on the diagonal points and placed in a clockwise direction of orientation. Correspondingly, the sbusidiary *vimanas* also have on the *grihapindi* figures but not those which have been recommended as appropriate to the divinities established into the sub-shrines in the following agamic period. For instance, the *agama* injunctions well followed say from the second half of the ninth century A.D., described the respective *vahana devatas* to be established as the animals or birds on the *grihapindi*, by which lion appears in Durga shrines, Garuda appears in Vishu shrines. Elephant appears in Karttikeya shrines and so on. Here, however, the subsidiary shrines also continue, where extant, to show mainly *yaksha* or *gana* figures on the corners as part of the partly decorative or internal element. This would perhaps emphasise the fact that the very feature of subsidiary shrines was not yet undergoing a sea-change during the time Krishna's monolith was carved.

The main *vimana* of Kailasa, as observed above, is of *chatustala samachaturasra triratha* lay-out with *astasra griva* and *sikhara.* The *vinyasasutra* line follows a very subdued *pancharatha* in the ground *tala*, with the *triratha* character emphasised somewhat more in the upper *talas*. As regards the overall size of the *talas*, the ground *tala* decidedly much taller compared to the other *talas*, while the last two *talas* are practically of the same type, the second being half of the size of the first. In opting for this stature or *talachhanda*, more than one consideration might have prevailed. Firstly, the ground *tala* appropriately could not be lesser than the solid *bhumitala* in height and, this being so, the upper *talas* have necessarily to be in their turn worked out within the scope of rock available from the *sikhara* downwards. Since the solid *bhumitala* or plinth and the ground *tala* of the main *vimana* would be equal. A question would arise as to why, these two could not have been made lesser and further, either the heights of the upper storeys could not be appropriately increased or even the *talas* themselves increased in number. It would be essential to point out that all these facts would have been duly taken into account before the monolith had been designed. The *first* important dimension (of the 'Southern' *vimana* order) that would have been established when the monolith was started, would be the dimension of the topmost *tala* and accordingly the *sikhara* that will come over it. It is necessary to understand that the topmost *tala* is the real *alpa vimana* whose measurements bear the direct relationship with the dimensions of the sanctum or the shrine chamber at the ground floor. This fact gets nearly blurred in later temples in the mediaeval times but is well maintained in the earlier temples by which the topmost storey is essentially the superimposed and self-contained unit forming the shrine proper and the additional *talas* convey a direct relationship in their turn with the scope of the total thickness of the shrine wall which would accommodate the expanding width of the *talas* working downwards. Since a shrine consists of the thickness of the wall, or the *bhitti* carrying the *hara*, the *alinda* or the passage that would be allowed for circumambulation in an *anarpitha* kind, the *antara bhitti* or inner wall representing the width of the upper *talas* and finally the *griva* and the *sikhara*, representing the *grihapindi*, the total thickness should be divisible into these four main component parts and the basal storey in its width should be able to accommodate the multiples of these components in relation to the height of the storeys. Krishna's Kailasa, of course, is of *arpita* kind where the *hara* is applied to the *pada* of the next *tala*. But the basic applicability of the formula continues, since appropriately the ground *tala*, which in *anarpita* temples, might have been *sandhara*, would be *niradhara* in *arpita* shrines, *i.e.*, not having a covered passage around the cella. Applying this rule, it would be seen that *chatustala* stature of Kailasa is well maintained over the distribution of the width of successive *talas* working downwards from the top and beyond the basal dimensions of the top *tala* which would represent the sanctum. In other words, the projection of the *hara* of the three lower *talas*, added to the thickness between the *griva* and the top *tala* wall, would indeed give the total thickness of the ground *tala* wall around the sanctum chamber, and this what has happened. In order to achieve this, it is essential to keep the *talas* of a particular height, since the height also in its turn would bear a proportion of the thickness of the wall. The significant additional consideration is that during the time of Krishna, there was nowhere a temple erected taller than four *talas*. In fact, the texts prescribe a limit of a normal *jati vimana* as four *talas*, and any *vimana* which is of more than four in its storeys would be calssifiable actually as *mukhya vimanas* and *mukhya vimanas* are rare. The texts themselves give only abstract measurements of *mukhya vimanas* higher than four *talas* up to 18 *talas*, which is the limit of the *mukhya vimana* stature. Therefore, during the time Kailasa was carved out, there was no possibility of raising *talas* higher than four in number and operating under this disability Krishna's craftsmen starting from the top taking into account the total height of rock available and careful to highlight this great edifice from outside by providing the solid plinth or *bhumitala* and desiring to be in conformity with the ruling of having the first *tala* equal to the plinth or *bhumitala* and making the *talachhanda* of the *arpita* shrine that they were rasing and working out satisfactorily after providing a reasonable passage around the main *vimana* for access to the subsidiary shrines and for its own *pradakshina patha*, could not nave arrived at a more perfect designing of the temple they wanted than the one they actually carved. In spite of this remarkable achievement of perfection amidst the difficulties of the situation, the fact that the component elements of the temple itself are reasonably simple, goes far to show the designing capabilities of Rashtrakuta carftsmen. That they should have carried it out on the rock-cut media where the slightest mistake or mismanagement would throw the entire work into a state of irregular, a typical and disterted scheme, is a perfect vindication of their sure adherance to texts which had given elaborate measurements for component elements.

In between these two massive pillars the main access to the temple comprises a non-functional lower *tala* whose external wall face alone is carved and which bears a second *tala* shrine as *nandi mandapa* of the longitudinal access. This solid first *tala* pillared *nandi-mandapa* shows above an *upana* and *jagati* or plain character, a plain *kantha* nearly 3' high carved with a series of *mithuna* couples and followed by a *kapota*. Upon the *kapota* the wall space is divided into three main parts each of them further divided into a *pancha ratha* lay-out. The lowest course above the *kapota* is the rafter frame work with the projecting end indicated by animals and the lateral ends by *makara* terminals. Upon this, the central part of the wall spaces is further divided by a thin narrow projecting screen-like pilaster wherein the elements of the pillars are shown in an abrreviated form with the shaft part carrying on a *gajamunda*, a rearing *vyala* with riders and outriders, surmounted by boldly relieved human figures representing celestials up to the top part of the shaft. The cornermost part further has the full rendering of the pillar almost exactly similar to the larger *dhvajastambha* in the courtyard. With this difference that on the top of it is a heavy *gana* squatting and supporting, like a caryatid, the weight of the superstructure. The *kapota* above is very massive and is followed by a like arrangement of division of wall space in which the major difference is that in the place of the *yakshi* or semi-divine figures shown on the pilasters, it is the *kinnars* and *kinnaris* and the like that are shown indicating the different strata of spaces. The wall spaces on the solid lowest *tala* show the figure of *tandava* Siva in the centre and *Ardhanari* and *Visnu* to the proper right and left.

The corresponding upper *tala* has the central part done in the form of a door-opening surmounted by a *makara torana*, while the sides are rendered in the form of *dvarapala* attendants. The niche frame work of the *tandava* Siva is in the main similar to those of Ganesa and Durga mentioned earlier.

Over the second *tala kantha*, again, come the rafter courses, followed by the *alingapatti kantha* and a slightly narrower *kapota*, surmounted by a more rafter courses and the *vidhana phalaka*. This first floor or second *tala nandi mandpa* is given access to the main shrine by a passage rears a *mandapa* carrying a *vedi*, on either flank, and connecting the *nandi-mandapa* with the main shrine. The entrance staircase into the main shrine itself is provided on either side of this lower open *mandpa*, under the passage by flight of steps running east-west, and then turning north and south from either side. This lower *mandpa* is decorated by two major panels facing each other on its inner and outer faces, the central figure being Siva as *Mahayogi*, in the case of the western facing panel, and *Gajantaka* in the other one. The *Gajantaka* figure is a massive composition with the God having ten hands, carrying the elephant tusk, *trisula, damaru* in the three of the right hands, *kapala* in one of the left, two more left hands engaged in being placed against the waist and in pacifying Parvati seated on the lower left. The remaining hands support the elephant skin whichh as been worn around the God, the head of the elephant itself being prominently shown to the proper right. There are two *ganas* (*Pl. V*) shown in *vismayahasta* in the outer zone on either side of the *Jata* of the God whose locks stand on their ends in vertical curls. The chest of the God is thrust forward and there are a number of figures shown below, of which the *matrs* with their *lanchanas* are visible in a row to the right end—*Bhringi* dancing in the centre, below the God's striding legs, with *Bhringi* again shown to the left leg of Siva. The dancing figure of Bhringi has cusped projections of the *trisula* on the head.

The opposite figure of Siva as *Mahayogi* is surroundded by *ganas*, *rishis* and *dikpalas* of which from the right are *Varuna*, *Vayu*, *Agni*, *Isana*, *Indra*, *Yama*, *Kubera*, *Nirutti*. The main figure of the God again is eight-armed, with the right arms on the lap and broken with *akshamala*, *naga* and *vyakhyamudra*, left arms carrying lotus and in hand palm up on the lap corresponding to the *vyakhyamudra* and the remaining two being broken. The figure is considerably decorated in its *jatamakuta* and on the body and shows on both ears *nakra kundalas*. The figure is shown as seated under a tree. It is interesting to note that some of the *yogis* depicted are very meagrely clothed and have very pointed beards and side whiskers, indicating they were votaries of *pasupata* cult, perhaps.

The two entrances to the main shrine in the upper *tala* have been camouflaged by a verandah carved into a series of pilaster spaces complete up to the *salasikhara*, while the side faces have been engraved with narrow miniature panels of the Epics. Above them the actual *mukha mandapa* of the main inner shrine occurs, borne upon a *vedi* having an *east-west* facing elephant *kakshasana* dwarf pillars, corbels and *kapota* with the *prastara* taken up to the next *kapota* but not showing any *hara* of *kutas* or *salas* on their top and showing only rearing lions in the corners. These *haras* of *kutas* and *salas* are reared on the main *maha mandapa* of the temple, which occurs immedialely within this *mukha mandapa*. Externally this *maha mandapa* beginning is indicated beyond the panel of epics as over a lower *adhisthana* part comprising *upana*, plain *jagati*, two receding *pattikas*, *padma*, a bold *kantha* part which have been relieved by a series of elephants, *vyalas*, leogriphs and lions and succeeded by the real *adhisthana* part of the main shrine lower above the *upapitha*. This *adhisthana* has an *upana*, high rectangular *jagati*, a recessed *kantha*, a *tripatta kumuda*, another *kantha* with two courses representing *uttira* and *vajana* followed by the *kapota*. Over the *kapota* comes the *vyalavari* followed by the *vedi* upon which the actual temple rises with the corners of the *maha mandapa* having projecting shrine units externally indicated, but internally non-functional, complete with shaft, *potika*, *uttira*, *vajana* and *kapota*. In these corner parts above this, there is a second narrow corner shrine unit which is again with its own shaft, *potika*, a *valabhi* having *malavahaka* type, followed by the *kapota* whose *prastara* carries the *kuta-sikhara* in the corner above its *griva*. There is a recess immediately adjoining these corner parts which are *karnakutas* which are followed by a slightly projecting part, whose central section is completely projecting forward in the form of a balcony and which, however, carries all the details similar to the *karnakutas*, except that the balcony is an open pillared balcony and the unit upon the pillared balcony is a broader rectangular unit, unlike square corner unit. The space flanked by the balcony opening is left plain except for occasional relieved carvings of *Vidyadharas* or 'cut-in' sculptures probably carved later, while the recesses between the *karnakuta* and the *madhya sala* show in their lower parts openings provision of *gavaksha* windows. The top of the *prastara* above these *karnakutas* and *madhyasalas* have, as already mentioned, the *kutasikhara* in the corner, and a *harantara* of *trisakha* intervened by single *nasika* in the *bhadra sala*. The *nandi-mandapa* has double pilasters at the corners at right angles pointing at each other. These are complete from *pitha* to *potika* followed by a double *uttira*, *vajana*, one above the other, and followed by a *valabhi* another *vajana* and a ceiling. The *nandi*, which is at present found here, had been apparently fixed later, since it is not monolithic nor does it have its dimensions commensurate with the stature of the temple.

The superstructure above the *mukha mandapa* has its *bhadra* part provided with a *triratha* projection while the end parts have been provided with *nasika panjaras*, the pilasters in the *pada* part being carved with female *nayikas*. The *kapota* of this *mukha mandapa* is very elaborately provided with *madhya* and *konapattais* of considerably completed scroll work.

The ceiling of this *mukha mandapa* has a lotus medallion and has been apparently very elaborately painted *pada* on the top and on the sides much of which is well visible, testifying to the high water mark of excellence achieved in the painting skill. The door frame of this *mukha mandapa* leading into the *mahamandapa* has *dvarapalas* placed as part and parcel of the bold inner pilaster of the *mandapa* on the side faces, with the result that the *dvarapalas* are actually facing each other, but have been bestowed a body which relieves much of their heaviness. Within these the door rises in a *pancha-sakha* scheme with the innermost *ratnasakha* and the *sakha* of human figures and *mithunas* of main pilaster and the *padmasakha*. At the lowest zone are shown Ganga and Yamuna with dwarf attendants and female accompaniment. Above the lintel of the door frame, is a series of *bharaputras* shown supporting the main *uttira* above, which is thin and flat followed by a *vajana*, *hamsa valabhi* and a *kapota*, over which there is a narrow *kantha* with a ceiling resting upon it.

The *maha mandapa* is divided into a scheme of five bays

longitudinally and transversely with balcony projections aligned to the central transverse bays. The pillars show considerable variation in their composition, the alternate series being of similar character, the two broad divisions being that of the southern unit consisting of the *pitha* shaft, *kalasa*, *tadi* and *kumbha* and of the northern type carrying above the shaft of *ghata pallava* type. The *potikas* are of a simple curved type with median band also shown plain. The central *ankana* shrine ceiling has a *tandava* Siva, presumably on *apasmara* with Parvati standing nearby, whose shoulders being touched by one of the hands of Siva, with a *gana* playing on the drum to the left on the left lower part. The central longitudinal and transverse bays are broader, while the two end bays on either side are narrower, resulting in a rather poor inter-columniation, thereby, the corners cluttered with too many pillars leaving the spaces in the upper zone considerably dark. It was perhaps intended as a natural reaction to the need, though non-functional, for supporting the lintels and the ceiling slabs, notwithstanding the monolitic character of the whole composition.

The *ardha mandapa* in front of the shrine chamber is a square borne upon rectangular end pillars two inner pilasters, adjoining but not attached to the inner wall, upon which the ceiling is supported, also resting on the side screens flanking the door frame and the *uttaranga* of the door frame itself. The two side walls of the *ardha mandapa* have sculpture composition in niches, whose *adhisthana*, in the form of a simple *mancha*, is borne in its *kantha* part by a series of four *ganas* in the case of the southern wall and upon which, within a pilastered niche complete up to its *salasikhara* is found a *vrishabha-rudha somaskanda*. (*Pl. LVI*). Behind the Somaskanda composition are shown two *chamaradharinis* and two *dvarapalas*. Uma is seated in the left lap of Siva which is flexed straight while his other leg is hanging down the caparisoned back of the Nandi, while on the right lap, whose leg is hanging is seated Skanda showing *suchi hasta* of his left hand, the *Jagatpati*. The right hand of Uma is clasped around the neck of Siva resting on his right shoulder while the left hand of Siva is jointly holding the waist of Uma. On the northern wall, the *adhisthana* is much more boldly projecting forward, essentially of a same *mancha* composition, the *kapota* part showing the bull (apparently

Nandi) with a number of *ganas* playing with it or fondling it. Above the *adhisthana* is seen what is the remaining part of a broken composition in which the torso of Uma is seen seated with the left hand resting on the left lap and much of the right hand and leg broken. The other figure which should have been Siva is totally missing and a socket is found in his place. In between Uma and this socket is found a platform like *pitha* upon which the dice board is delineated.

The main shrine has Ganga and Yamuna shown in a very bold fashion on either side on the side pilasters while the main shrine door frame itself also shows Ganga and Yamuna with attendants, together with the *dvarapalas* in the lowest part of the jambs.

The sanctum is a square chamber, whose height is almost equal to the basal width and in the centre of which is placed a detachable *linga* borne on a rock-cut *pitha* of circular cross section and having a very long water-chute projection or *varimarga*, integrally cut into the live rock across the chamber and the shrine wall, and emerging out in the form of a *pranali*. The water-chute projection is one piece from floor to its channel-led top. The *linga* stone would seem to be sandstone, while the *pitha* being monolithic and integral with the rock is trap. Only the side of the *linga* has been smoothly finished, while the top has been chiselled and but not ground and polished. The way in which the *linga* is fixed rather with a tilted shaft indicates that it is not integral with the *pitha*, even in its original. The *linga* does not have any indication of its orientation also by the incurving of the *madhyanadi* and *brahmasutras*. Much of the *pitha* had also been later reconstructed in dressed stone masonry added to what would have been originally a damaged monolithic *pitha*. Whether the *linga* shaft was even in original, however, integral with the *pitha* cannot be assessed in its present condition. The analogy of the other caves at Ellora would seem to show that the *pitha* alone was cut out of the live rock and the *linga* installed separately. This is a variant of the Chalukyan made in rock cut caves where the *linga* and *pitha* are together integral parts of live rock although this type where the *pitha* is cut in live rock and *linga* is perhaps separately fixed as also found in the Badami cave group. A slightly earlier occurrence of this type is also noted in the Udayagiri caves next Bhilsa.

The dwarf pillars of the balcony are of the *ghata-pallava* type. Outside the doors leading to the balcony on either side are also found *dvarapalas.*

On the *prakara*, the exterior wall of the shrine is dividedinto five spaces by three projections and two recessions, the recessions have niche shrines not rising up to the top, but about two thirds high, complete from plinth to the *nasika* on top. These units two on each side represent *nasika panjaras* or *kapota panjaras* and since the shrine units represented inside their *kudus* are excepting in one case of *dvitala chaturasra vimana* models. The solidary remaining examples are showing *astasra, dvitala* model. It is possible that these are actually representing the *sukanasas* attached to such temples. The main projections in the centre and in the corners have two vertical divisions formed by carved niches which are supported at the bottom by the *bharaputra* and which carry above a *mayuratorana,*, itself having the figure of Gajalakshmi at either end; in some places. it is *makara-torana* also. The central *torana*, however, is with human head and the floriated tails of a *makara* above this in the upper zone right in the centre are relieved figures of *Vidyadharas.* The pilasters in each of these cases are double pilasters in each of these cases are double pilasters, one projecting outward and the other sideward, and rise up to their full stature up to the entire height of the *tala* with a series of bands at successive intervals connected by *patralata* vertical band work and surmounted by the scheme of *kalasa, tadi, kumbha, padma* and *phalaka* and *potika* and *uttira*, the *valabhi* zone is of the *bhutavari* type with garlands being carried by these *bhutas.* Over the *kapota* is the rafter composition, animals like elephants and vyalas, standing for the projecting rafters and over this *alingapatti* the vedi comes up followed by a *kantha*—like recess which forms part of the *prastara*, and stands for the *griva*, above which rises the *hara* of *kutas* and *sala sikharas* with *nasika kudus* in between the central *nasika* of the *harantara* being larger than the side ones. Above this *arpita* (applique) *harantara* rises the *pada* of the second *tala* and is similarly divided into five sections the *bhadra sala* and the *karnakutas* with the *kapota* in between where there are no integrally surmounted *nasikas*, but only those which occur on the *kapota* just above with which they are connected by regular pilasters. The *karna* brackets of the projecting parts of the wall spaces are further relieved by rearing *vyalas* at the angles. The *valabhi* of the second *tala* is a *hamsa valabhi* and over this above its *kapota* and *prastara* again there is a *hara* of *kuta* and *sala* with *nasika* intervening on the *harantara*. The third *tala*, much narrower than the second is rising on the *harantara* and has only three projections and two recesses without the *nasika panjara* in view of the reduced dimensions, the projections carrying the *kuta* and *sala sikharas* on the top. Above this, the fourth *tala* rises following the pattern of the third *tala*, but without any *hara* of *kutas* and *salas* above the rafter frame work of its *prastara*, but only having the *pidhana phalaka* which closes the superstructural composition and bears the *griva* and the octagonal *sikhara* above. Thus, the temple is a *chatustala vimana* of the *samachaturasra* type with octagonal *sikhara*.

The *pranala* of the main shrine is of the *vyalamukha* type and is set upon the topmost part of the *adhisthana* which comprises an *upana*, a high *jagati*, *padma* and a thick *prati* in place of the *pattika* and the *pranala* is resting upon this *prati* in the main *pada*, the receptacle which will receive the *abhisheka* water out of the *pranala* is shown integrally cut on live rock in front of the *pranala* in continuation of it, so that under the *pranala* projection, the rock is shown as one piece right down up to the flooring. This is an echo of the usage prevalent in the rock-cut examples wherein immediately below the water-chute projection of the *linga-pitha* a depression either rectangular or circular in the from of a rock-cut cistern is cut to receive the *abhisheka-jala* and this should, therefore, be taken as a transition in monolithic medium to the presence of the cistern placed immediately below comparatively in structural temples and directly aligned with the terminal of the *pranala* perhaps by a suitable bracket figure motif carrying on its outer face a cut joinery for leading the water into the cistern. The subsidiary shrines are single shrine chamber units without even a *mukha mandapa* and have in the chamber, a monolithic pedestal, integral with the live rock cut back-to-back with the rear wall in a rectangular way with the water-chute projection provided on one of the sides and with a socket hole in the centre cut in such a way in a stepped fashion in order to receive a statuary. The moulding of the pedestal are ***upana*, *padma*,** *kampa*, *kumuda*, *kantha*, a series of two *kampas* standing for *uttira* and *vajana* followed by a *kapota*, a *prati* upon which is a heavy *pattika*. The shrine has double pilastered corners showing complete unit from *pitha* to *potika* and the *uttira* and the upper mouldings as well, and are approached by a *sopana* with *surul-yali* balustrade. One of them has a socket depression on the floor at the corner immediately adjoining the corner pilasters and intended to receive the *abhisheka-jala* from the *nala* which is cut on its *prati*, which has got a quadrantally drooping water-chute further beyond the limit of the *kapota* reaching down to the *kantha* level.

The arrangement of the topmost tier of the *maha mandapa* shows that the central *sala* above the projecting balconies on its rear wall were much higher than the remaining *salas*, one on each side which are of the same height as the *karnakutas*. These central *salas* which are shown only on three sides, excluding the east, are in addition, shown higher on the western side than on the northern and the southern sides. Therefore, even among the *salas* three different heihgts had been worked out depending upon whether the particular *sala* is on the front, side of the temples, on the sides of the temples or in the side *haras*. Thus, to some extent they have attempted a progressive heightening of the members of consecutive units of the entire complex by which, starting from the *gopura*, the *sikhara* on the *gopura* is less high than the topmost part of the *nandi-mandapa*, which itself is lower than the top of the *mukha mandapa* which is lower to the central *sala* on the western part, which has its *sukanasa* attached to the main superstructure and behind which the superstructure of the shrine itself rises much higher. The idea was to get as much out of the declivity of the rock here, as possible, since the rock itself is, in its contours, seen almost touching the tops of the units mentioned above. Therefore, they had concentrated only upon the frontal aspect of the shrine. Even so, they had shown the main shrine, its *ardha mandapa*, *maha mandapa* and *mukha mandapa* as integral parts, and a front *nandi-mandapa* and the exterior *dvara mandapa*, as two isolated units, although connected by a passage. The intention in providing for a very massive non-functional solid ground floor, which is but a glorified *upapitha* to the *adhisthana*, is itself to lift the profile of the temple and its skyline as high as possible, and this, combined with the fact that they had almost followed the topmost contours of the whole solid slope would show very great care had been exercised in laying out the temple.

The roof of the *mukha mandapa*, *nandi-mandapa* and the *gopuradvara* show certain features, which may be briefly referred to here. The *gopuradvara* as is necessary, shows a *sala sikhara* on the top with the *sala* disposed north-south and *nasikas* provided on four faces. It has, however, been scooped a little in its core, perhaps to insert the series of kalasas in one piece in the socket here, and left, as it is, after perfecting the sides of the *salasikhara*. The roofs of the *nandi-mandapa* and the *mukha-mandapa*, however, have *pithas* with *kalasa* and *stupi* in the centre and the *nandis* in the four corners immediately outside them, in the case of the *nandi-mandapa* and a series of receding *padmadalas* ending in a *padmakesara* at the centre with two rearing lions on the front corners. These again were expected to heighten the profile of the temple and in addition to introduce certain elements, which were prevalent in the northern style of temples in their *sikharas*. The roof of the *maha mandapa* similarly shows rearing lions alone around its central *kalasa* and *stupi pitha*. The most important feature of the composition, however, is the *sukanasa*, itself attached integral with the main superstructure of the *vimana* proper at its upper *tala*, and has a projectional depth equal to the *ardha mandapa*. This *sukanasa* has actually an arrangement of a pillared shrine supporting a *salasikhara* placed upon the typical *prastara* of the lower *tala* of this pillared shrine. This, unlike the *sukanasas* which are attached to the northern style temples, even in the Deccan, which follow the peculiar arrangement of overlapping quadrantal tiers with frontal *mukhapatti* and *sakti dhvaja* on top forming harmonised parts of the sale to which they belong, is actually a Dravidian pattern of the typical *sukanasa*, and is merely repeating in a longitudinal way, a *sala* frontally over a small shrine chamber. Thus it indicates the indispensability of *sukanasa* for this region, a feature which is totally absent in the Tamil country. The fact that the *sukanasa* is adopted to the *sala* of the main shrine, whether northern or southern, is itself an equal proof of its ritual necessity in this region. The *kapota* of the *sukanasa* composition is aligned to the *kapota* of the second *tala* of the temple and the top of the *sukanasa* itself is reaching the top of the *kapota* of the third *tala*. *Nandis* have been placed on the corners of the topmost *tala* below the *griva*.

Outer Corridor of Pradakshina Patha of Kailasa

The first panel shows a *linga* with square *pitha*, while the pithas found in Kailasa and in Dasavatara cave are of circular section. It shows the mouldings of an *upana*, *padma*, *kantha*, *kumuda* and *pattika*.

The third panel again shows Siva holding together with Parvati a *linga* on a *pitha*. This would appear to be a variant of the other types found in Ellora, Aihole, Pattadakkal etc., in the Deccan and Kanchi, Melapazhuvur, Kodumbalur–Siva carrying a *linga* on his shoulders. The *pitha* here is again square but has the mouldings of *padma*, bold *kantha*, with *kampa* above and below, followed by a *kapota* and a *prati*. A slight projection on the western side of the *pitha* is shown, apparently standing for the water-chute. The *linga* and the *pitha* would seem to be of almost equal height.

An interesting sculpture in the remaining series is the lingodbhava panel directly aligned to the longitudinal strike of the main temple. This Lingodbhava is facing west as it should according to established southern canons—and is flanked by the figures of Brahma and Visnu in *Anjali hasta* standing near. This is an almost exact replica of Lingodbhava type at Kunrakkudi cave in the Pandyan country and this possibly helps us to date in some form the latter, as we know very well the date of Kailasa cava. The nature of the orientation of the Pandyan Lingodbhava, however, would show it as an earlier specimen and if so Kailasa merely recapitulates the southern variant of this iconography with orientation well fixed, thus perhaps making this Kunnakkudi cave datable to mid eighth century A.D. if not slightly earlier.

Of the sub-shrines, the one at the north-west corner forming integral part of the *Karnakuta* of the *sabha mandapa* is intended for Ganesa, as suggested by a large sized carving of Ganesa in the deep niche inside. The reason why it has not been carved into a shrine is because the thickness of the wall did not permit it. This niche shrine is provided with outer corner cantoning pilasters rising from the level of the *prakara* floor, on the *phalaka* of which at the corners of the intersecting corbels rising Vidyadhara figure is shown as à bracket supporting the *kapota* in between the turning of the *bhutavalabhi* course. The niche itself is cut in the centre of the wall space within and shows a seated Ganesa with right leg flexed laterally inwards and left leg flexed vertically, fore-legs being very short and provided with *kinkinis.* The God is four-armed, the two left arms are holding as *vajra* in the upper and *modaka patra* in the lower, while the right arms hold a *parasu* in the upper, and, though broken, might have held the broken *danta* in the lower. The *mastaka* does not carry any regular crown except a full plain *padma* placed on the top, while the ears show sprouts of lilies and are well spread laterally with curved pointed tips. There is a broad *kanthi* with bells around the neck, *keyuras*, *udarabandha* of *naga* and *yajnopavita*. The trunk from what remains of it was seemingly turned to the left and so short because the chest of the figure is intact. The right leg shows its toes bent inwards realistically. The figure is seated on *padmapitha.* It is quite typical of western and eastern Chalukyan Ganesas, and forms the interesting type by itself, in its simplicity of decoration, realistic body rendering and massive character. This sub-shrine is facing east.

The next sub-shrine corresponding to the *bhadrasala* of the main *vimana*, but broader than that is an *ayatasra dvitala* shrine with *salasikhara* represented by a ground *tala* borne upon a plinth having the mouldings of *upana*, high *jagati*, *padma*, and *prati*, over which a set of four pilasters, the corner one being of the cantoning type dividing the wall section into three parts of which on the southern side direction in which the temple is facing in the centre is cut a door frame aligned with a flight of steps below. Flanking the door frame are shown two female door keepers. The pillars show all the elements of a prevailing square section up to *phalaka* above which the corners of the narrowly set intersecting corbels are shown rearing *vyalas* supporting the *kapota*. Over the kapota occurs the *prastara* consisting of the vyalavari, and *vedi* followed by very attenuated *kantha*, representing the second *tala pada*, showing the *uttira*, *vajana* and *valabhi* and also showing rearing *vyalas* in the corners. The fact that this *pada* further emphasised by the representation of a *kapota*, *panjara* rising from the top of the *vedi*, on pilasters with a *kapota* and *vedi*, further stunted pilasters harmonising with the *nasikas* on the main *kapota* of the second *tala*. The broader side shows a regular *bhadra* projection on the *pada* with two wide set pilasters and rearing *vyalas*, just outside them locating the *kapota panjaras* in the *karna* part. Over the second *tala kapota* occurs the *vyalavari*, *vedi* and main *griva* followed by the *salasikhara*. The *griva* itself is very narrow and the elaborate *nasikas* as the end faces of the *sala* are supported on their terminal underside by obliquely set human figures from the point where the *makara* terminals of the *vyalavari* meet. The central part of the *sala* has also a prominently projecting *nasika* like a *sukanasa*. There is only one *kalasa* extant on the top mid rib, although the total number would have been three as suggested by the three *padmadala* seatings. The three faces of the *sala* ends show representations of Surya as riding on his seven-horsed chariot on the western face and as standing in *samabhanga*, with two lotuses in the arms on the eastern face. This might tend to suggest that this shrine might be intended to Surya, although the shrine proper is facing south. It might also be appropriate that there were female door-keepers holding lotuses in their arms for the shrine, as already mentioned. There are two additional such representations between the two corner pilasters of the shrine front wall showing a mithuna couple in each in tight embrace. The remaining three walls are bare of sculptures. Important character of the sub-shrines consists in its not having a *hara* of *kutas* and *salas* in its *talas* either in both or in the lower one. This is repeated in the other two cardinal *sala* shrines as well are the only instances in this period of this type. The fact that the *kapota-panjaras* are repeated prominently and *haras* are eliminated would show that this seemingly formed a shrine so earlier proto-type would be the temple such as the upper Sivalaya at Badami. This shrine has been followed also in certain Eastern Chalukyan temples as at Biccavolu. Here it is employed to divide these *sala* shrines as close from a square sub-shrines in the rear corners.

The next sub-shrine, which is set in the north-east corner is of *samachaturasra tritala* with an *astasra griva* and *sikhara*. It has its plinth well mared out by *bhadrasalas* and *karnakutas* and two salilantara recesses, the latter showing double pilasters by their relation with the adjoining pilasters of the *karnakuta* and *bhadrasala*, while the corner pilasters of the *karnakutas* are of the cantoning type. The plinth shows a slight variation from the northern sub-shrine by having a *upana*, a *jagati*, a *padma*, a vritta *kumuda* and *prati*. Rising from the top of the *phalaka* in the *karna* as well as the *bhadra* parts are shown rearing *vyalas* supporting the *kapota*. The *nasikas* of the *kapota* show human faces. The *prastara* shows *vyalavari, vedi*, a narrow *griva* and the *hara* of *kutas, salas*, and *harantara*, the *harantara* unit well set apart, with three additional *nasikas* embellishing the *harantara*. The *pada* of the second *tala* shows a pilastered *bhadra* part and *karnas* in addition to the corner pilasters being provided with the *kapota panjaras* in the middle, aligning with the corresponding *nasikas* of the *kapota*. On this account the *prastara* shows *vyalavari, vedi* and the *griva* followed by the *salas, kutas* and *nasikas*. Over the *kapota* or the *harantara* of this *tala* rises the third *tala* to a height, almost the same as the *prastara* of the second provided with a pilastered *bhadra* unit ending with the *kapota* not showing the wall in the centre and the *kapota panjaras* aligned with the *nasikas* of the topmost corners. Over this would have risen the *vyalavari* and *grihapindi*, followed by an octagonal *griva* and *sikhara*, but much of the last *tala* and the *griva* are badly broken. The central *nasikas* of the *harantara* of the ground *tala* and the *kapota panjaras* of the successive *talas* show figure work inside the pilasters. The *bhadra pada* of the ground *tala* shows a *stambha-torana* consisting of pilasters up to the *phalaka* over which a *torana* rises almost continually. The pilastered niche shows almost standing divinity with the parasol above in *samabhanga*, with both the arms drooping at the side, left arm holding *kundika*, while within the *torana* a seated figure of a *yogi* with *lakuda* in one hand and what would be the *matulunga* fruit on the other hand is shown. He is also provided with a parasol. This figure is most likely to be Lakulisa, and would represent a standing figure of the same divinity further below.

The interior of the shrine is square provided with double pilasters above the corners surmounted by members up to the *valabhi* and its own *vajana*, both of square character. Against the eastern backwall of the shrine is a rectangular *pitha*, showing a moulding of *upana*, *padma*, *kampa*, *vritta kumuda*, high *kantha*, *kapota* and *prati*. On the top of this *prati* in the centre is cut a socket for seating the image. To the proper right towards the north cut on the *prati* and provided with a channel spouting descending up to the level of the kapota over the *nala*. The underside of the *nala* is unfinished.

The third sub-shrine at the cardinal eastern point is approximately similar to the corresponding northern sub-shrine excepting that it shows double pilasters in the *bhadra* projection of its corner side has *bhadra* projections on the breadth side as well enclosing a niche shrine surmounted by a *salasikhara* within on the southern side and a *nasika* on the northern side and has the carvings of *dvarapala* inside the pilastered *makara torana* in the corner parts of the front face. The other details are approximately similar. This *dvitala ayatasra* shrine with *salasikhara* has its *sikhara* badly broken, though retaining one of the *kalasas*. The dvarapalas are in *abhanga* and carry straight swords in the right hand and with the left hand in *kati*.

The interior is rectangular and has its pedestal unfinished.

The next sub-shrine in the south-east corner is one of the best preserved and shows similar to the north-east a *samachaturasra tritala vimana* with *astasra griva* and *sikhara*. It is, however, provided with double pilasters for its *bhadra* as well as *karna* parts making for a prevailing *pancha ratha* pattern of the base, which, like the north-eastern shrine shows on its plinth the *vritta kumuda* as well. The interesting additional features of this well preserved shrines are as follows :

(1) Its front face which is westwards shows *dvarapalas* on the wall space flanking the door frame, four-armed of whom one is a caryatid-like *gana* and is holding a mace at the ground level, right leg upon a seated caryatid *gana* and is having his *gada* at the ground level below which his left leg is entwined. They are shown within a *makara toranas* rising out of the inner double pilaster unit. The other *dvarapala* also four-armed is resting both his legs upon a caryatid-like *gana*. Two of the hands of the *dvarapala* hold *naga* and lotus; the other two are in *kati* or holding *gada* respectively. The *karnakuta* wall

of this space adjoining the *dvarapala* is decorated by another figure work of a male attendant at the northern end, holding what seems to be a cornucopia. He is two-armed and is having a *naga* hood above his head. Below his foot is shown separately in a small niche a later sculpture of a dancing figure with *naga* in one hand, with a female attendant in erotic posture. The figure to the southern end is a divinity in *samabhanga*, the left arm on the *kati-bandha* and right arm in *abhaya*, with the head in *jatamukuta*. He is standing upon a caryatid-like *gana* holding a *padma-pitha*.

(2) The pilasters flanking the door frame are different from others and show a square-sectioned shaft, a *malasthana* octagonal, followed by a *ghatapallava*, another *malasthana* of a receding octagonal and multi-fluted character, succeeded by *kalasa*, *tadi* etc., of curvilinear section upon the *phalaka*.

(3) The side walls show representations of *pancharatha sala* and *gajapristha vimanas*, the latter shown with the *nasika* on top and rising to *dvitala*, stature, all of them shown as *alpa vimana* units and the *hara* of *kuta* and *sala* below the *griva* and members of the *prastara* well emphasised and contributing with the height of the model. This is the only place at Kailasa, where (a) *alpa-vimana* models show haras as well; and (b) where in the *alpa-vimana* model, we have the *gaja-pristha kriti* also depicted, since otherwise the top of these lateral models should have shown a *sikhara* behind the *nasika*.

The third *tala* shows in the corners of the *bhadra*, a full *alpa-vimana* unit of *chaturasra* type complete with all the elements of the *prastara*, but without the *hara*. The *karna* parts of this *tala* which also show double pilasters display carved figure sculpture within trefoil recesses wherein even the *dandika* projections are shown by the *kudmalas*.

The interior is a square and shows a more or less square pedestal or *pitha* against the back wall displaying the mouldings of *upana*, *padma*, *antari*, *vritta kumuda*, high *kantha*, *kapota*, and high *prati*. This *prati* has been cut on the northern side in the form of a water-chute or *nala* and abruptly its projection is stylised. Below on the floor against the double pilaster a rectangular depression is provided.

In the centre of the pedestal top is a narrow socket for the seating of the main figure of worship.

The next sub-shrine on the cardinal southern direction is almost exactly similar to the corresponding one on the north excepting that on the front side, viz., the northern side the central section flanking the door ways is immediately flanked by double pilasters, leaving no gap for any figure sculpture in the northern one. The end sections, however, are relatively broader in their niche providing wherein *dvarapalas*, two-armed, are shown, one of the arms resting upon a mace and the other in *vismaya mudra* in the case of the western one, while in the case of the other, the hand is broken at the end. The wall spaces on the other side do not carry any sculpture. The superstructure is almost similar to the northern one in all essential details. The interior of this shrine provides for a continuous narrow pedestal, along the three sides of the wall, wherein seven sockets have been cut against the back wall on the pedestal probably intended to the seven *matra* sculptures. While the western pedestal extension shows two more pedestals, apparently for *kala* and *kali* or *Ganesa* and *Kala*, while the eastern extension only one socket, apparently intended for *Virabhadra*. The double pilasters are shown as rising only from the pedestals.

The last sub-shrine, corresponding to the Ganesa sub-shrine at the north-west corner and integrated with the *karnakuta* of the *maha mandapa* shows only a niche similar to the Ganesa shrine, but apparently the image (that of Karttikeya) was fitted loose for which a socket hole is available in the centre of the floor of the niche.

The main Kailasa *vimana* in its superstructure presents a *chatustala* tower in clear outline, notwithstanding the many artistic devices it employs for surface embellishments. The usual entablature mouldings comprising the *vyalavari* and the *vedi* are shown in appropriate proportions to the height of each *tala* and in viewed prospects. In a similar way, the *bhadra sala* is given the dimensions that would be appropriate in relation to the *bhadra kapota* sections of its own *tala*, so that the picture presented is always that of a miniature *sala vimana* at each step. The same could be said of *karnakuta* and in order to separate the two very clearly, the recessed wall section between the *bhadra-sala* and the *karnakuta* is provided with the *kapota panjara,* this *kapota panjara* itself further continuing with its own harmonised projections of the *vyalavari, vedi* and *nasika* of the *harantara.* This *nasika* in each of the *talas* is slightly larger than the adjoining *nasikas* and in the topmost *tala* it is only a *nasika.* Thus a visual effect is created while looking at Kailasa *vimana* from the sides of vertical lines being emphasised notwithstanding the fundamentally horizontal and tiered lay-out of the *vimana.* Conventions like the presentation of the *bhuta-valabhi* at the ground *tala* and an interesting *hamsa-valabhi* in the upper talas had also scrupulously been maintained. The *valabhi* itself has been given a new life by presenting in pure architectural members of the rafter composition in each section whether *sala, kuta,* or *salilantara* recess only the *makara* terminals being really provided in figural pattern, but at the same time the architectural features, highlighted by the representation of two elephants in combat face to face with each other. Seen in front of the *vyalavari*, the elephants themselves almost resting upon the *kapota.* Even at the higher levels, the size of these combating elephants, though reduced, is well maintained. The *salilantara* recess, however, here and there shows the actual *vyalas* in lateral profile insofar as sculptural ornamentation is concerned. There is again consistency with which the wall sections of the *sala, kuta,* and the *harantara* are provided with full scale standing sculptures and certain innavations like making the sculptures on the *kapota-panjara* almost three-quarters relief and making them stand almost on the *kapota* level are also adopted. The *nasikas* of the *prastara* above the cornice in the *harantara* stages as well as in the *sala* and *kuta* stages are again fully embellished often with the presentation of the *vimana* models either square or octagonal or even circular or alternatively with figure work. In the case of the *madhyasala* of the first *tala prastara* actually the *kapota-panjara* is integrated within the *nasika kudu.* Coming to the *griva* and *sikhara* of Kailasa *vimana* it is important to emphasise that they conform to the chaste outlines of a '*Dravida*' *sikhara.* The neck part is too over-powered, being a very narrow *kantha* and the presence of the neck itself is suggested mainly by a series of free-standing double pillar units cut from the *vedi* level to be harmonised with the *nasikas* on the eight facets of the *sikhara*, the *nasikas* themselves carrying *chaturasra* or *astasra vimana* models, in addition to these free-standing pillars of diminutive character, but of definite shapes, the *hamsa valabhi* that is shown on the visible *valabhi* horizon, just below the horizonal chamferred underside of the *sikhara* edge also heightens the individuality of the *sikhara* and keeps the irregular *nasika* apart from the *griva*. The *sikhara* piece itself is devoid of any spctacular flange, but is of prevailingly drooping profile with the edge imperceptibly flanged and with the *konapattais*, not too floridly emphasised, but the ribbing itself, on the other hand is not well brought out. The *nasikas* are again not unduly prominent in the *sikhara* in order that they may not vitiate the smooth drooping hemispherical outline of the *sikhara* piece. It could be noticed that this *sikhara* is in keeping with the same of the earliest *sikhara* types of the octagonal forms known to us as in the structural temples at Badami like Melegitti Sivalaya, or in the structural temples of the early Pallava Rajasimha period as at Mahabalipuram Shore temple. This desire to keep the *sikhara* free from flamboyant decoration is the very essence of the virtuosity so notable in the Kailasa *vimana* and the *stupi* that goes over it again does not rise too tall in order that it might not distract the outline of the *sikhara*, but just sets it off.

The figure sculpture of the niches of the super-structure show secular as well as truly iconographic forms, and it would seem that the main niches are of importance in this respect, particularly, in the first two *talas*, since in the subsequent *talas* there is hardly any space for a full-dress figural representation in the central niche, though this might not be said of the *karnakuta* or the *salilantara*. In these latter two cases, as one goes up, sculptures are displayed in seated posture, so that they reduce dimensions of the body, might be in getting provision available for the onlooker.

Sculpture on the northern side of the Mahamandapa

The northern side central niche figure of the second *tala* is that of Kubera. The central niche of the first *tala karnakuta* shows a *vrishabhantika* Siva, four-armed, the left arm resting on the bull which is itself having its head to the left and body behind the god, and facing frontally. The left upper arm is in *abhayahasta.* The right upper arm is flexed upwards against the shoulder, while the right lower arm is bent against the chest *kartarihasta,* The figure of the god is in *abhanga.*

Sculpture on the second tala of the karnakuta

The figure shows a standing Siva in slight *abhanga* with the left leg bent slightly forward and heel raised, right arm resting upon a *gana* squatting by his side and the left arm placed under the *katibandha* elbow. The left upper arm is holding a *damaru* and the right upper arm is holding a *naga.* The hair-do is of *karanda* type of *jatamukuta* and the whole body is slightly turned away at an angle and this is almost in three-quarters relief from the wall. The recessed sculpture shows invariably *vidyadharas* in pairs flying in the air, with their legs flexed backwards in flight. The size varies with the place and the position they are located in.

Projection of the wall space to the west of the northern porch

The sculpture panel corresponding in the level to the first floor of the *karnakuta* and the *gavaksha* window is that of Durga as Mahisha-mardini. The whole panel has been studded in action and at the same time telling the story in consequential pattern. It straightens with the left leg stemmed below vertically and the right leg bent and resting upon the body of Mahisha who is himself shown in forms one to the proper left where he is shown with the buffalow head squatting on the ground with the hand held on the mace and attacked by the goddess, while the proper right mauled by the lion mound of the goddess and again shown in kneeling position, almost in with the left hand planted with his bent legs to the front. The demon is shown in human form. The rest of the place is entirely occupied by the eight hands of the goddess holding different weapons.

Corresponding sculpture panel to the east of the northern porch

This shows Andhakari form of Siva. The figure of Siva practically occupy the whole of the panel with his *sula* becoming a diagonal measure and mauling the Asura who is shown just outside the outer corner of the panel. The demonic forms which *Andhaka* was to take are awesomely depicted just below the flying figure of the demon in a kind of mask of a demon with a grinning canine in his mouth. By the side of this mask is shown, the *gajamunda* representing the Gajasura whom the god vanquished first and depicted second is his own garment. Two of his hands themselves are holding the hem of the section on the upper part of the panel. The figure of Kala or Chamunda holding up a *raktapatra* under the trunk of the *gajamunda* to prevent the proliferation of demon out of the blook split, is represented with high realism. The face and body of the Chamunda is a fine study of modelling. The figure of Parvati shown seated just outside the panel under in *ardhaparyankasana* with the left leg taken over the right leg on the right thigh and left arm placed ove the shin; the right arm resting upon the ground, shows the outer in front with which Parvati is viewing the whole fair. She is having a becoming *jatamukuta*, *kundalas*, *graiveyakahara*, *yajnopavita* which runs in between the breasts, *keyuras* and *kankanas*. The raised left foot of the god is itself respectively borne by a seated *gana* upon the *padma* held by the left arm of the *gana* over his head, while between the legs of the god is shown another *gana* dancing in glee. The god himself is holding by his other hand sword, a *kapala* in two of his arms, his two more arms engaged in holding the edge of the elephant skin, one right arm holding a spear and the corresponding left arm is holding the spear further up near his shoulder. While the remaining left arm is kept on the *kati*. The head of the god is thrown back and the *jata* is a very substantial and well coiffeiured mass. The god is provided with a *yajnopavita*, an *udharabandha*, *kati bandha* and *kativastra* falling in heavy loops across the thighs and *kinkinis* at the calf. This is one of the finest representations of Andhakasura Vadhamurti here or elsewhere and in artistic merit even surpasses the earlier Chalukyan representations.

The ground tala panel of the north eastern karnakuta

The panel represents Gajendra Varada Visnu riding on Garuda shown in human form flying in the air, but with the wings on either side. The figure is four-arme, with the two arms resting on the thigh, keeping the balance, while flying in the air, the dangling legs themselves being well supported by the two hands of the Garuda, while the two remaining arms hold *sankha* and *chakra* in the left and right respectively, the latter being lifted up in the aspect of discharge. The face and the body is turned to one side somewhat in tune with his action and the aspect of the face is downwards. A lotus pond is shown full of flowers and stalks in which elephants are flowing one of which is being held by a crocodile and is crying out in agony with the trunk and head raised high. The face of the Garuda is pressed and steady and conforms to representations of *gana*. The central niche in the rear wall of the eastern cardinal shrine carries the sculpture of Surya standing in *samabhanga* with lotus in two hands.

The panel facing south on the ground tala of the southeast karnakuta of maha-mandapa

The sculpture represents Narasimha in a pose just prior to the demon being vanquished by him. It represents Narasimha in an unusual pose having his back to the demon with the right leg stamped vertically and left leg bent slightly and itself placed upon the body of the figure who is apparently one of the attendants of the demon, and who is fallen down by the very impact of the appearance of the god from the pillar. There is a drama in the way in which the god has turned his body three-quarters around, while the demon himself is almost hanging on his hip one of the right leg flexed inwards and flying in the air, as the god bent forward and lifted him off his feet. One of the right hands of the god shown diagonally towards the corner of the panel is drawn out to give the terrific and fatal blow, while the face looking at the demon by the corner of the eye shows tremendous power and rage. The right hand of the demon which is itself lifted high in an effort to attack the god with his sword is seen limp with the sword itself drooping downwards. The sculpture at Ellora, whether of the Vaisnavite or the Sivaite kind, had been very significant for new syirit of resurgent Brahmanism that they represented, and the innovations that they innovations that they introduced in the presentation of well known Puranic legends are to be viewed in this light and this Narasimha form is one such and of considerable potency and spirit.

The Next Panel to the East of the Southern Porch

This would have been its own extension just below it owing to the inadequacy of the panel space to represent the event selected. The panel proper shows the fight between Vali and Sugriva and it presents too many figures in human body looked in combat, one of them facing frontwards with the leg wide apart, while the other is trying to pour him down by entwining his left leg around his right thigh and his hands around his body. As it is, it would seem that the frontally facing figure is that of Vali owing to the remarkable subtlety that his stance is showing. Below the panel in an extended space, separated from the main panel like inset is shown the sequel to the combat providing a scene of great pathos wherein the victorious as well as vanquished are all in deep sorrow. It shows Vali lying on the ground very renderly supported by Sugriva from behind and his face means of agony, while at the other end figures of Rama and Lakshmana are shown in the pose of hermits with *jatamakuta* and with bow in hand. Rama shown a little ahead of Lakshmana. It between are two female figures, one standing in front of Vali and looking at the fallen hero, while the other had fallen at the feet of Rama. Apparently the two figures are of the same and represent the two moods and stages of Tara, Vali's wife, one witnessing the fall of her invincible husband and the other supplicating before Rama, giving him the blessings for reaching Punyaloka. It is very difficult to present these themes and in having done full justice to the important episode in Ramayana, the Rastrakuta artists had not only brought out their great skill in figure moulding, but also in their complete mastery over the theme by presenting it at the appropriate angle.

Kailasatolana scehe on the soild ground tala: level of the southern side beow the southern porch of the mahamandapa :

Before this very important and major panel in Kailasa is described, it is necessary to state that the sculpture has been carved with great deliberation and pre-miditated design. This was fully indicated by the fact that the two pilasters rising upon the lower plinth mouldings proper are perfectly finished and the plinth mouldings themselves return inwards and continue only to show the cavernous depths of

Kailasa into which Ravana had applied his trial of strength. It is thus appropriate to assume that the architects had planned ahead to reserve this space for a special panel and to provide the setting by returning the mouldings of their *adhisthana* and the pilasters to emphasise this.

A feature of some importance which does not normally hit the eye of the casual observer is the fact that the south side *mahamandapa* porch of Kailasa is dissimilar to the northerly one. The difference consists not merely in dimensions which could well be the fortuitous occurrence in rock art, but also further in its very composition. This southern projection does not return in completed form with its *kakshasana* parapet on its southern side as in the corresponding northern one. It shows, on the contrary, a tendency for the *kakshasana* to continue further south from beyond the corner pillars of the porch. This, however, is only suggestively preserved in view of the fact that the rock mass on the edge of the porch had been only irregularly existent. Examining, however, the context in which this southern porch could have extended northwards, one may very well accept the probability that it was a direct sequel to the occurrence of the important rock-cut tableau scene of Ravana shaking Kailasa immediately below. In order to give the appropriate dramatic effect to the cavernous character of the scene in relation to the Kailasa above, Krishna's architects should have thought of a device by which a bridge like projection is continued from the southern porch further south almost up to the original cliff face of the courtyard. It is necessary also to understand here that the triple storeyed cave now seen thus from the opposite side of the southern porch would not have been in existence at that time and had indeed been created more than a quarter century later and when this happened, its architects had removed this overhanging bridgelike piece projecting from the southern porch, to adjust the facade elevation of this triple storeyed cave, leaving it more or less in the condition in which we see it now. This apart from the highly imaginative device originally adopted, seemingly by the creators of Kailasa in regard to the setting of the Kailasa-tolana scene at this place, would almost furnish an internal evidence to the very anteriority of the Kailasa in relation to the triple storeyed cave—which is proved by other independent factors also—and of the contemporaneity of the Kailasa-tolana tableau with the Kailasa monolith itself. It would thus underscore the justification for the appellation 'Kailasa' effectively although the valuable and picturesque original evidence of this is unfortunately now lost to us.

The panel represents in the lower half in almost more than life-size the figure of Ravana kneeling on the ground with his back to the audience, but with his bunch of ten heads in symmetric row around his single neck like a heap, labouring with his 20 arms to shake the mount Olympus of the Indian myth—the Kailasa abode of Siva. His right leg bent and planted in front of his body and his forest like arms radiating in all directions gripping the cavern, have all been brought out in deep relief in order to relate it to the scene that is depicted in the upper register. This very register itself is of two sequences—the lower showing the representation of scene in the mountain, the rocky character, the play of animals like monkeys, the activities of *ganas* carrying above their work and the two *dvarapalas* or attendants, seated on either side with their gorgeous and profusely matted hair, one of their holding to the proper left a *trisula* and the other to the right holding a *gada* between the crook as leaf like edge, which he has taken over the right. Above these *dvarapalas*, who are themselves carved in deep relief and thus provided a foil in the form of the scenes above the clouds, on either side wherein divinities, *dikpalas* and others are shown on their proper mounts, bearing witness to this stupendous spectacle. The central figures of this trump are, however, three in number, firstly the female attendant of Parvati shown to the extreme left of scene is absolutely arrested with fear by the quake in Kailasa and is flying off panick-stricken with her head turned to portray, her dismay and body almost 45° angle on her toes to flee from this scene of parade. The next is Parvati, herself most comfortably and in a leisurely way halfreclining against Siva, extending her right leg to full length upon her left leg slightly and taking it under the right holding the right leg in position by raised heel part. She is differentiated from the frenzied attendant and in keeping with her dignity she is presented as having been overcome by a sudden feeling of distress at the tremour caused by Ravana's shaking and naturally and casually holding unto the body of Siva by gripping his left arm at the elbow and with her left and by throwing her right arm over his right shoulder from around his body. In relation to the fine bow-like bend of the body wherein the legs, navel, breasts and the face, have all been given their subdued modelling, the face itself a poem of great dignity; the stance of Siva himself who is the main target of attack by this false show of heroism in Ravana is interpreted and has hardly been affected by the tumultous spectacle around him. He is shown seated in *ardhaparyankasana* with the left leg dangling and right leg taken under the left in a homely and comfortable fashion, the leg itself placed upon the head of one of the demons who is playing upon the drums below his seat. His body is almost erect and we may even suspect the very taughtness of the body reflects his awareness of the root-cause of this whole distress; his left shoulder raised slightly owing to the vertically drooping left hand placed upon the seat, while the right shoulder is gently sloping down due to the extended right hand resting upon his right knee. In order to further emphasise the deep concentration of Siva, even a *yogapattai* fastening his hip with his right knee has been bestowed. The *lolahasta* of his right arm and the bent knee, *yogapattai*, all contributing to the deep concentration of the figure. His other right arm is carrying a *Parasu* by a tip of his fingers, while his upper left arm has been placed reassuringly around the shoulder of Uma, but has unfortunately broken. Both the figures of Siva and Parvati compared to that of Ravana are smaller, but compare favourably with the figure of the attendants seated on either side at Kailasa. It is this balance in figure work by placing four major figures in the four diagnol corners and distributing the scene in the remaining parts and above allowing the action of the picture to emerge from the bottom and the reaction to be rendered from the top appropriately, that the sculptors had achieved complete success. It would be impossible to find a parallel to this depiction notwithstanding the many examples of this theme that have been available.

Jatayu's gallentry

The panel to the west of the porch represents the scene of Jatayu the great eagle king attacking Ravana, (*Pl. LVIII*) while the latter was in flight after carrying away Sita. This had been another interesting theme presented by the sculptors at many places, almost the exact parallel of this being available at Pattadakkal in the Virupaksha temple monument supposed to have inspired Krishna for carving his Kailasa, and shows an unusual event in the epic of the Ramayana a piece that has apparently been selected because it gives scope to the presentation of an event where movement is the central theme and where the might of Ravana is brought against the might of a lesser being like a bird, and where there is panorama caused by the presence of a third party, viz., Sita as a helpless witness to the unavailing gallantry of the bird. Thus, the three elements of the picture are : Ravana confident, over-powering and ruthless, Jatayu outraged and brave, and captive Sita almost overwhelmed by the events and standing on the chariot board. The dominant figure of Ravana is almost shown across diagonally in the panel with the right leg bent and right arm raised in the posture of attacking the eagle king, the left arm holding the scabbard. The left leg is itself planted upon the ground to give momentum to the act, notwithstanding the rear part of the panel having been left bare and is fully taken in by the figure work.

The ground tala south-west of karnakuta of the Sabha Mandapa (Pl. XLIX)

This panel shows a standing figure of Lakulisa on *padmapitha*, four-armed, the two lower arms in *kati*, the upper right arm holding a *lakuda*, and the upper left arm flexed high and placed against the shoulder of the hairlocks. The figure is in *samabhanga*, practically without any ornamentation and seemingly nude with the *urdhvamedha* or the *membrum virile* held erect, a characteristic feature of Lakulisa figures.

It is interesting to note that its parallel also in the Virupaksha temple at Pattadakkal has been placed more or less at the same place on the south-western corner of the western face of the temple there.

The western face of the same tala karnakuta

This panel represents the figure of Brahma seated on *padmapitha* four armed, the upper arms holding *kundika* and srk the lower right arm holding *akshamala* and the lower left which is placed upon the lower lap and which should have held *Pustaka*, being damaged. The figure has three heads, the central head wears a pendant bead, has a necklet *yojnopavita*, *udarabandha*, *bahuvalayas* and *kankana*; the hairdo is, that of a tapering *jatamakuta*.

The panel adjoining the western door frame leading to the Sabha Mandapa

This panel shows a famous *lingodbhava* wherein it is interesting to note that the central shaft itself does not appear to have been defined either at the base or at the top, but, just merges with the top and bottom. In the centre of the shaft is a lenticular slid within which is shown the figure of Siva standing and visible above thigh, two-armed, right arm in *abhaya*, lower arm in *kati*,, with an attractive *jatamakuta*. The attendant figures are five in number, viz., the two standing figures of Brahma and Visnu to the left and to the right respectively in *anjali hasta*, four-armed, each of them holding appropriate weapons in their upper hands, viz., that of *akshamala* and *pustaka* and *sankha* and *chakra* respectively. Next lay the two figures of Visnu in the form of Varaha, body held upside down, legs bent trying to bury into the ground at the foot of the shaft, and Brahma at the diagonal corner fiying in the air with arms again in *anjali-hasta*, three-headed and not shown like a swan corresponding to the boar. In the corner above Visnu, there is two-armed Vidyadhara figure flying in air in *anjali*. The most interesting part of this figure is the central shaft, and all others show variations of representations of the theme elsewhere at Ellora and thus, it might not show all the details of the shaft insofar as it does not represent a symbol of *linga* with a well defined base and top, thus well in keeping with the fact that the *lingodbhava* itself is representative of the primeval pillar rather than a male organ.

The corresponding panel on the northern side of the door at the head of the stairs shows Gangadhara sculpture; represents Siva standing to one side of the panel on the back of a *gana*, in *abhanga* with right legs slightly bent forward, left leg planted straight, one of the left arms endearingly taken around the figure of Parvati standing cross-legged, both the legs resting on lotusses, whose own right arm is holding the left arm of Siva. This endearing action is for mutual understanding in view of the fact that the descent of Ganga and the acceptance of Ganga by Sive on his matted locks introduces elements of rivalry in his domestic household. The upper left arm of Siva holds *naga*, while the corresponding lower left arm is on *kati*. The upper right arm is touching one single matted lock from his head to absorb the torrential flow of divine *ganga*, who is shown in *anjali* pose on the top of the panel with stream line like carving, her flow. In the upper corner is shown Bhagiratha in diminutive figure performing penance, as a consummation measure of which is the site. But the panel does not rest with the depiction of Gangadhara alone. It also shows the whole story and thus it shows the flow of Ganga. It represents a *rishi* seated in the upper right middle who is apparently Janhu, whose *asrama* was engulfed and who drank Ganga up and again, on supplication by Bhagiratha, permitted Ganga to be released through his cars, as suggested on the panel by the release of Ganga's stream from the ear of the *rishi*. Even after that presents an elephant trying to hinder the flow of the stream as part of the story is also represented by the elephant, and a prancing horse are shown behind the elephant, apparently stands for the *asvamedha* horse in process of the protection of which the Sagaraputras were reduced to ashes by Kapila and the descent of Ganga was called for. These Sagaraputra figures are shown in multiple form at the bottom and Ganga is shown as flowing apparently over them and giving them *punyaloka*.

The panel on the karnakuta of the ground tala north-west

This represents the scene of Kalari or Kalakala of Markandeyanugramurti. It shows the figure of a linga and peculiarly enough, this linga has been placed upon a square *pitha*, whose mouldings are *jagati*, *kantha*, *kapota*, and *prati*. From the top of the cylindrical *linga* of the shaft, the figure of Siva is shooting up and with his left leg giving a kick to the figure standing by the side, who is apparently the god of death. As suggested in this panel by the chain which he has in his hands stands standing for the *kala-pasa*, (knots of death) he wanted to take possession of Markandeya's life on the expiry of the allotted sixteenth year of life has been the theme. With two of his hands the figure of Siva is also thrusting his *sula* at the breast of Yama, making it clear in no uncertain terms to the disciples he has with this act of demerit on behalf of Yama to intend to acquire such devout Sivabhakta like Markandeya. The figure of Markandeya whose head is unfortunately gone is shown as kneeling and clutching at the *linga* as his only solace. The remaining two unengaged hands of Siva are in mood and holding a *damaru*. The figure of Yama who is shown in a far from terrific and obstacle placing fashion in *samabhanga*, is also represented as being equal on the uptake as suggested by his right hand raised in *vismayamudra* in this privately blessing spectacle of Visa countermanding his own orders.

Main vimana

The *ardha mandapa* recess-last level on the top of the plinth figure without any niche against the wall in deep relief standing on a *gana* kneeling down as is a common pattern all over the temple, for, all figures of divinities the figure is two-armed, is in *abhanga*, the right arm is resting on the thigh and the left arm which is unfortunately broken is flexed up and taken against the chest. The figure is in *jata-makuta*. The figure is apparently an attendant.

Karnakuta niche of the main vimana

The figure in the panel over a seated caryatid *gana* holding a *padma-pitha*, shows Vrsabharudha Siva, *Vrishaba* being shown in simulation with the head to the proper right; Siva shown as seated comfortably on it, but unfortunately both his legs are broken. Two of his hands are also broken but all upper hands are shown as raised high without holding any weapon. It is just possible that it is representing Siva not in ceremonial procession but seated at leisure in Kailasa. His body is thrust forward; his head thrown backwards and it is a fine statue in three-fourth relief. Above the figure over the *mayuratorana* is shown seated representation apparently of Saraswati with lotus buds in two arms. The figure is shown with the breasts bare and with a parasol over her head and two *chauris* represented on either side of the figure.

In the harantara inside niche

Siva standing in *abhanga*, two lower arms in *kati*; two upper arms holding *Sula* and *naga*; body slightly thrust forward and shoulder slightly turned; head thrown backwards; *jatamakuta* shown in distinctive but compressed character with the *kativastra* hanging in hips on either side *mukta yajnopavita*, *udharabhanda*, *graiveyakahara*, *keyura* etc., forming the ornaments.

The bhadra niche over the pranala

Standing figure of Siva in *samabhanga*, upper arms holding *damaru* in the right hand, lower left hand in *kati* and the lower right hand broken. *Kativastra* done in loop which hangs up to the knee, *yajnopavita* running over the elbow.

Above the panel in the *torana* loop is shown the figure of seated Siva, four-armed, with *naga* in one of his upper hands, lower arms in *kati* and the left on the knee and flexed on the right; body slightly bent and thrown backwards; hairdo done in *karanda* type of *jatamakuta* and face slightly thrown backward. An interesting figure of Vidyadhara with a garland in hand shown upside down hovering in the air above this *torana* higher up is to be noted.

Next harantara niche panel

Standing figure of Siva in *abhanga*; upper arms holding *parasu* and *sula*; lower arms in *kati* and apparently *abhaya-hasta*, but broken with an elliptical nimbus behind the head; the hairdo done is *karanda* type of *jatamakuta*. The whole figure is of considerable balance of grace in slimness and subdued modelling. However, Siva figure is shown in dimunitive forms in front of the octagonal *sikhara* of the temple; on the *nasika* is that of a *lingadhara* Siva bearing a *linga* on his shoulder by one of his upper left arms, the provenance and antiquity of such *lingadhara* froms having been already dealt with else-where.

The karnakuta figure adjoining north-eastern corner

Figure of Ardhanari, *abhanga*, four armed on the Uma side, lower arm in *lola hasta* upper arm raised high and bent towards the head, apparently for balance over the left arms; the hair-do none in a rising coiffeure, though of *jatamakuta* on the left side and of normal reclining type to the right. The body, shoulders, single breast, the ornate *udara-bandha*, graiveyakahara, and *mukta yajnopavita*, the drapery shown as hanging down to the shin on the left side and unfortunately not visible on the right owing to the damage; the right leg bent in tune with the skilled modelling.

The figure above the *torana* shows Gajalkshmi seated on *padma* with lotus bud in two hands, with two elephants on either side discharging *abhisheka jala* on her head. A parasol is found over the head. Around the corner adjoining the panel is that of Tandava Siva in *chantura* pose with the feet got wide apart above the floor, almost rather equally; eight-armed, the right arms respectively in *kati*, *danda-hasta*, holding a *sula* and with a corresponding uppermost left arm holding a *naga*, behind the head in a loop. The left arms in *kartarihasta*, holding a *naga*, and hanging down, in *lolahasta*. The slight frontward turn of the body and the back of the head, pointed *Jatamakuta*, and the assured countenance are all notable

The figure on the *torana* above this shows a seated central figure, apparently Siva as two-armed and the *torana* animal motif itself is a hybrid with human face and feathery tail. In the figure within the niche, is a standing from of Siva in *abhanga*, with left leg kept slightly apart, right fore-arm, the upper arms, holding *naga* and *trisula* in the right and left, the lower arms in *kati* and *abhaya*, the *abhaya-hasta* having been broken.

The main niche figure of the Bhadra

The main niche figure of the *bhadra* is an interesting standing Siva figure in an arresting pose, with the two upper arms holding *naga* and *parasu*, the left lower arm in *kati*, with the arm itself turned twisted inwards and the fingers touching the *kati bandha*. The right lower arm hanging down in holding a rolling cobra in his hand, the body thrown slightly to the side and forward complementary to the right hip raised, the head thrown well backwards and tilted, having a heavy *jatabhara*, ears sporting *patra* and *nakra kundalas*, and the lower garments forming an *ardhoruka* tied by a *kati-bandha* as well as a *kativastra* in multiple loops and the free hems of the knot falling on either side up to the shin level.

The figure above this *torana* is even more interesting in the form of Siva-lila dance of the *padaswastika* pose; body gyralling and turning three-fourths around; the head tilted backwards, facing up; One of the hands playing with the curls of the hair; the other hands holding *trisula*, and other weapons, the figure almost in the round with great beauty.

Next panel shows the figure of Parvati standing in *abhanga*, two armed, left arm in *kati*, right arm in *abhanga* broken in the forearm; the hairdo in beautiful *sikhanda*, with the breast bare, with the body decorated with necklet, *graiveyaka hara*, *yajnopavita*, *keyuras*, *kankanas*, *udarabandha katibandha*, falling in single loop in the middle of the legs and drapery. Of the lower part of the body running across the calf in the free hem *padasaras*.

The south-east corner niche showing Vrishabhantika Siva, four-armed, in *abhanga*, right and left upper arms holding *damaru*, and *trisula*, right lower arm in *kati*; left lower arm in *lolahasta*, holding a cobra, over a nimbus behind the *jatabhara*, with the body almost tending to be in *tribhanga* though in *abhanga* by 'S' twist. The fore-legs of the bull and its head and hump are shown to the proper right of Siva. Above this niche there is a seated figure playing on what looks like a Veena, perhaps Siva as Vinadhara, though two-armed. It is also flanked by hybrid *torana* figures of human body and floriated tail.

The panel round the corner shows a dancing Siva, apparently of the *bhujangatrasa* type, as shown by the rolling snaka, held in one of the left arms with curved hood, hanging below. Siva is dancing on a goblin below as is usual himself playing with snakes. This is also in *padaswastika* pose. The two upper arms holding *ghanta* and *halahala*. Two more right and left arms flexed towards the body and reaching the chest, and forming a balance; one at left shoulder level, the other from a half raised elbows. The remaining right arm is hanging across in *danda-hasta*, corresponding to the left which is holding a snake which is rolling. The hair-do is gorgeous, with the *jatas* over-flowing behind like a crocodyle. The head is thrown slightly backward and the right chest just thrown forward. The right part of the body is unfortunately damaged. To the proper left bottom is shown a Nandi seated and playing on the drums.

Above this figure on the *torana* is a seated figure of Sarasvati with lotus in the hands, with two female attendants by the side of a parasol over her head.

The next panel inside the niche shows apparently a devotee or a divinity, if the nimbus is of any significance In gracious but mild *tribhanga* the right arm slightly raised and the left arm holding a flower in its flexed and raised fore-arm, the right arm in *kati*, *yajnopavita* flowing over the left hip, slightly bent backwards and the lower garment reaching up to the calf. The hair- do is in pointed *jatamukuta*. It might even be a portrait sculpture.

Main Central niche

Figure of Visnu in *samabhanga* on *padmapitha*; four-armed, the two lower arms in *kati*; the two upper arms holding *sankha* in the right and *chakra* in the left hand against the usual reverse position. The head wears a *kirita-mukuta*, *nakra-kundalas*, on both the ears, ornamentation of a subdued character, and the drapery forming a wavy hem at the calf level. The *kativastra* forms a heavy loop at the sides with the free ends falling up to the heel.

The figure above, though two-armed is apparently a divinity in view of the showing hybrid human figures of the *torana* holding *Vismayamudra* towards the figure.

Next figure, Siva standing in *abhanga*, four-armed, two upper arms holding, *naga* and *parasu*, and *trisula*, two lower arms in *kati* and in *ahaya*, perhaps broken on the right side; the hair-do in delightful *karanda makuta* type; both ears sporting *nakra kundalas*.

Next figure an unusual character of Siva in dance, with the left leg planted firmly on the ground, with the right leg flexed and bent up to almost chest level in *parsvojanu* style. One of his right hands taken as *dandahasta* across the body, unfortunately broken, but one of his left hands correspondingly bent and taken across below the right knee, but also broken towards the end. The left upper hand in *abhaya hasta* resting just above the raised knee; the right upper hand holding a *damaru* well aloft; the hair-do done in a bold *jatapasa*; face tilted towards the left and inward contemplation. It is one of the most interesting of the dancing Siva pose. *Yajnopavita* is shown as raising high on the back up to the right upper hand. The *kativastras* are dwelling in loop in the midst of the dance. Over the *mayura torana* of this figure, is the form of a seated Saraswati on *padmapitha*, with right leg flexed horizontally on the *padmapitha*. Left leg slightly raised and flexed obliquely; the right arm on the right knee; left arm flexed high *abhaya hasta*. The head gear is in *karanda* type of *jatamukuta*.

The last figure in the *ardha mandapa* wall is a standing figure of Siva, four-armed, with *naga* and *trisula*, in the upper arms, lower arms in *kati* and *abhaya*, but the latter is broken. The figure is in *abhanga* and has an elliptical nimbus behind its head. The figure is badly eroded and weathered.

The Vidyadhara figure shown just above this sculpture in the upper level in three-forth relief along the wall surface is almost repeating the type of dance that Siva was showing in the previous panel, with only two hands that he possesses. It is to be compared, thus, with the previous sculpture for its beauty.

On the rock wall opposite across the open court-yard to the front of the south west corner of the *maha mandapa* is an unfinished sculpture depicting, Andhakasura Vadhamurti where only the upper part of the body of Siva with his face, shoulder, chest and his shoulder mauling Andhakasura have been completed. Two of the upper arms of Siva hold the edge of the elephant skin. Two pilasters have been shown on either side in the upper part. The figure is more than life size and from the fact that they have been at a rather inaccessible upper level insofar as the caves on either side are concerned. It might be appropriate to presume that they have been carved when the rock mass was being removed to provide for the *pradakshinapatha* and well before the present *pradakshina* level was reached. If so, they will from part of the early stage of Kailasa excavation and indeed the face of the God forms a delightful sight, which can compare very well with some of the Chalukyan cave sculptures.

Miniature frieze panel on either side entrance stairs of Kailasa : Northern side

The lower two panels represent scenes from Krishna Lila.

Starting from bottom right, they show the birth of Krishna; the representation of Krishna and Balarama, the latter shown clutching the palm-tree which is his *dhvaja*. Some more figures who are shown might be attendants and to wrestlers Mustika and Chanura, supported by temple model of the *sala* type. The next scene shows Krishna with his shepherd friend enter Gokula. looting homes for curd and butter.

The next shows scene from Gokula where apparently we have the cattle in different postures and the shepherds also in different postures are shown but partially unfinished. The representation of a *banyan* tree with its shades is very realistic.

Rural scenes of churining milk for butter and husking grain on the quern are also shown. The next figure below is also in continuation of the cattle friends with Krishna shown in the middle. Adjoining that and almost in the same zone is the figure of Krishna tied to the de-husking stone and toddling along to steal butter from the pots.

The next figure shows Krishna sleeping on the cradle and integrated with this are scenes showing *Baka* or crane which has attacked him and (representing Bakasuravadha) and showing Putana ogress by the side (representing Putanasamhara both). It does not show Putana-suckling Krishna.

The next scene to the right shows the figure of Durga with her various weapons, almost shown hovering in the air, perhaps apothesis of the scene where the 7th land of Sarasvati was *Yogamaya*, who has to be equalled with Durga. Her lion mount is standing by her side, one of its forepaws raised and tail twisted.

The last figure to the right shows again an intergrated scene, firstly Krishna astride between the wheels and the cart, broken apart axially and thus representing Sakatasuravadha and holding another demon by his locks of hair and ready to smash him with his right hand. This represents Kamsavadha rather than Kesi-nishudana since the demon is holding a sword and a shield, and there is a large audience of men, women and children witnessing this.

The upper five friezes represent episodes from Mahabharata.

The relief panel on the southern side depicts scenes from Ramayana, starting with the divine god into the world as Rama from Vaikuntha, going through the various scenes, like Viswamitra Yagya—Samrakshana, Ahalya sapa-vomochana, Tatakavadha, Subahu, Marichivadha, Surpanakha-mana-bhanga in the second panel, Mayamriga being desired by Sita, destruction of Maricha by Rama, Ravana arriving as Kapata Sanyasi; kidnapping of Sita by Ravana; Jatayu attacking Ravana, and Ravana killing it, and Lakshmana in search of Sita and meeting Hunuman in the third panel. Rama establishing his friendship with Sugriva; Rama killing Vali and making Sugriva king; Sugriva sending warriors in different direction in search of Sita; Hanuman crossing the sea and meeting Simhika, Lankini etc., destroying them and arrival back and handing over *Chudamani* to Rama; the *vanasarenas* proceeding to Lanka; Angada king as ambassador meeting Ravana etc., in the next two panels and the last two panels showing Rama and other *vanarasenas* on the sea where *Sethu-bandhana* is performed and during the battle; Sanjivi Parvata. is being brought by Hanuman and ultimately Rama vanquishes Ravana The last part of this panel is left incomplete and apparently should have shown the crowning of Rama. (*Pl. LX*).

Sculptured panels along the cloister walk of the Kailasa from the middle of the northern side to the middle of the southern side.

Panel No. 1 : Ravana offering his heads, in place of flowers in worship of Siva; nine of his heads arranged like a garland around the *linga* placed upon a square *pitha*, whose mouldings are *upana*, *kantha*, *vritta kumuda*, and *pattika* and *prati*. Ravana himself is shown below in the act of cutting off his last head, at which moment Siva is supposed to have been pleased and granted him the invincible sword Ravana is seated in front of the sacrificial fire.

Panel No. 2 : Uma-sahita Siva, in Kailasa in *utkutika* posture; Uma stretching her right leg leisurely towards the side. Lower panel below shows, probably Siva with a figure standing in frount, four-armed and likely to be representing Karttikeya because of his boyish character.

Panel No. 3 : Siva-Parvati in Kailasa; Siva holding in his left hand a *linga* mounted on a *pitha* of *mancha bandha* capped by a *kapota* moulding, square-sectioned, Parvati is also supporting it by her right hand. Nandi bull is shown in the lower register. This should be compared with other *linga*-bearing Siva figures here and elsewhere, referred to in the text.

Panel No. 4 : Siva-Farvati at Kailasa. Siva in *ardhaparyankasana* with the *yogapattai*, taken across his waist and flexed right leg. Nandi bull is shown in the lower register. One of Siva' upper arms is supporting *Jatabhara* of Parvati.

Panel No. 5 : Vrishabhantika Siva standing in *samabhanga*, four-armed, upper arms holding *akshamala* and *naga*; lower arms in *abhaya* and *kati*; bull shown to the proper right.

Panel No. 6 : Unfinished panel Siva-Pårvati seated, facing each other, apparently, playing dice. Parvati's right hand is holding dice, while her left hand actually flexed in and resting her chin on it, shows deep concenstatron. Siva shown as two-armed; lower register not completed.

Panel No. 7 : Standing figure, two-armed, apparently that of Daksha or attendant; with the head-gear. which is like a conical cap, below which curly *Jatas* are hanging, is carrying. Sachel over his shoulder, apparently holding some article in it. The right hand is dangling by the side and in what appears to be *varada-hasta*, though the figure is not a divinity. If it is a divinity, it might be an unfinished figure of Bhikshatana Siva in which case, the stick on the shoulder would represent the bundle of bones. The posture of the figure and walking movements of the legs would suggest this icon. The figure is, however, only two-armed.

Panel No. 8 : Kailasa *tolana* by Ravana; Ravana in lower register and unfinished Siva and Parvati reacting to the shaking of Kailasa; Parvati by entwining her arms, around the left arm of Siva and Siva by facial reaction looking at Uma, apparently consoling her; Siva is four-armed. One of the arms taken around the neek of Parvati. He has the *yōgapattai* taken around his right knee and hip.

Panel No. 9 : Unfinished, Siva-Parvati in Kailasa Siva is Playing on *vina*. Parvati seated by his side. One of Siva's four arms taken around the neck of Parvati. The lower register shows Nandi bull within pilasters.

Panel No. 10 : Next, Siva and Parvati in *aksha-krida* Lower zone--Siva holding dice; upper arm in *suchi-hasta*, warning Parvati not to violate rules of the game.

Sometimes taken as also representing that he has won. One of the left arms of Siva clutching the right hand of Parvati; when she is just to leave the game. The lower register shows a full complement of *ganas* frolicking around the Nandi bull, playing around at different parts of his body. There are as many as 12 figures shown in the picture.

Panel No. 11 : A tall standing figure, apparently of Siva, four-armed, upper arms holding *naga* and a weapon which appears to be *pasupata astra*; the two lower arms in *kati* and left arm in *varada*. The two relatively smaller figures are kneeling to the proper left, one larger than the other. Both of them in *anjali hasta*. Only the lesser figure is holding bow. It is just possible that it is a sequential representation of kiratarjuniya Siva in the act of Siva bestowing *pasupatastra* to Arjuna.

Panel No. 12 : Kalarimurti—Siva shown as emerging and sanding out of a cylinderical *linga*, whose *pitha* is not shown and shows one of his bent left legs against the kneeling *kala*, who is himself in *anjali hasta* Markendeya is shown in between, worshipping the *linga*. Siva is four armed with his body and head thrown a little backwards. Two of his hands are also holding *sula* which he is thrusting against Yama. Yama is two-armed

Panel No. 13 : Around the corner wall, starting the eastern row—Kalyanasundara Siva—Siva four-armed with two upper arms holding lotus flower, both apparently in tune with his pleasing his bridegroom. His left arm apparently touching the right shoulder of Uma, while the right arm is placed over the right palm of Uma, the left arm of Uma in *lolahasta*; Siva in his casual bending forward towards Uma in Imperceptible *abhanga*, while Uma is in gracious and mild *tribhanga* with the toes meeting each other and rubbing against each other in bashfulness. The figure of Brahma, the official priest of the marriage in between points at the bottom in seated posture in front of the sacrificial fire. Brahma has three heads, and four-arms, the arms holding *akshamala* right holding *srk* in the act of offering *havis* to the fire. This representation is absolutely unconventional owing to the placement of Siva's palm over Parvati, unlike the normal function of the bride-groom holding the brid's hands. It is probably an innovation suggesting that he is completely giving himself up to Uma in the act of marriage.

Panel No. 14 : Andhakasuravadha Murti combined with Gajantaka. The Gajan taka shown to the proper right with the trunk dangling, has been taken around the body of Siva, whose right leg planted vertically and left leg raised give momentum to the mauling of Andhakasura with his *sula* held by two of his hands. Diagonally across the body, two of his upper arms are holding the edge of the elephant skin. The other arms are holding *damaru* and *raktapatra*, just below the demon. The additional figures show a *gana* supporting the raised leg of Siva. Kali as Chamunda straddled under Siva's leg in emaciated frame and gleeful face, holding also the *rakta patra* accompanying to the small carrion vulture adds to the grimness of the scene. To the left bottom on a seat Paravati is seated in *utkutikasana*, calm and quiet.

Panel No. 15 : Siva as Tripurantaka, standing on the chariot board with his foot well into the chariot and not visible in the act of discharging an arrow from the bow held extended by one of his left hands and the bow strings stretched to the maximum up to his ears. The figure of Siva has double *tunira* on his shoulders. His other arms are *halding* a *sula*, and *halahala* in the two right hands, the hand holding the *sula* bent down and *sula* held vertically along the panel. The other hand flexed towards the ears over the *tunira* and holding the *halahala* by the opposing in the hand. Two of his left hands holding the Nandi panel in the lower raised against the left thigh Nandi himself shown as the capital piece over the *phalaka* in couchant from adjoining by the panel below, while the other hand flexed and taken under the extended left hand, holding the bow and in *suchihasta*, pointing at the trig. A frontal aspect of one wheel which is spokeless and flat is shown and Brahma, the charioteer is seated on the front urging the horses.

Panel No. 16 : Siva-Parvati in Kailasa seated in *ardhapparyanka-sana* and in *lalitasana* respectively; Siva four-armed, two of his upper arms holding *Sula* and *damaru*, the lower arms in *Varada* and taken around Parvati's body. Parvati herself is partially resting against Siva's slap with right hand placed on the lap. Nandi bull shown in the lower register.

Panel No. 17 : Standing figure, apparently in the form of Laku-lisa as suggested by the *urdhvamedha*, unfortunately damaged, which is rising right up to the naval. Siva is in *samabhanga*, four-armed, the upper arms holding *kundika* and *damaru*, lower arms in *kati* and holding the famous *lakuda*, a characteristic of Lakulisa.

Panel No. 18 : That of Lingodbhava, representing the *linga* shaft whose terminal is well defined and lotus is placed on the top with Brahma and Visnu standing on either side in *anjali*, while Visnu is as Varaha also shown burying under and Brahma in his own form flying up on the top left. The tip right shows Vidyadharas in *anjali* pose. From the lenticular slit in the centre of the *linga*, the figure of Siva shown up to the ankle, emerges. Two-armed arms in *abhaya* and *kati*.

Panel No. 19 : Gangadhara panel—set within a *makara-torana*—figure of Siva standing in *samabhanga*, four-armed, two lower arms in *abhaya* and *kati*; the two upper arms holding a *naga* and left hand releasing a lock from the top of his *jatamukuta* by the right hand. Along side this right hand the descent of Ganga in wavy pattern is shown, Ganga herself shown in full figure over the head of Siva in *anjali* pose, hovering in the air. The one on the course of Ganga in the middle right certainly ends where the sage Janhu is shown seated. As a sequel to the story, the right arm of Janhu held against the ear reveals the release of Ganga through the ear of Janhu, got her the name of Janhavi. Further below is the elephant also in the story shown trying to obstruct the course. Bhagiratha is not shown but Parvati is shown seated at the bottom corner on the lap in a comfortable *utkutika* posture with the left leg dangling.

Panel No. 20 : Also within a *torana*, apparently this would have been a completed scheme in all the panels. The figure shows Vrishabhantika in *samabhanga*, four-armed, upper arms holding *naga* and *sula*. Lower arms in *kati* and *abhaya*. Bull is shown in proper right in frontal aspect, while a *gana* is shown to the proper left kneeling.

Panel No. 21 : The central axial point of the temple lay-out is reached now and three panels successively showing Visnu on the north in *anjali* pose in the figure, and Brahma to the south in the same point and Siva in the middle forming an interesting harmonisation with the temple orientation. All the figures are four armed. The figure of Visnu is having an attendant, apparently Garuda, kneeling to the proper right, whose upper arms holding Chakra horizontally in *prayoga-hasta* and *sankha* in the left. The figure of Siva has a *naga* and a lotus in the upper hands, the two lower hands in *kati* and *abhaya*. He is shown as Vrishabhantika in *samabhanga*. The figure of Brahma is shown with his upper arms holding *akshamala* and *kundika*, and lower arms in *kati* and *vyakhyamudra*, is also in *samabhanga*, three-headed and to the proper right corner. Below is shown his mount Hamsa.

Panel No. 22 : Is also Vrishabhantika, shown very stunted and low. Siva four-armed, upper two arms holding against the shoulder in gracious bend and in almost feminine posture, usually attributed to Parvati; the two lower arms in *kati* and *abhaya*.

Panel No. 23 : Siva again shown in *abhanga*, as Vrishabhantika, two-upper arms holding *naga* and *damaru* lower arms in *kati* and *abhaya*: The left leg is slightly flexed forward and feet apart. There is a *gana* attendant standing to the proper left in *anjali* pose.

Panel No. 24 : The figure of standing Siva, just with his body turned slightly towards the proper left, the form is that of Bhikshatana with the body almost casually drapped by an *ardhoruka* and *kativastra* with a *dandika* taken across his chest and right shoulder, apparently carrying a — thus being canonical *dandi*. The right arms in *kati* and holding *damaru*. The left arm in *abhaya*. There is a figure of Parvati in acute *abhanga* 'standing to the proper left, almost under the extended arm with begging bowl of Siva shows offering held in her hands, in *kati* and holding a flower. There are two Vidyadharas hovering in the air in deep corners, as the hip of Siva is taken slantingly to one side.

Panel No. 25 : Siva dancing in the form of *Urdhvajanu* left leg bent diagonally and placed firmly on the ground, right leg bent and flexed almost horizontally across meeting behind the left knee against which the toes are resting.

The two lower arms in *danda hasta* for the left across the body and *kartarihasta* for the right bent and taken over the rest of the left, the remaining two arms holding a *sula* on the left and *damaru* on the right. Apasmara is shown under his foot. The body is in *tribhanga* curvature with the head thrown a little backward.

Panel No. 26 : Siva standing in *abhanga* with left leg little apart, four-armed, the upper arms in *kartari hasta* and holding a *sula*, the right and left lower arms in *kati* and *lolahasta*, the figure of an attendant is shown to the proper left stading.

Panel No. 27 : Standing figure of Siva in *abhanga* with the right leg taken a little apart, though straight, figure four-armed and head slanting a little to the left, the *jatamukuta* carefully done with the upper arms holding the *sula* on the right and affectionately touching the dhammilla coiffeure of the figure of Parvati standing to the proper left. While the two lower arms left just in *lolahasta* is held against Parvati's right breast, while the right lower arm is in *kati*. Parvati herself is in *abhanga* with the right arm in *kati* and left arm in *lola hasta*. This apparently is a form of Chandrasekhara and if the fondling of Siva tresses of Parvati is any additional criterion, this could be even taken as Alingana Chandrasekhara.

Panel No. 28 : Shows Siva with one leg stuck in the lotus pond and held by a *makara* and *kurma*, the right leg placed outside and slightly bent, the body is of slight *abhanga*, the hip thrown backwards, two upper arms holding *sula* and in *vismaya hasta*, two lower arms in *kati* and for the right and the left being allowed to be occupied and filled out by Parvati standing in *abhanga* to the proper left. Parvati is shown with left hand dangling. The scene is clearly a representation of Siva as Brahmacharin, before he reveals himself as Lord for whom Parvati is performing penance.

Panel No. 29 : The central figure is that of Siva standing in *abhanga*; face is in four-armed, two lower arms in *kati* and *abhaya* for the right and left respectively, the two upper arms holding *sula* and in *vismaya hasta.* The figure of Parvati is shown standing to the proper left with right arm in *kati* and left arm in *lolahasta.* Parvati is having a dhammilla coiffure.

Panel No. 30 : Around the corner starting the southern wall series shows Siva as Vrishabhantika Ardhanari; the bull shown to the proper right frontally. The figure is four-armed, the upper arms holding Parasu and in flexed upwards and towards the shoulder like *Vismayahasta,* forming the feminine Uma part. The two lower arms in *kati* for the right and *lolahasta* for the left. The left which is shown pressing the left side on the thigh and leg shows feminine drapery; right side *ardhoruka.* The hair-do is also similarly distinguished, though forming massive *jata-bhara.*

Panel No. 31 : Siva as Vrishabhantika; Vrishabha shown rather stunted in the right corner frontally, four-armed and in mild *tribhanga,* lower arms in *kati* and *lota hasta* and upper arms holding a *naga* and in *vismaya hasta.*

Panel No. 32 : Shows a *linga* shaft around which another figure is held encircled his arms. The figure is having his left leg stemmed on the ground slantingly and right leg bent and it is placed upon another small *linga.* The figure is four-armed. The other two arms holding a sword and shield. The figure is shown with at least three faces, one of the side faces well marked out. This is sometimes taken as Ravana in the act of trying to pull the *linga* which he had placed on the ground against promise and which (*linga*) comes rooted at the spot preventing displacement from there further.

Panel No. 33 : Narasimha placing the body of Hiranya on his left thigh in the semi-standing posture and ready to open the entrails. The god is four-armed, the two arms in the act of tearing the Asura's body, the two upper arms in *ascharyamudra* and holding the *sankha.*

Panel No. 34 : Visnu as Anantasayi reclining on a single transversely twisted coiled body and under the seven-hooded *naga* head. Visnu four-armed, the two lower arms bent and taken along the body respectively; the two upper arms resting his head and holding the stalk of the lotus respectively. From the top of the stalk of the lotus which emerges from the naval of Visnu, the figure of Brahma is depicted seated. Below Seshasayi, five figures are represented of which one is apparently female, together forming *panchayudhas*, the *chakra-sudarsana*, *sankha-panchajanya*, *gada*, *kaumodaki*, *asi*, *handaka* and *dhanush*.

Panel No. 35 : Shows the straddling figure with left leg raised up and placed on a *padma pitha*, borne by a *gana*, with a number of cattle shown in diminutive form at ground level, and a devotee in *anjali hasta* to the proper right corner. The god is four-handed, two of his hands supporting the load of the top, while the remaining two of his hands are in *suchihasta* and on the left lap. The figure is obviously that of Krishna as Govardhanadhari.

Panel No. 36 : Trivikrama, right leg planted vertically, left leg taken above the level of the shoulder, one of his right arms is also shooting forward in the same direction. His arms holding *gada chakra*, and *khadga*, the last just across the thigh on the right and *sankha* and *khetaka* and *suchihasta* on the left, thus making only six. The figure of a devotee is shown to the proper right bottom, probably, *garuda*, while to the proper left below is shown the scene of *Vamana*. as a dwarf Brahmachari with a parasol in hand requesting for three strides of land of Bali who is offering it with water of libation. The figure near Bali is probably that of Sukra, his preceptor.

Panel No. 37 : Garudarudha Visnu seated comfortably on the shoulders of Garuda with his leg supported by the two hands of Garuda shown in full human forms, with bird's wings is the act of hovering in the air with bent legs. The two lower arms of Visnu held on the lap and in *suchi-hasta* respectively pointing below in which case which is only part of the scene which is intended as Gajendra Varada. Correspondingly one of his upper arms of Visnu is discharging *chakra* downwards to save Gajendra, while his left upper arm is holding *sankha*, although Gajendra is not shown. This is Gajendra Varada panel.

Pahel No. 38 : Bhuvaraha, right leg planted vertically on the ground, left leg bent and supported by a *naga*, right upper arm holding the *chakra* and left upper arm holding the *sankha*, right lower arm bent and taken against the chest, complementary to the left upper arm which is also raised above the shoulder with the fore-arm bent towards the chest and holding the crook of the arm of 'BHU' in *anjali hasta*, while the head of the god thrown backwards is smelling the goddess with his snout.

Panel : *No. 39* : Figure of Krishna the right leg planted in the ground vertically, left leg flexed and placed in the chest of Kalinga which is shown with his sword in hand with five hoods. The right lower arm of Krishna is holding the tail of Kaliya and the right upper arm is in the act of giving him a blow. His left upper arm is holding the snake, while the left lower arm is in *suchi hasta*, pointing to his destruction. The curved and bent body of Kaliya who is hardly managing to support it by placing his left arm in the Kalindi pool and his utter subjugation have been well brought out in a rather unconventional portrayal of Kaliya-damana-Krishna with Kaliya having the sword and Krishna's leg not placed upon the hood of Kaliya.

Panel No. 40: Standing Visnu, four-armed, the two lower arms in *varada hasta* and holding the *sankha* on the left the two upper arms holding a long and heavy mace on the right against the body, of which at the bottom is shown Gadadevi in *anjali haste* in relief. The left upper arm holding *chakra*, the figure to the proper left corner is that of Garuda kneeling and in *anjali hasta*.

Panel No. 41 : Standing figure of goddess is *sama-bhanga* with upper body of it entirely bare, without ornamentation, but for a *graiveyaka-hara*, with the head carrying a *jatamukuta* with the upper arms in *varada* and holding a *kundika*. The figure is obviously a representation of standing Saraswati in view of the three important diagnostic elements held in the hands. This is again an unconventional representation of Saraswati.

Main vimana of Kailasa : The figures of the *bhadra* on the second *tala* of the main *vimana* : On the south the figure seated on a stool with one of the legs dangling and the other leg flexed and vertically kept on the side. There is what appears to be a *makara* shown by his side. It would thus be Varuna. On the east the figure seated apparently on the elephant, is therefore, Indra.

Among distictive types of their kind in the Kailasa (*Pl. LXI*) sculpture are to be noted Surya below Makaratorana with Aruna on top; (*Pl. LXII*) Parvati with mirror and clad in channaira, on the side walls of the front porch in the court; (*Pl. LXIII-LXIV*) the two amorous couples, in full stature in postures of osculation.

6

The Panchayatana Complex on the Southern Side Roof of the 'Kailasa'

The superstructure of the triple-storeyed excavation to the south of Kailasa would suggest that it was intended as a continuation of the lower excavated storeyed temple and to integrate the monolithic trends into it. It is interesting that this trend should have occurred at all at this stage because correspondingly such a trend had occurred elsewhere as well in the eastern Chalukyan region apparenly influenced by these Rashtrakuta efforts as at Vijayawada and Undavalli. The scheme that was adopted here had no direct relationship with the type of excavation that had gone off below, and at the same time has involved many concepts that make it not merely important, but as a type also, chronologically related to the other monolithic efforts at Ellora itself, for, it is obvious that this monolothic superstructure over the triple storeyed cave has come off towards the close of the time when or well after Kailasa had been carved out. This is suggested not merely by the reasonable proposition that to carry such a monolith with intricate details would have been achieved only after the major assignment of Kailasa had been completed, as also by the internal evidence of the evolutionary relationship between the feature of this monolith and others found in Ellora.

The monolith takes the form of a four porched regular *triratha* patterned structure enclosing a central chamber and providing around it for a *pradakshina patha,* whose four corners carry *chaturasra alpa-vimanas* with square *sikhara* or *kutas*, while the cardinal points at least insofar as they are preserved in three directions, namely, the east, north and south, carry *dvara salas* of which the one to the east cut out in 3/4 or almost full relief from rising cliff wall at the back makes it out as the most important of these *gopura dvaras*, thereby suggesting that the entrance of this subsidiary temple was from the east. Between the corner shrines, and the *gopuradvaras* run parapetted battlements or prakara walls providing a minimum primary pathway around the central shrine. The central unit which, as already been mentioned, is a *sama chaturasra* shrine with four projecting porches in *triratha* pattern, but serving purely as adjuncts in relation to prevailing straight line of *vinyasa sutra*, as clearly indicated by *bhadra* parts and *karnakutas* on the main units, stands at present only to one storey height. But, if the slope of the rock and the availability around it is any criterion, there was any great possibility of its having risen higher than a single *tala*, if at all it had been completed, as it is in truncated glory over this *tala* which is preserved practically up to the *harantara* top.

The porches have been made to carry roofs simulating a *sukanasa*. Entrance into the shrine has been given only from the west, thus making the porches in their present appearance false porches, but it is likely that ultimately they would have been either provided with *jali* windows or full openings—probably the latter—in view of the large scale *dvaragopura* carved on the eastern end. It is not clear at all if, on the other hand, this unit was mainly to serve as an entrance tower and further continuation of a major temple was to be cut into the mass of rock available towards the east. But in its present apparently rugged and unfinished character, particularly in regard to the return of the *prakara* walls into the major *sala gopura* on the eastern side, it would be proper to consider this as a finished unit in itself, and not a part.

It has been mentioned that the porches on the four sides represent *sukanasa* projections on their roofs. These are different from the *sukanasa* applied on Kailasa monolith in the main *vimana* and are nearer those of Chhota Kailasa and Chaumukh. They have a common and organically extended *kapota* with the mass of the main unit rising over their pillars, corbels, *uttira*, *vajana*, and *valabhi* of schematic simple workmanship and are provided with a *vedi* of a narrow type and a equally narrow *kantha* with pilastered divisions and nasika proper. The *nasika* is having a basal spread along the sides in the form of a foliage coming out of the *makara* just outside the horse-shoe shaped or cusped *mukhapatti* and within the *mukha patti* trefoil *kudu* is provided with pilasters supporting *dandikas* and a narrow niche in the centre within which figure carving is shown. The *simha lalata* is not too high over the *mukha patti*, but just over the outline of the flange barrel back of the *nasika*. The side flanges carry a *nasika kudu* one on either side in the centre.

The main unit, however, is divided into *bhadra salas* and *karna kutas* raised over a simple plinth of *padma* and *prati* and separated by a set of three cantoning pilasters in the course of *karnakutas* and two in the case of *bhadrasalas*. Their pillars show greater details than the heavy simple pillars of the porches by representing a thin square shaft, a *malasthana*, just blocked out, an undifferentiated *kalasa* with *ardha mandapa* blocked out on the sides, *tadi*, *kumbha*, *padma*, *phalaka* of square section, a narrow square *virakanda* and rather small, smoothly curved intersecting corbels with *vajanas* and projecting *uttira* members, also intersecting, and surmounted by a *vajana*, *uttira* which ties down the *uttiras* by overlapping at its corner angles. The *valabhi* and the *kapota* as mentioned above are common to the main unit and the porch. The *kapota* has been carefully decorated with *konapattais*, *madhyapattais*, *nasikas* with lotus medallions inside at regular intervals and on it is resting the rafter course, *not seen in Kailasa*, but found in Chhota Kailasa and Indra Sabha, Chaumukh, namely, a series of reasonably closely placed rafters of quadrantal chamferred front, running both axially and transversely, thus getting tied. These are to be the *lupas* and *jayantis* of the basal rafter frame work which supports the load of the superstructure and are not usually repeated at each *tala*. The regular *vyalavari* runs over them in the form of transverse and longitudinal rafter stretches tied individually by the *karnakutas* and *bhadrasalas* but not across the recessions which run like a *vedi*. Over this occurs the *vedi* proper formed by a *vajana*, *kantha* and *urdhvapadma* or *pratikapota* followed by the regular *griva* or the *hara* consisting of *salas* in the centre and *kutas* in the corners and the *harantara* of the well-flanged *kapota* with *nasikas* resting directly upon pilasters of the *kantha* below. The *sukanasa* projections of the porches come up to the level of the *harantara*. The *kutasikharas* show a perfect flange where fully preserved, as in the north-east corner, and are well festened by *konapattais* and decorated with *nasika*, complete with the *kudu*, *mukhapatti* and *simha lalata*, rising high and a single *padmadala* on the top resting perhaps below the *kalasa* which is, however, missing. The *dvaragopuras* on the north and south are simple *toranas* with pilasters on either side followed by integrated *uttira*, on them, a *vajana*, a *valabhi* of simple offsets, *kapota*, a *kantha* and oblong *sala* embellished with the *konapattais*, *nasikas*, in the centre, and *kudus* on their side faces showing *kudmalas* on the trefoil *dandika* points. The one to the north is complete, though truncated and with its *sala*, while the one to the south is complete from top to bottom but without the door opening cut into it. The eastern *sala* is magnificient insofar as it goes and has been completed only up to the level of the *kapota* of the intermediary *tala* and was apparently intended to rise in dvitala stature, to the basal *tala* of the same height as the porch projections of the main unit. It is obvious this section was also broadly similar in that over this basak *kapota*, the projecting *nasika kudu* running up to the next *kapota* was approximately of the same dimensions as the *sukanasa* of the main unit porch, though slightly smaller and does not have corresponding *nasika* projections on the northern and the southern sides, where the *kapota* runs. The return of the *bhadra* part of the *kapota* has been indicated at point where the regular wall rises. Over this second *tala* occurs the rafter course similar to the one described for the main unit, consisting of reapers with chamferred ends closely placed *makara* run over by the regular *vyalavari* and surmounted by the *vedi*, *griva* and *salasikhara*, whose *sala* is more massive than the other *dvara toranas*, and rise in the base of its *sala* height equal to the top of the main unit, the *sala* itself to having a relationship to the superstructural form, originally conceived for the main unit. This *sala* has within front face prominently relieved *nasika kudus* and *konapattais* and its side faces are carefully worked out with pilastered scheme inside the multifoil *kudu*, showing the close door-leaf between the pilasters within a framework, in addition to representing the *dandika* points of thereof interior on the frame of the vault as *kudmalas*. Since this lowest *nasika* rises above the level corresponding to the *kapota* of the main unit porch, it is clear that truly *dvitala* form was intended. Otherwise, the *nasika* cannot descend to this level. By the same token it is apparent since it is conceived as the main *dvaragopura* of this unit, the main unit itself would be of the *dvitala* stature only consistent with the availability of the rock here. The height of the projecting *mahanasika* facing west to this eastern *dvara gopura* ground *tala*, as already stated, corresponds well with the ground *tala* of the main shrine and thus would have seemingly been provided with regular passage opening across it east-west, when ultimately this *dvaragopura* had been completely carved out as a monolith. The fact that the plan the upper *tala kapota* shows only one *karna* and *bhadra*, but not the inner *karna* together with the fact that its *vyalavari* and *vedi* and even *griva* shows a *bhadra* and *karna*, would show that in the completed form after the rock is pushed back further, there would be a corresponding *bhadra nasika* projection towards the east at the ground *tala* level. This pattern of an almost intersecting *sala* type of *dvaragopura* has been obviously modelled after a typical cross *sala* door unit of the *dvaragopura* of Kailasa, although there the *mahanasika* and *salagopura* are not distinguished as in the present case. This is indeed a distinguishing feature stylistically between this monolith and Kailasa and makes it nearer to Chhota Kailasa, where the projecting *mahanasikas* at each level of the superstructure are unrelated to the *hara* series but placed somewhat below them. This feature described earlier harmonises with the four projecting *mahanasikas* of the main unit of this monolith. This evidence, therefore, is of considerably comparative value in fixing the age of the monolith and the Indra Sabha Chaumukh in relation to Kailasa.

The completed characted of the lay-out pattern of this monolith is further enriched by *kuta* units on the corners of the *alpa-vimana* type showing the *pada* of plain walls, without any corner pilasters, run over by *uttira*, *vajana*, *valabhi* in continual *kapota* similar to the *kapota* of the main unit, followed by a rafter frame work with chamferred ends similar to the other described in the *dvarasala* and the main unit *vyalavari*, *vedi*, *kantha*, and *chaturasra sikhara* slightly larger in size than the *kuta sikharas* of the main unit.

The perfect symmetry of the whole composition forming complete unit in itself would show that it is deriving its ritual directive from a *sarvatobhadra* shrine, additionally of *panchayatana* form and, if so, it is perhaps the only instance of such a type in the Dravida style. It is not known what the *sikhara* of the main unit was conceived as, but taking the cue from Indra Sabha Chaumukh and to some extent from Chhota Kailasa, it could have been largely of the old octagonal type alone, if not of the square type. The relationship of this temple would seem to lie midway between Kailasa on the one hand. Chhota Kailasa on the other and it is an interesting intermediary or transitional stage, which would not only help in projecting the stylistic evolutionary stages of lapse of time between this and the others. It has already been noted, while dealing with the cave temples with the triple storeyed shrine below, that because of its internal features, it might have been of the time of Indra III and probably not much later than the first quarter of the ninth century A.D. The presence of this temple unit of the *monolithic* type integrated with the cave temple underneath, shows that this could have been later to the cave temple below, and as such should have succeeded the cave temple in point of time. Thus, the age of this monolithic unit itself could be properly around the same period, viz., first quarter of the ninth century A.D., and if so, it helps us to visualise that Chhota Kailasa and Chaumukh themselves would have been somewhat after that period, but well within ninth century A.D., perhaps around the middle of that century. Thus, by the occurrence of its style, viz., *sarvatobhadra-panchayatana* type, by its integration of the cave and monolithic styles, by its propinquity with the great Kailasa and by showing features, some of which are not shown in Kailasa, but in Indra Sabha Chaumukh and Chhota Kailasa alone this unit is a valuable creation helping a better understanding of the monolithic enterprises of Rashtrakutas at Ellora.

The interior of the main unit carries a lotus medallion pendentive on the ceiling of the central *ankana* and shows below on the side walls the beam a canopy like architrave. The recess, the very character of its pendentive ceiling and the fact that its floor has been cut to integrate it with the cave temple below would show that notwithstanding the monolithic model that it forms on its exterior lay-out, which is finite and empirical. The interior was attempted to be converted into the clerastory of the cave temple below, particularly considering the cusped *gajatalu* like ceiling below the opening. The opening however is not of a deliberate, furnished or organised character, but is just a break-through. The significance of this monolith is not a little due to its location, so integrally close to Kailasa, by which token its basically Brahmanical character is high-lighted, although its architectural formulations have left very little scope for sculptural or iconographic affiliations. All the same, it is hardly to be expected that such a monolith would have been the handiwork of the Jain religion as the Indra Sabha Chaumukh and the Chhota Kailasa are as we find them today. This again would place the excavation closer to the Kailasa, but one does perceive the sharp diversity, though Kailasa and this monolith which is the very integration of *panchayatana* type of lay-out with the *vimana* type of temple units, whether of the *sala* or *nagara sikharas* would show a cross fertilisation of impacts, although it should be emphasised that the Rashtrakutas had deliberately aligned themselves with the southern *vimana* order under circumstances when their own political contacts with North India in their victorious campaigns had kept them up to strong influences of the *rekha-nagara* order of Upper India. Indeed the consistency with which they had reared monolith after monolith at Ellora, all attuned basically to the *vimana* order would show that the Rashtrakutas were traditionally hide bound and stuck to this individuality. Even on this structural plane, there are a very few Rashtrakuta patronised temples of the *rekha-nagara* order in Southern India. Thus, the Ellora *panchayatana* shrine is yet another instance of controlled ecclecticism than traditional limits in architecture under the Rashtrakutas additionally it has achieved, though in miniature form. Not even the great Kailasa had not been provided with the complete prakara unit with *dvaragopura* set on them and to this extent it is actually to serve on the post-script to the formulations implicit in the Great Kailasa monolith.

The top of the *sikhara* had been badly damaged by a cleavage caused by a block lamination of the rock and has slid towards the front perhaps, as suggested by the slopy face of the lamination still extant on its top front. It is unfortunate that this should have happened, since otherwise, it would have preserved one of the most interesting super structure known to us from Ellora.

Appendix

A Conjectural Reconstruction of How Kailasa was Executed

It is inevitable that the excavation of the magnitude of the 'Kailasa' should evoke not merely wonder and perplexity but also attempts at the possible reconstruction of the technique and methodology. Several scholars had given various suggestions including Dhavalikar who had specifically dealt with his view of the *modus operandi,* which opts for a facial attack in stepped phases, to put it briefly. However, it is the belief of this author that this, though not totally unacceptable, is not yet satisfactory and in any case does not render technical justice to the fact that temple building had certainly revealed certain first principles of architecture, of its own which could not but have been brought into play in such an enlarged endeavour, through the ken of the *sthapati* and his knowledgeable associates. It is also inherent from the parts of the sculpted architecture and the uniform common level to which the primary part, of the *Vimana* upto the porch of the *sabhamandapa* and the isolated *nandi mandapa*, and the secondary part of the entrance with its *dvara-sala* tower, that they should have been separated into three successive blocks before setting about shaping them into the required individual organic and traditional temple parts, with a solid surbase in the case of the main first phase and with hollow under-passages for the remaining axial parts. The manifest familiarity with the quantitative geometric and symmetric principles of massing, besides the obviously necessary principles of down-cutting are evident in this process. This was indeed the case and in order to follow the stages of this excavation work, one should turn back therefore to the first principles of architecture of the *Vimana* style, as we are dealing with here.

In the first instance, either a possible eroded rain gully cutting or one deliberately provided from the front, on either flank for access to the transportation of men and materials, should have been worked out to the level at which the architects and artisans had to operate for a reasonably long first phase. At the upper most surface of the hill also the corresponding deep shaft which would broadly have been as wide as the outer circumambulatory open court wenow see between the cloister and the main complex, would have been cut out. (Fig. 1 & 3)

From this stage onwards, towards the west, a ramp cum steps would have been maintained down to the proposed outer front entrance where the scarp would have been vertically cut and the toe part of the front hill eliminated to form an open ground level-front court to the complex. Thus, a marginal shaft all around the intended monolithic design area would have been isolated, to be precisely and effectively reduced to the ultimate layout and *urdhvachhanda* of the eventual 'Kailasa' in the next phase. (Fig. 1 & 2).

The actual apportioning of the cutting work would not, however, have been undertaken all the sama time; and indeed the 'fixed points' of each solid mass required for the design proposed, would have to be arrived at by taking a series of *datum lines* on the hill top, after it had been cleared of its defects and declivities in the area which would verily be the *vastu-purusha-mandala* zone. This process would be based on the same principles as the *manasutra* and *vinyasasutra* lines of a structural temple, horizontally and vertically for the required basal plinth area, which would have marked out on the cleared hill slope. (This would be almost similar also to the way an archaeologist would fix datum lines for a slopy ground, as in a rampart wall, before it is excavated and afterwards for drawing its excavated section.) This downward cutting thereafter would also have been *tala* by *tala* and to start with for executing the *sikhara*, *griva* (Fig. 2) and the entablature of the uppermost tala proposed. Axially, this work would go for the main *vimana* separately and the *sabhamandapa* with its triple projecting porches (*bhadravalokanas*) and similarly separately for the *nandi mandapa* block and the *Dvara gopura* roof level parts, but all the datum lines fixed in a series and work simultaneously overseen for proper level and component correlations. This would, in other words, mean that the level of the upper axial series from the main shrine to the *gopura* roof level was kept at a firm horizontal datum, almost until this entire work was completed. For this the horizontal level would place the projecting porches or the *sabhamandapa* would have been] at the same plan as the Lankesvara cave temple, on the northern flank (upper level) of Kailasa complex, and similarly the cornice and *vedi* of the ground floor of the triplestoreyed cave on the southern flank (which had however been conceived of towards the later stage of completion of the monolith.

It is here that we have to digress on the stage and date of lankesvara cave. This excavation, from its own internal evidence and the developed nature of its *sabhamandapa* and *vedi* parapet of the nave, not to mention the two differing sets of wall panel sculptures, was clearly built in two distinctive stages of time. The earlier of these two would have involved only the main *sandhara* sanctum, its *chala-linga* and Mahesa panel on the sanctum rear wall and the *antarala* ending perhaps one bay more into a south-facing verandah facade, facing into possibly an access that had been scooped out from the western toe of the hill. At one time of the Kailasa main temple down-cutting, therefore, it would have been linked with the Lankesvara, in the same way as we find a link bridge vestiges on the south side of the projecting porch, even now. At that stage, the facade of the main Kailasa complex, fixing out the *prakara* wall and entrance point would have been organised so that the clear axial orientation of the temple complex could be constantly before the eye of the artisans.

It is relevant at this juncture to note that: (a) in the entire range of Rashtrakuta cave temples or others at Ellora, Lankesvara alone shows a *sandhara* cella, all the others being *nirandhara*; (b) similarly, excepting here, in no Rashtrakuta creations at Ellora, a square *linga pitha* has been seen, all the others being of circular type; (c) the innermost wall flank leading from the *antarala* of Lankesvara towards the edge of the outer *prakara* court pit of Kailasa, contains a large *Tandava* Siva panel which is distinctively different in style from all the rest of the inner northern wall panels flanking the *sabhamandapa* of the present Lankesvara layout and are coeval in style in the latter with the inner pillars *vedi* carvings and the nandi also at the western end in a scooped chamber; (d) if the main Lankesvara cave had been carved, on the other hand, in one continuous effort, much later to the completion of the Kailasa monolith, all the above features, (a) to (c) would not have obtained or been even stylistically relevant; the shrine would have then been *nirandhara*, the *lingapitha* circular, it would not have had the Mahesa panel (Kailasa itself does not have it, nor Dantidurga's Dasavatara cave cella; and the carvings would have all been of the same type as the tale carvings around Kailasa complex. The Siva *tandava* mentioned is indeed comparable in style to the Narasimha panel on the outher *prakara* wall of Kailasa entrance exterior, which shows that this single Siva *Tandava* panel on the edge of the floor had been executed when the main temple cutting had been operating in that level, in the porch of the *sabhamandapa*, and thus was part of the central stage of Kailasa execution and the cella and *antarala* of Lankesvara had then been pre-existing. All these factors are sufficient to draw the inference that the main Lankesvara cella and *antarala* were early Rashtrakuta or perhaps even pre-Rashtrakuta, but the rest of Lankesvara was contingent upon the completed Kailasa complex and the stairway approach, the *nandi mandapa* and the *sabhamandapa* were all of a piece in a much later addition, and on the other hand, the fact that the cloister showing some remarkable range of ritual iconography, has been commenced from the very point of the ground floor periphery where the Lankesvara cave sanctum above is located, showing that the latter was pre-existing.

Once the work of the main temple had been completed at the upper level horizontal plan held at the axial line and the transverse line, the matter of down-cutting further, to the level of the present courtyard pit, would have commenced, cutting the massive surbase or *upapitha* upto the point of the main upper level porch, beyond which by the exigencies of the sloping hill, the ground floor level below the *nandi mandapa* and the *Dvara gopura* had to be lower than the *prakara* court and the underpassages for the above two axial units were designed which could also provide solid north-south screen walls for display of the magnificent Gajalakshmi panel and the provision of the covered flights of steps one on the north and south leading to the porched upper entrance variously, whose side walls were ultimately to be embellished with the narrative story-telling rows of miniature friezes from Ramayana and Mahabharata, bestowing some food for thought and satisfaction to the common man. (Fig. 3)

Thus, the main upper complex of temple parts was cut down and finished in three stages: firstly, for the main *vimana* proper which was designed as an *ashta-parivara* scheme, then the *sabhamandapa* with its three porch projections and subsequently for the *nandi mandapa* and the *dvara gopura.* What was commenced and mostly carried out during the time of Krishna I, uncle of Dantidurga, was completed possibly by the time of Govinda in the 9th century. The plan, levels, sculptures, pillar types all bear this out.

The Kailasa monolithic complex, thus, was most plausibly cut downwards, on first principles, and was certainly not a telescoped or stepped progression strictly, but the execution, on the ground, of a fully pre-meditated strategy of action by architects already inured to a well nigh century-old familiarity of *sthapatya* and *vastu vidya,* and is clearly all the more endearing to the art-historian thereby, since creative art is indeed all about conversion of a conceptual vision into a perceptual reality.

KAILASA MONOLITH
(STAGES OF CUTTING)

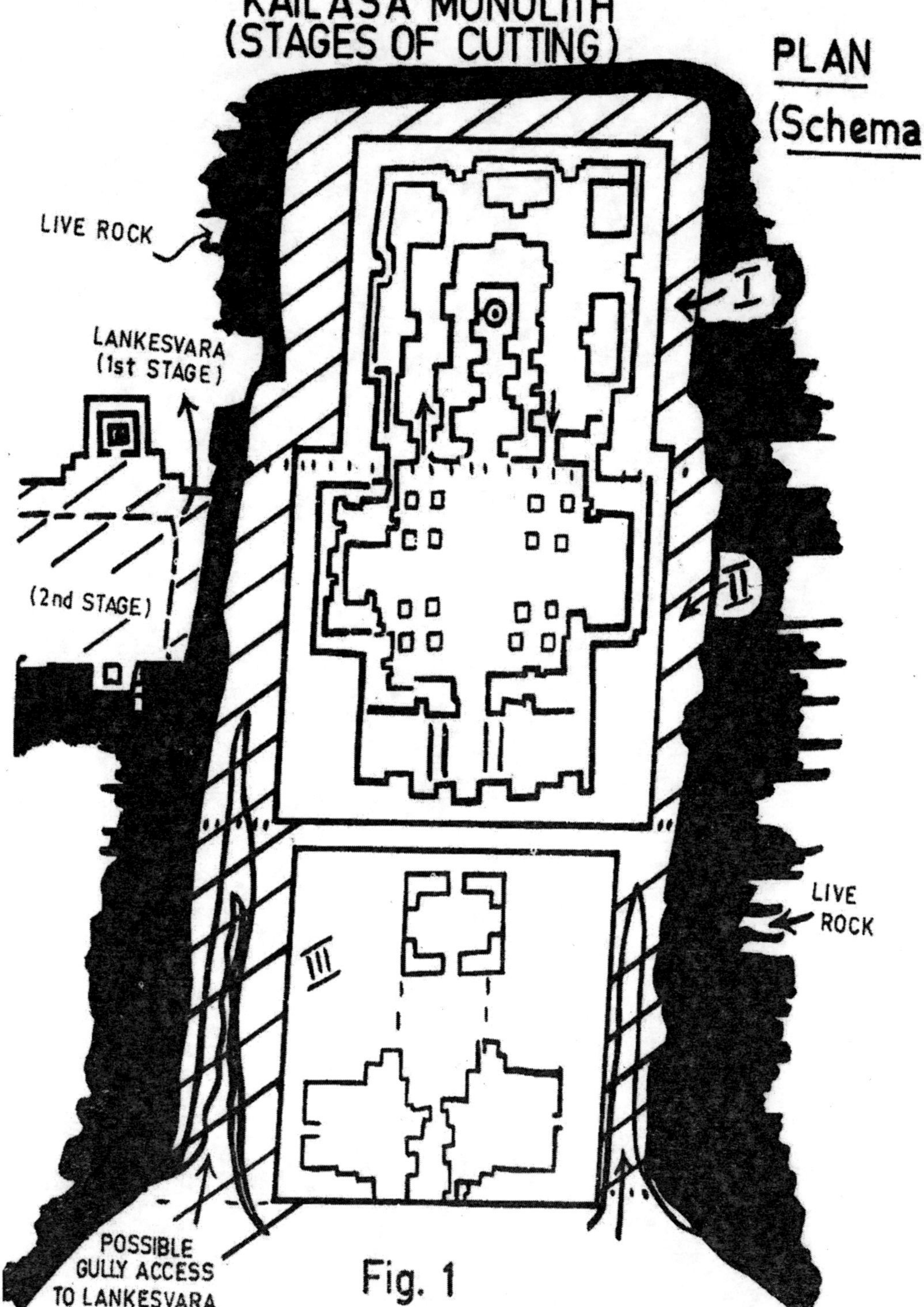

Fig. 1
(Appendix)

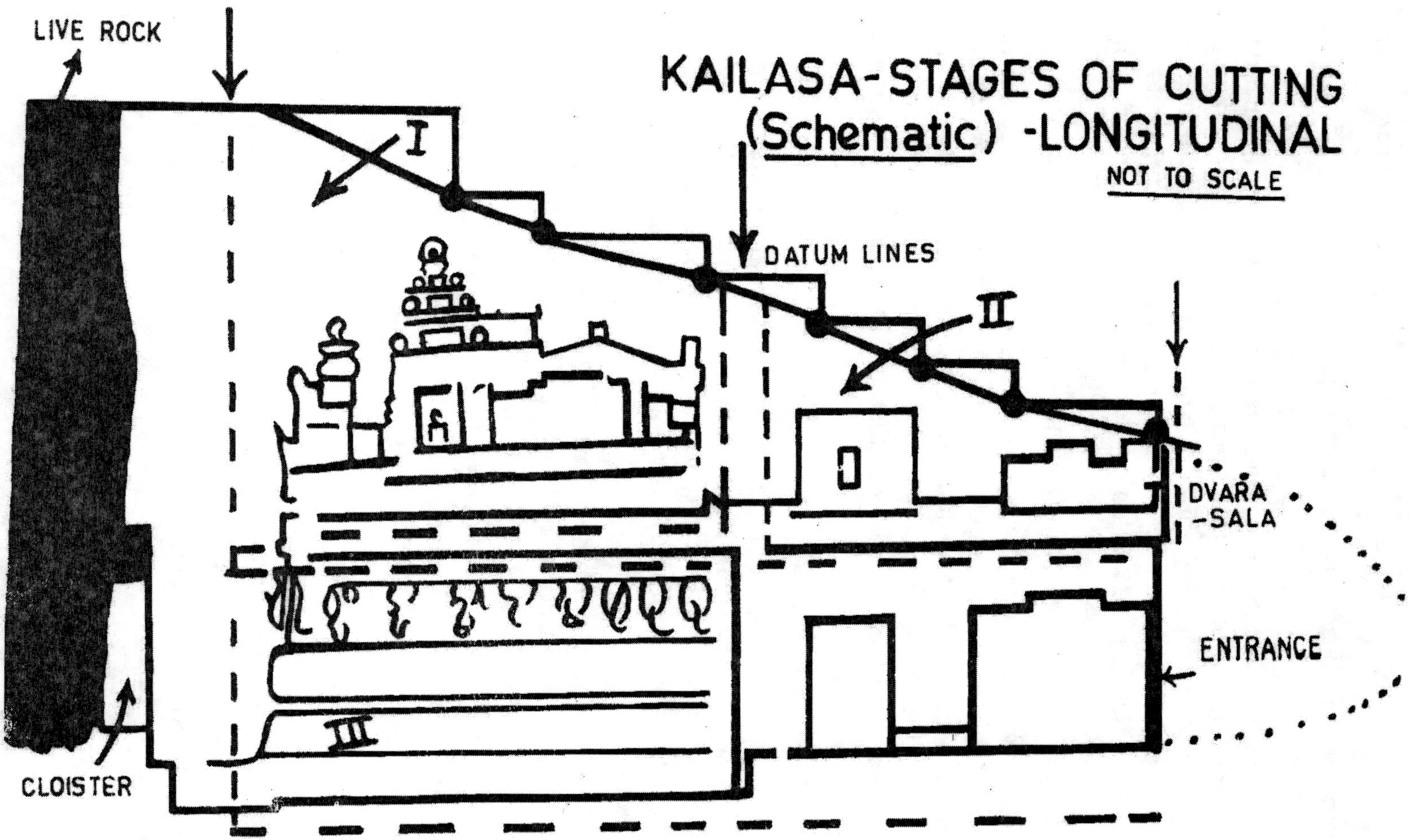

Fig. 2
(Appendix)

would be called the mukhamandapa, or when very narrow, a praggriva.

Arpita : Signifies in a southern temple, the hara units over each tala, and prastara, not of free-standing nature forming regular parapets for the pradakshina passage of successive talas, but rather applied to the next following tala. Its counterpart is anarpita which is generally an earlier form, indicating rudimentary provision for pradakshina at each tala level. The passage involved is actually the alindra of the southern architectonics.

Arshalinga : A type mentioned in the early texts to represent a linga shaft which has only a square-sectioned lower half and a cylindrical-sectioned upper half, the latter of which is thinner at the base and bulging at the top. Typically noted only in the Chalukyan early caves of the Deccan, as at Ellora, Elephanta etc.

Ayatasra : Rectangular in plan.

Bandhna : Signifies a horizontal patti or band running across the exterior wall of the temple, more than once in some cases as in the Central Indian Chandela temples, where the vertical registers by such divisions are in harmony with the horizontal lay-out of the rathas.

Barandika : Represents the topmost part of the bada of the orissan temple, showing cornice above and occurring over the bada inan Orissan temple.

Bhadra : Essentially means the cardinal opening or projection. In northern or southern temple plan it represents the cardinal ratha, and signifies a temple open on all the four sides, when used as a sarvatobhadra. In south, such a projection is also called mukha bhadra.

Bharani : Represents the capital part of a pillar in northern usage, corresponds to the padma and phalaka of the southern usage.

Bhitti : Represents the wall part of a temple and corresponds to pada of the southern usage, jangha of the northern usage, bada of the eastern and Kalinga usage and mandovara of the western

Gujarati usage : is found in this form in the earliest northern texts.

Bhumi : Literally, a vertical division of the super-structure, but essentially employed in non-functional storeyed forms as in the Nagara rekha sikhara, where it roughly stands for each of the nodes of the vertical profile, delimited by a karnamalaka.

Cchanda : A term used in relation to other terms like jati, vikalpa and abhasa and generally meaning certain gradations of the super-structural units, and probably also divisible in the form of free-standing temples, full relieved temples, partially relieved niche models, and painted specimens respectively.

Chalalinga : It is different from the svayambhu as well as achala. This represents the category of all the lingas which are detachable from the pithas and are not fixed naturally.

Chaturasra : Square in plan, representing one of the three major fundamental architectural plans of temples, the other two being ashtasra (octagonal), and vritta (circular). There are also ayatasra or rectangular and Vrittayata or apsidal forms, the square essentially pertaining to the northern temples. Ashtasra (octagonal) plan relates to a Dravida temple in its pure form, but relates mainly to the form of its sikhara and griva.

Chatushki : A complete mandapa unit found integrated with the balcony porch of the sabhamandapa the pillars being four in number and carrying decorative forms on the ceilling above.

Chitra : Generally meaning a picture or engraving, but in architectural texts intended essentially to mean a sculpture in the round.

Chitrabhasa : See chitra and chitrardha. The terms means a depiction, in paint, of a divine form.

Chitrardha : It is different from Chitra. This means carving in relief—a bas-relief.

Devakoshtha : Stands for the niches containing shrines of divinities in stipulated forms and directions, as enjoined in the texts.

Dharalinga : One of the early linga forms in the south. It represents a shaft with multi-faceted or multi-fluted exterior meeting at the top which is usually mildly flattened. In such cases, it does not have any pitha or any visible pindika. Later dharalingas show divisions of the vertical part into lesser and greater flutes. Dharalingas are considered to be the best form of the lingas.

Dravida : One of the three major divisions of temple styles often used in Silpa texts, the other two being Nagara and Vesara; it is essentially restricted in texts to designate the octagonal diagnostic sikhara feature, but has considerably more component features, for identifying a temple as Dravida in a clinching way.

Dvara : Means gate-way, and it is divided into many forms in early texts, such as dvarasala, dvarasobha, etc., and contains the germs for latter day gopuradvaras. One of the earliest dvaras in South India will be seen around Kailasanatha Shrine at Kanchi and the Shore Temple, Mahabalipuram facing east.

Dvarapalas : These are the door keepers or pratiharas as known in northern usage and could sometimes by dvarapalikas as for Durga, corresponding to pratiharis. They are generally found on the door frame of the cella in Deccan, and North where they are also accompanied by Ganga and Yamuna along side on their respective mounts, namely, the makara and the kurma. In the south they are generally placed outside the main temple unit, be it ardhamandapa or mahamandapa in its most original lay-out and, as a result serve to indicate the original limit of the temple, by their location. They wear ayudhas reflecting and personifying the Sivaite or Vaisnavite or Vaisnavite main deity.

Dvarasakhas : These are the overdoors of the main doorway entrance into the cella. While these sakhas vary from a single one to elaborate panchasakha units, they also differ in their lay-out and details, and are slightly orr-setted in Deccani usage, while they are horizontally spread out elsewhere. The important sakhas of the southern door frame are nagasakha, patrasakha, stambhasakha and pushpasakha. They are usually encased in a framework of padmakosa. The lower southern Indian practice is that of a plain featureless door frame.

Dvyasra : A term used apparently to denote a rectangle ending with an apse. It could thus be well called a vrittayata, although the latter could equally well mean the elliptical form. It is a prevalent view that dvyasra has become 'vesara' in the terminological jargon.

Gajatalu : A component element of vitana decoration consisting of integrated depressions at successive courses forming a series of kosas or coffers, relieving the projections in between the two.

Gavaksha : Pierced window-openings for ventilation and light.

Ghanadvara : This represents a large grill-window or a pilastered niche provided on the cardinal points of the main shrine on its outer walls. It implies essentially a false door. It is flanked on the outside by two free-standing pillars. Such types are generally seen in the Nagara prasadas of the North and the Deccan.

Ghantasamavarana : Miniature turrets running along the radial limgs of the exterior roof over the sabhamandapa and the chatushki, of a northen temple; shaped in the form of a ghanta or a bell complete with a thin amalaka and a kalasa on top. A host of such is a samvarana, receding courses of such rise in a stepped form on a roof of the ancillary walls of the temple.

Griva : The nick of the super structure. See also table under section IV(a)(i)

Hara : A string, literally, and connotes the string of shrine-miniatures that runs over the parapet of each tala (generally excluding the last, except in very early contexts) and comprising kutas at the corners, and salas in between. Sometimes panajara units are also displayed in the hara. See under panjara.

Harantara : The recession between kuta and sala in the southern context and the bhadra, anuratha and kurna in the northern where it is also called the salilantara, since it facilitates storm water drainage.

Jagati : See under padma. It is a recurrent form in southern temples at the base of the adhishthana above the upana and is plain vertical right angular moulding; it is different from the jagati of the northern temple where it signifies a spacious structurai terrace upon which the main temple is erected.

Jangha : See bhitti.

Jativimana : It is a type differentiating it from jatitara types and from a mukhya vimana, and representing temple model which has upto four talas.

Kailasa : A primary form like Vairaja etc., and representing a circular plan.

Kakshasana : A seat-back provided above the vedi on the inner side of the sabhamandapa along its outer limit, particularly in the cardinal projections of the balconies.

Kalasa : The most important and topmost part of a temple structure, showing a properly consecrated pot form usually encased in copper metal. No temple is fit for or deemed as in active worship without its being in position.

Kani : Known also as Karnika. This northern term is essentially depicting a flattened kumuda-like moulding rising above the padma on the plinth. It is very typical in Gujarat architecture.

Kapotabandha : An adhishthana form whose top member is a kapota; unlike that of padabandha and pratibandha, which have a patika. A kapotabandha further should normally have a vritta-kumuda, but occasionally tripatta; typical of Chalukyan region and used early only once in the south, in Dharmaraja ratha.

Karna : Signifies the corner unit of the plinth and wall carrying its on superstructural elements in harmony with the main temple style.

Karnamalaka : Represents the end of each bhumi on the super-structure of a nagara rekha sikhara.

Karnatilaka : Represents a miniature Nagara sikhara unit placed at the joinery between the main sikhara and the antarala on the side profile; not found in the southern usage.

Kati : The term employed to represent pada or bhitti or jangha of slightly later usage and is so mentioned in Visnudharmottara.

Kshipta : A vitana type wherein the designs are cut-in in an integrated mode, the patterns laid one within the other.

Kudyastambha : The pillars which additionally support a pada and are placed at regular intervals on the exterior of the wall over the plinth.

Kumuda : An important moulding of the adhishthana; see under pattika. It has two classes, the vritta kumuda and the tripatta kumuda, which are self explanatory. In Chalukyan country, we have a multi-faceted kumuda also, in early usage, as at Aiholi, Nagaral etc.

Kuta : A 'sikhara' unit in the 'southern' style, which has a square plan and is basically capping an alpa vimana or single-storeyed unit, but stands for miniature or kshudra alpa vimana part of the multi-storeyed temple. In these, it occupies the corner (karna-kuta) of the parapet, above the entablatures, of each storey or tala.

Kuta-chhadya : Essentially northern in connotation. It represents the plain projecting externally ribbed chajja-like cornice overhanging main beam on the top of the jangha. Temples without kuta-chhadya are often found in the north, particularly in Eastern India.

Lalatabimba : This represents a small ritual carved tablet located in the centre of the lintel of the cella door. It is popularly taken as a cognizancc of the religious affiliation of the deity within, but could indeed be a merely auspicious common motif, employed more on a regional pattern than anything else. The usual lalata-bimba devatas are Gajalakshmi, Ganesa, Garuda, Lakulisa, Anantasayi etc.

Latina : A term found in some northern texts to represent the highly intricate and over-lapping Jalaka patterns on the rekha sikhara of the northern temple.

Linga : Originally meaning a mere symbol or a formal criterion, having the same sense as chinha, later appropriated to Sivaite usage and taking the form of a vertical shaft of stone either plain or faceted. It is also relieved with figure work in the earliest instances. In such a case, it is called a mukhalinga and may have a single mukha or five mukhas. These are mounted directly on the square base and thus vertically support the originally iconic character of Siva turned into the symbolic pillar form subsquently.

Manasutra : The vertical plumb-line delimiting the projections of the kapota or cornice and essentially coalescing with the projection of the upana of the lowest moulding of the plinth in southern temples, but not necessarily so, in the northern temples. In northern temples, particularly in early medieval stages, the plinth flares out much wider off than the drip line of the cornice.

Manchabandha : An adhishthana type of the simplest kind in the form of a high kantha, with an upana below and a pattika or kapota above. A very popular chalukyan usage here it has a kapota top.

Mandovara : See Bhitti.

Manika : Of the same group as Vairaja and Kailasa. It represents an elliptical form.

Mulabhera : The main deity, usually of stone (Sila), brick and stucco (Sudha) or in wood (daru) or in paint (Abhasa), and both in iconic and aniconic forms.

Mulamanjari : The main tower found within the encircling urahsringas or miniature half-turrets applied to it. In the earliest northern usage of the term as in Visnudharmottara, in the form of manjari, it represents the superstructure itself.

Mukhapatti : Horse-shoe shaped or trefoil barge board of sukanasa or even smaller nasikas. These are decorated in the former with side cusps bearing nagas and with resette series along the border, representing nail heads.

Mukhya vimana : Signifies a temple which has more than four talas. The text prescribes that a maximum number of talas for most of the mukhya vimanas is between 12 to 15 and in any case, could not be more than about 200 ft. in height. The term is essentially of southern usage. The Great temple at Tanjore is an outstanding expression of the highest example of the mukhya-vimana with 13 talas.

Nabhicchanda : A major type of vitana in a northern mandapa consisting of receding annular rings on the ceiling, ending in a pendentive and supported by brackets rising from the pillar corbels and decorated with madanikas as bracket struts.

Nagara : Generally taken to mean 'northern' temples owing to their sharp divergence from southern or Dravida; stands for a square —sectioned temple, whose sikhara is of the rekha type surmounted by an amalakasila sometimes. It is, rather obscurely, taken to represent any temple, in early Tamil literature.

Nasika : Representing small dormer windows on kapotas, prastaras and sikhara roofs; shaped essentially in the form of the original Buddhist chaitya dormer, owing to their peculiar projection forward, they are known as such. In the most significant and larger-sized projection at the base of the Sikhara on the main direction of orientation of the temple or all the four cardinal directions, they are called sukanasa or mahanasika respectively.

Nirandhara : As opposed to sandhara, this has a single wall for its main temple cella and the pradakshina is to be made around it on the open court or terrace. Generally a characteristic of southern temples.

Oma : Basal pitha of a pillar—generally found in the Deccani and Northern series, but not in a temple of Tamilnadu until mediaeval times. Its use is also noted in some texts only.

Pada : Wall part, above the adhishthana or plinth and below the cornice, in southern context.

Padabandha : One of the adhishthana types of early southern temples, differing from the other important form, namely, pratibandha in the two features, having a vritta kumuda and often not having a prati.

Padma ; Standing for the cyma recta of western usage and usually found in the northern or Deccani usage and in the later southern temples. In the earlier ones its place is assumed by a plain jagati or rectangular high moulding.

Panjara : Meaning a cage and representing a nasika supported by pilastered frame work at the lower levels of the tala and generally located in the recessions of the harantara or salilantara portions of the wall face. Where it is having a regular sikhara miniature, as sometimes in evolved pre-mendieval Deccan usage, it is called sikhara panjara. Where it has the base of the pilaster a large kumbha and overflowing foliage on the top, as in the mediaeval southern usage, it is called a kumbha panjara, and so on.

Parivaradevata : A subsidiary deity, which is subordinate to and attendant upon the main deity or mulabhera of a temple, in a given sectarian context.

Pattika : Heavy oblong-sectioned topmost moulding of the adhish-thana in the southern temples, the other parts being kantha, kumuda, padma or jagati and upana. It projects over the kantha. In Tamil texts called 'agrapattiyal'.

Phalakalinga : A form mentioned in the texts suggesing a linga made out of a rectangular or flattish block or nodule of rock. Some of them are early. We have interesting specimens of this kind, though slightly later, at Gudimallam, where, however, it is relieved with figure carvings.

Pindi or Griha pindi : The coping slab, single usually, that seals the superstructure below the griva level; also stands for the wall immediately surrounding the main deity in the cella.

Pindika : This is essentially the support or platform or pedestal, upon which either the linga or the image is placed. In the former case, it could be called a pitha where it rises fairly high; and where it is kept very low almost close to the floor-and often in a single slab, it may be called pindika.

Pishtika : Stands for jagati of the northern usage and upapitha of the southern usage and is employed in Kalinga architecture.

Praggriva : Represents an incipient mukhamandapa or antarala terminating the temple unit, the only other part being the cella. Not used in the south.

Prakara : The wall erected around the main temple unit, leaving open space around for perambulation of the deity as well as the devotee. It is intended as a measure of protection as mentioned in the texts and employed mainly in the south.

Pranala : This signifies the provision architecturally made for discharge of a abhisheka water from within the garbhagriha to the prakara both for drainage as well as for ritual utilisation by the devotees. The earliest temples in the south upto the time of the early Cholas generally do not have the pranala projections. In these instances it is just a water channel (where found) essentially cut on the topmost member of the adhishthana. In the Deccan however, there is a mixed usage of pranalas as well as plain slab-cut water channels or nalas, running at the level of the inner sandhara prasada and provided with a reception opening within the cella. The pranalas according to texts should be cut in the form of simha-vaktra (iron face) and should be ridden over the nandi or ganas. The terminal is either in the form of a makara or a vyala or an elephant trunk in the evolved cases. The pranala is essentially different from varimarga or ambumarga.

Prasada : A term generally employed to signify palace in civic architecture in early times, but coming to mean temples subsequently, of the northern type more commonly as a Nagara Prasada. The southern usage prefers the word vimana although Prasada is used.

Prastara : Entablature, namely, the parts above the pada or wall part and below the griva or the neck part in the southern context. For equivalent terms in other regions see under section IV(a)(i).

Prati : The topmost course, cut or placed on the pattika or kapota, as the case may be, of the adhisthana; it signifies the level of the garbhagriha floor and is a basic level for compulation of elevational portions. It is from this word that the Tamil word padi for step is derived.

Pratibandha : An adhishthana type of the southern temples tenerally having a tripatta kumuda and a bold prati; usually older in provenance than the padabandha type.

Pushpaka : Of the same class as Vairaja, Kailasa, and Manika. It represents a rectangular form.

Rajasenaka : A relieved figure carving shown on a band immediately resting below the vedika of the northern usage; it shows animated scenes of royal army etc.

Ratha : Graduated projections of a temple plan in the northern usage, where it could be triratha, pancharatha or saptaratha according to the evolution of the style. Each of the projections in such cases is also called rathaka.

Ruchaka : Square form as applied to pillar cross-section. Essentially employed in northern texts. The other forms of pillar sections are svastika (octagonal), vritta (circular), Bhadra (with pratirathas), Vardhamana or pancharatha, shadasraka, (hexagonal). It is interesting to note that these cover the Nagara, Dravida and Vesara forms also (respectively of square, octagonal or hexagonal and circular).

Sabhamandapa : Sometimes called the ranga mandapa. It is the most ornate outer vestibule of a northern temple, open on one, two or three sides and provided with a torana on the axial outer end; corresponds to the mahamandapa of the southern temple usually separate from themain unit; divided into nine compartment on plan by the pillar series and thus to be called a navaranga mandapa.

Sahasralinga : Evolved early mediaeval linga form wherein, tier after tier miniature lingas are picked out on the curved surface of the lingashaft. In the north or western India it goes by the name of Hazara linga.

Saktidhvaja : This signifies the upper part of the nasika face or front of a sukanasa; contains pennants and a simhalata or simha or vyala crest.

Sala : Similar in import and usage to kuta and is found in multi-storeyed shrines along with the kuta and alternatingly. It always occurs in the middle section in such cases, and never on the corners for the obvious reason of its being rectangular in plan.

Salilantara : Also known as Jalantara (northern term), it largely stands for the harantara recess of the southern usage. Its purpose is for the drainage of water from the superstructure roof through nalas, kept above the cornice in this recess, making them unobtrusive.

Samatala : A vitana type of a northern temple mandapa of almost level horizontal ceiling design.

Sandhara : A shrine which has a closed perambulatory circuit between the inner garbhagriha wall and the surrounding exterior wall. Essentially a feature associated with northern temples but rarely and not regularly found in the southern types.

Sardulas : These are the mythical leogriphs combining a lion and the griphon and employed as an embellishment not only in the salilantara recesses of the temple wall, but also on the roofs of the sabhamandapa and mahanasika, shown with one of their fore-paws raised.

Sikhara : In the 'southern' style denotes only the topmost major component of the temple elevation, above the griva or neck and below the stupi. In the 'northern' usage, it stands for those whose the superstructure of above the cornice level is.

Sringa : Miniature sikhara units placed all around the main superstructure at the lowest level, the corresponding upper units of similar chatacter are called Urahsringas.

Stupi : The topmost ritual part of a temple elevation. It includes generally the kalasa and the finial proper.

Sukanasa : Also called Mahanasika. This shows the integral projection of the basal part of the superstructure forming the roof of the antarala (or ardhamandapa). It is of two varieties, depending upon whether the structure is a Nagara prasada or a southern vimana. In the former, it is in the form of the mammoth trefoil nasika complete with the mukhapatti saktidhvaja and simahalalata. In the southern, it takes essentially the form of a front-on sala, reared upon a pada. The sukanasas are practically unknown in the temples south of the Andhradesa, but are a diagnostic feature of the Chalukyan genre.

Svayambhulinga : This signifies the natural form which have taken the shape of lingas and have been found fit for consecration and erection of temples in situ over them. Svayambhulinga, thus, is never planted.

Tala : Storey and generally involving a plinth, a pada, a prastara, a griva, over which in a series occurs a sikhara, as in the southern style.

Tarangabodhika : Wavy corbel with or without a median band. The caves could themselves be in simple series or in paired volute forms or with the corner rolls in involute type, or in double roll one above the other, as in the chalukyan monuments.

Torana : This is an ornamental device used either in a free-standing manner or in relief. In the former mode, it is located in front of the mukhamandapa, at the very entrance into the temple unit, and in the latter mode it is to be found in niche shrines on the exterior walls. The free-standing citra torana could be very elaborate, as in Gujarat where it is provided with two massive full scale pillars surmounted by double architrave beams with makara terminals and bearing a makara torana on the upper architrave. Without the architraves and forming a continuous curved arch over the pillars, it is found in Kalingadesa as at Bhubanesvar (Muktesvar). In the form of relieved outer frame work of niche shrines, it consists of two broad types, the stambha-torana and the makaratorana. The latter would itself be either a patra-torana almost entirely or makara-torana. Engaged toranas are also utilised as parts of the pillar frame work of the Sabha-mandapa in northern temples. In such cases they rise from the upper part of the pillar in the form of engrailed arches and are made to bear partially the weight of the cross-beams and serve essentially the purpose of brackets.

Trivishtapa : Of the same group as Vairaja, Kailasa etc. It represents an octagonal form.

Upana: The lowest and plain moulding of the adhishthana forming a basal preparation of the temple plinth.

Upapitha : The basal additional and optional functional part of the plinth below the adhishthana proper in a southern temple, often consists of a simple mancha bandha; generally employed only in evolved temples or in special contexts, where the shrine does not have sufficient elevated position.

Urahsringa : Miniature semi-towers which are applied to the main structure both in the bhadra part as well as on the ratha and are themselves receding backwards as they go up, and encase the mulamanjari—a typical character of the Central Indian Chandela and the Lata (Gujarat) temples of early mediaeval times.

Utsavabhera : The subsidiary to the image in the sanctum, and the main ritual image subjected to movement and abhisheka during festivals, and which is usually made of bronze and prevalent mainly in South India. It is placed either in front of the mulabhera in the sanctum, or in the mahmandapa on a portable mancha or table.

Uttaranga : The mouldings and architectural parts above the uttara of the main door frame of the garbhagriha. They usually carry miniatures of temple vimanas or prasadas, and in the latter northern usage have, in addition, the Saptamatras and Navagrahas, as in Gujarat and Rajasthan.

Vairaja : A primary form, one among the five, representing a square, and mentioned in early texts like Visnudharmottara.

Valabhi : This is the zone located under the cornice known as the kapota. It is essentially an overriding course connecting the uttara with the prastara and tying the cornice (Kapota) as a cantilevar. It is usually decorated either with a row of bhutas or ganas in which case it is called a bhutavari; or it is embellished with hamsa or geese. Usually in evolved contexts the valabhi is either having a simple padamatala motif or is left plain with mild curvature. Rarely, it is also of the bevel type. Etymologically, the valabhi would represent turret roof and it is probably in this context that this term is employed in the northern texts like Vishnudharmottara.

Varimarga : This is a channel provided partially within the garbhagriha and projecting into the thickness of the wall meeting the pranala for the discharge of abhisheka water. Early temples show essentially a varimarga, but no specific pranala. By reference to a ban on the cutting of the top moulding of adhishthana for a varimarga, the texts imply their provenance earlier. Early Pallava temples have, one and all of them, only varimargas cut on the plinth top. In the southern tradition during the circumambulation of the cella either in sandhara types or in open prakara type a varimarga is crossed to reach the front of the temple. In the evolved northern tradition, however the varimarga particularly is Siva shrines is not to be crossed, but the devotee is to retrace his step backwards to the nandi mandapa. Usages as ell as textual references up hold this.

Vedi : Represents a parapetting mainly divided into a series of pilasters and intended to provide an outer walling over the plinth. In the north, it additionally serves the purpose of having a kakshasana and a chatushki borne over dwarf pillars forming open balconies in the sabhamandapa of the temples.

Vesara : Notwithstanding the differences about its suggested connotation and its covering the circular cross-sections, also the term probably stands for apsidal structures of gajaprishthakriti in elevation and having a chaitya pent-house front for its superstructure, the area of its largest and prime incidence is the zone between Narmada and the Krishna rivers.

Vikalpa : See Cchanda.

Vimana : The full minimal shrine unit, covering from plinth to the spire (upanadi stupi paryantam). The term is used mainly to refer to a Dravida or southern temple type, as different from the word Prasada, which is used in the 'northern' context. (See under

Prasada). It is used only in religious and never in a secular context.

Vimanadevatas : Figures of divinities placed in koshthas on the cardinal points and sometimes on the vidiks also on the superstructure of the vimana at successive talas. The texts prescribe a specific vyaha for such vimana devàtas, appurtenant to Saiva or Vaisnava usage.

Vinyasasutra : An axial thread line indicating the norm of the plinth lay-out, the nature of the projections and recessions of the madhyasala, karnakutas and the harantaras at plinth level. The vinyasasutra line is generally dead straight in most of the southern temples, while in northern temples the projection of the central (Bhadra) part beyond the lateral parts in various ratha off-sets results in ratha-form becoming the norm.

Vitana : Literally a ceiling, either with free-standing pillars and canopy of part of the main structure or mandapa itself.

Vitanas : They are generally severely plain in southern temples. They are found with a navagraha grid and a central panel of god-head, in the Deccan, as in Chalukyan temples. But in the north, particularly in Gujarat, they are provided with infinite variations of patterns and are divisible into sama-tala and nabhichchanda types. These in turn have themselves many varieties of the kshipta type or kshipto-kshipta type, employing gajatalu or cusped teeth or moulds and pendentives in the centre.

Vyalavari : Literally the griphon course; it is a conventional structural blocking-course or rafters running both longitudinally and transversely and forming a framework, upon which the pada of each tala including its cornice is sustained. Usually in early specimens, it is embellished by showing the projecting rafter ends as vyalamukhas only or as vyalas in lateral full aspects, the corresponding cross rafters which tie them being shown as having makara terminals. The vyalavari is usually but not always found below the topmost member (pattika or kapota) of the adhishthana and correspondingly in the subsequent tales as the upper member of the prastara below the vedi and griva of the hara. In evolved architectural stages, the vyalavari tends to follow strictly the original wood techniques, and displays only plain rafter ends and terminals.

Yoni : Generally taken as meaning Avudayar (Tamil) or the pindika or the pitha in mediaeval usage, in relation to the word linga, particularly when such a pitha is circular and with a water chute projection on the northern side. But its originally meaning in the Silpa texts is that of a specific ritual orientation of the main image and its platform to be fixed according to Ayadi shadvarga formula, yoni itself being one of the shadvargas, the others being aya, vyaya, tithi, etc.

Index

Errata

Page	*Line*	*For*	*Read*
1	1	Ellora is	Ellora (Pl. 1) is
3	1	Coglong	Colgong
,,	17	in the previous	in a previous
,,	18	the Deccan,	Deccan' by the author
4	7	rather desperate	rather disparate
5	9	do not have	we do not have
8	21	known that	known by that
21	4	657 A.D.	875 A.D.
24	Caption	Monoliths	Monolithic
25 to 33	Folio	Monoliths	Monolithic
40	29	Chotta Kailasa	Chhota Kailasa
48	6	figures rendered	figures (Pl. VIII) renders
71	7 (from bottom)	top front.	top from (Pl. XIX).
72	17	the nidhis—	the nidhis (Pl. XX)—
112	19	(Pl. XLXII)	(Pl. XLVII)
124	6	second tala	second tala (Pl. LI)
,,	7	from	(Pl. LII) from
136	17	ganas (Pl. V)	ganas (Pl. LV)
145	5	kailasa	kailasa (Pl. LVII)

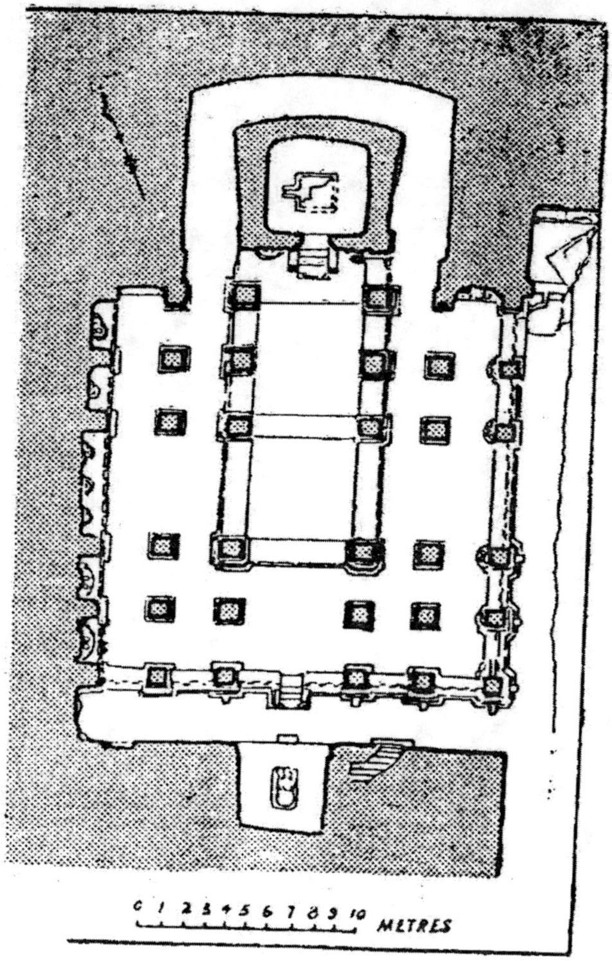

Fig. 1. Lankesvara cave (No. 16)

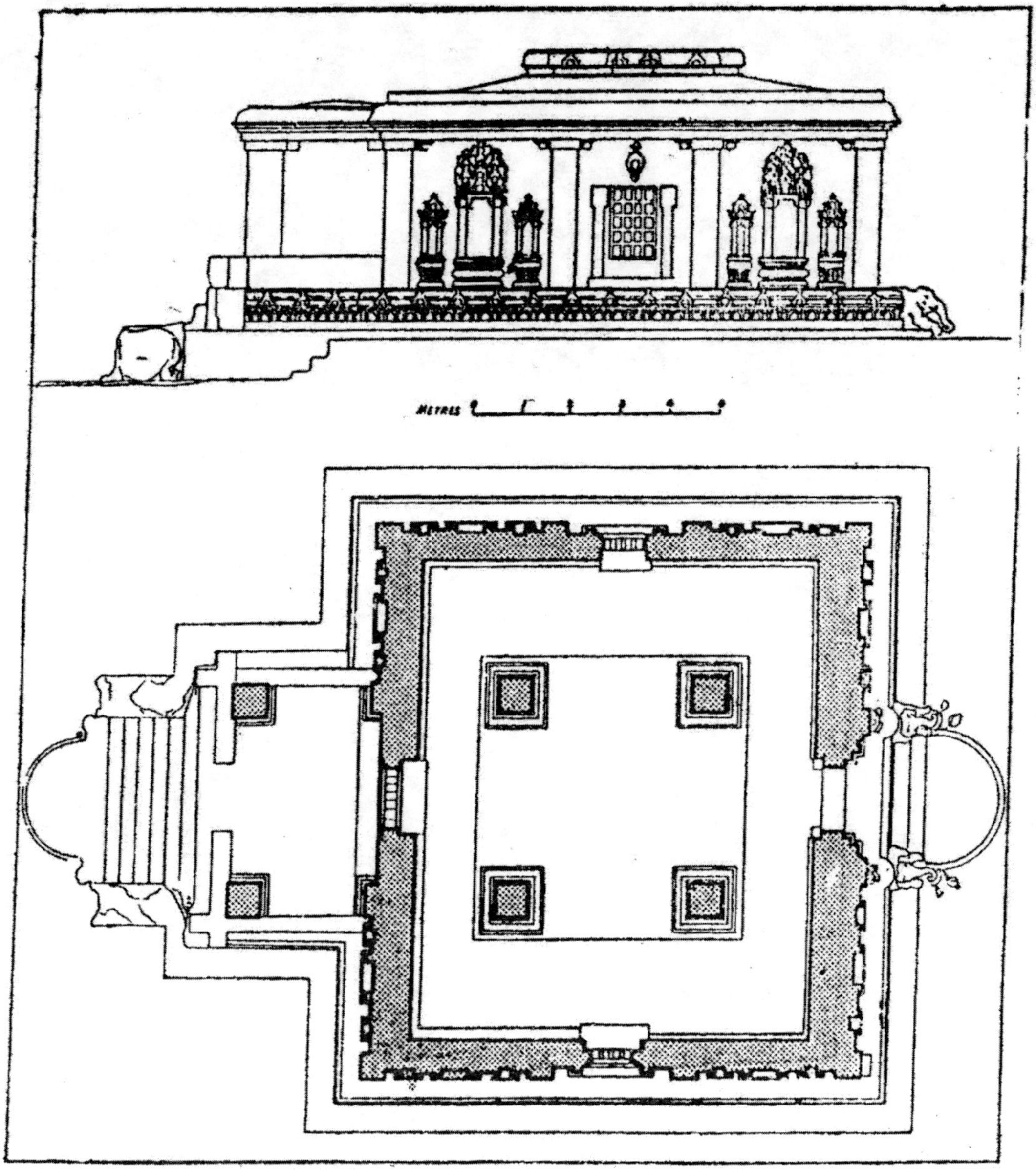

Fig. 2. Mandapa in front of Dasavatara Cave (No.15)

Fig. 4(a)–(c) - Details, (a) Door Frame and Pilasters

Fig. 4 (b) : Sukanasa.

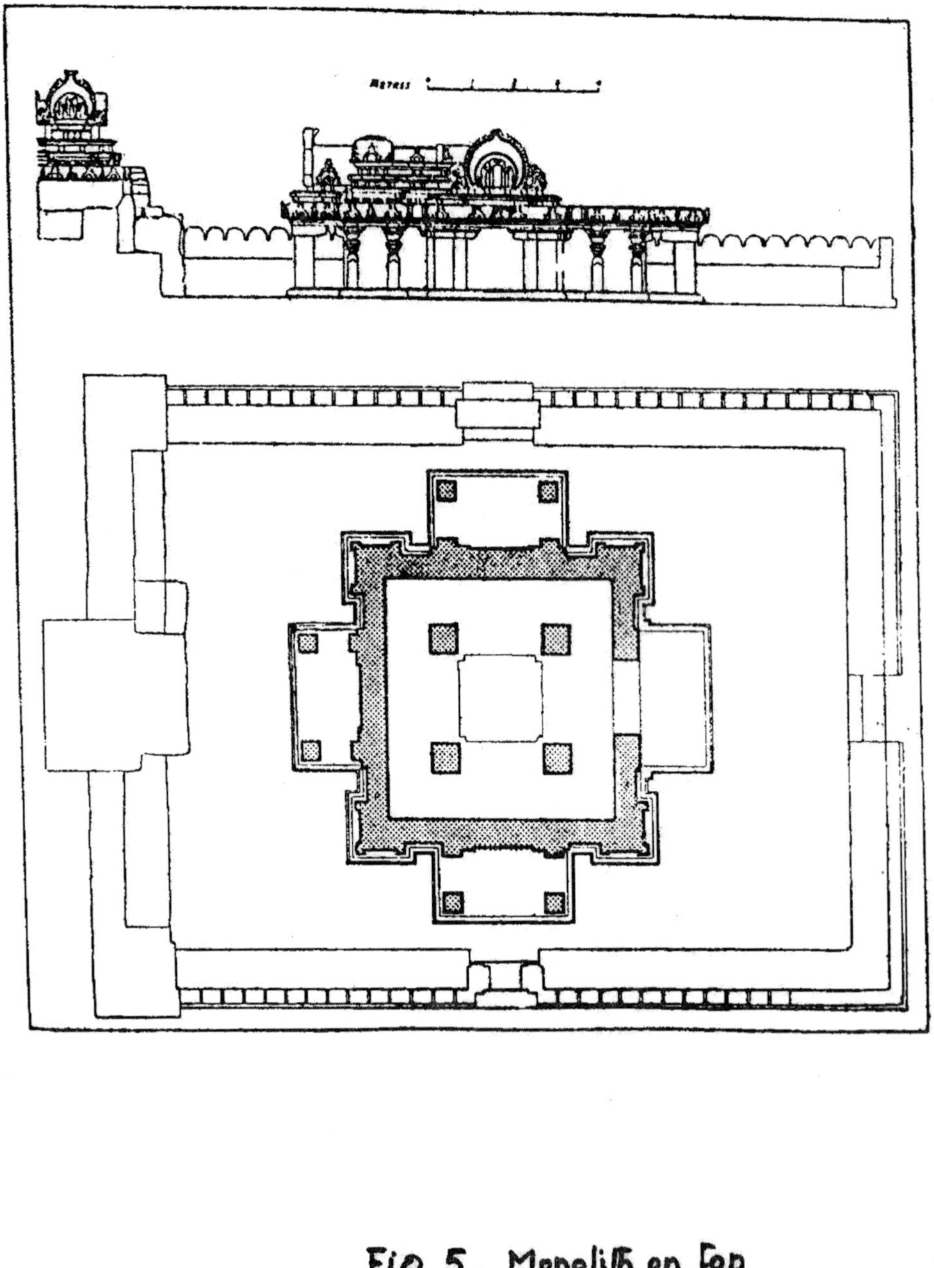

Fig. 5. Monolith on top roof of Triple-storeyed cave in Kailasa Complex (South side)

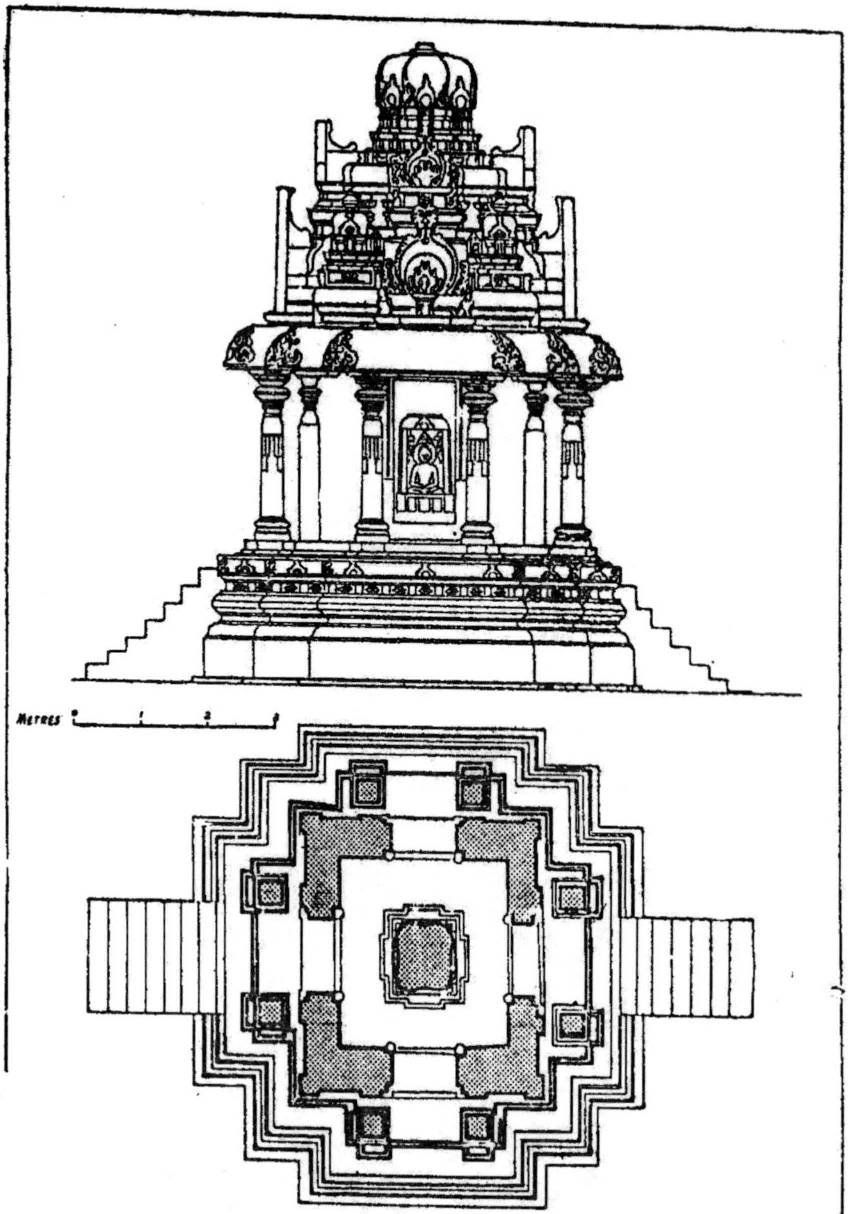

Fig. 6. Chaumukh monolith of Indrasabha cave (No 32)

Plate I—Ellora : Kailasa (Cave No. 16) outer most open front entrance outside the Prakara.

Plate II—Ellora: Cave No. 15—Dantidurga mandapa-western porch.
Full detail of Torana and the dvarapalas below.

Plate III—Ellora : Cave No. 15—Dantidurga mandapa-western porch-Torana over grill window.

Plate IV—Ellora : Cave No. 15—Dantidurga mandapa-recumbent elephant balustrade of eastern entrance steps.

Plate VI—Ellora : Cave No. 15—Dantidurga mandapa-Mithuna (Bacchanalian)-north-east corner pilaster, facing east.

Plate VII—Ellora : Cave No. 15—Dantidurga mandapa-female figure with vessel in right hand and gana attendant touched by her hanging left hand.

Plate VIII—Ellora : Cave No. 15—Dantidurga mandapa-Nayika mithuna-(Bacchanalian)-north-east corner pilaster, facing east.

Plate IX—Ellora : Chota Kailasa—Upper part of the Sukanasa projection and the unfinished lower part (north-east side).

Piate X—Ellora : Chota Kailasa—Main shrine tower scheme from the south-east.

Plate XI—Ellora : Chota Kailasa—roof of the sabha mandapa the showing same scheme as at the Kailasa (Cave 16) monolith, but in subdued and undifferentiated *hara* parapet and without any central miniature shrine crest or the animals in the round on the periphery.

Plate XII—Ellora : Chota Kailasa—Showing the south-eastern corner of the tower and the unfinished lower levels.

Plate XIII—Ellora : Chota Kailasa—Sukanasa front with the Sankha and Padma nidhis and with the tower scheme below. The Sukanasa contain a sub-shrine within it.

Plate XIV—Ellora : Chota Kailasa—View of the *Mukha*-chatushki porch of the front entrance.

Plate XV—Ellora : Chota Kailasa—View of the entrance from south-west, showing a part of the cloister and front flat-roofed dvaramandapa exterior also.

Plate XVI—Ellora : Chota Kailasa—Details of the triangular udgamas, pilaster scheme and the *Vidyadhara* couple.

Plate XVII—Ellora : Chota Kailasa—View of the Superstructural tower and the Sukanasa on the roof.

Plate XVIII—Ellora : Chota Kailasa—Roof of the Sabha mandapa with Sukanasa projection leading to the upper storey shrine within, and the damaged main tower of the monolith.

Piate XIX—Ellora : Chota Kailasa—General view from south-western side showing exterior of dvaramandapa, view of the inner temple and its tower against the steep hill scrap.

Plate XX—Ellora : Chota Kailasa—Carved detail of the *Padma-nidhi* type on the flanks of the *mukhapatti* of the *Sukanasa*

Plate XXI—Ellora : Chota Kailasa—Carving on the upper *tala* wall of the tower—a mithuna pair seated.

Plate XXII—Ellora : Chota Kailasa—General view of the south-western corner of the monolith.

Plate XXIII—Ellora : Cave No. 32—(Indrasabha)—General view from outside showing the *prakara*, *dvarasala* and the inner *chaumukh* tower.

Plate XXIV—Ellora : Indrasabha *chaumukh* monolith—Details of the plinth.

Plate XXV—Ellora : Cave No. 32 (Indrasabha)—Entrance from outside the *dvarasala*, through which the square pillar of the *chaumukh* within the courtyard is seen.

Plate XXVI—Ellora : Indrasabha *chaumukh*—View of the tower showing the *kernakutas* and *mukhasalas* and the octagonal sikhara.

Plate XXVII—Ellora : Indrasabha *chaumukh*—A full elevational view of the *chaumukh* tower scheme.

Plate XXVIII—Ellora : Cave No. 32—Indrasabha *chaumukh*—Full general view of the setting against the scarp of the hill and the technique of cutting a shaft for creating the monolith. Conch-blowing *ganas* are seen on the corners of the griva of the monolith.

Plate XXIX Ellora : Indrasabha *chaumukh*—Monolithic elephant carrying in the front court.

Plate XXX—Ellora : Cave No. 16 (Kailasa)—Western *Prakara* face showing panels of Kartikeya, Agni and Vayu in pilastered wall sections.

Plate **XXXI**—Ellora : Cave No. 16 (Kailasa)—Western *prakara* wall showing full Panels of Agni on ram (left) Vayu (on deer) centre and Varuna on Makara-(right.)

Plate XXXII—Ellora : Cave No. 16 (Kailasa)—Western prakara wall; full panels of *urdva-tandhava* Siva and Brahma.

Plate XXXIII—Ellora : Cave No. 16 (Kailasa)—Siva panel on the exterior western face of the front *prakara*.

Plate XXXIV—Ellora : (Cave No. 16) Kailasa—Upper part of the Tandava Siva panel on the west face of the Prakara exterior.

Plate XXXV—Ellora : Cave No. 16 (Kailasa)—Narasimha panel on the western face of the prakara exterior.

Plate XXXVI—Ellora : Cave No. 16 (Kailasa)—Ground level western axis-Gajalakshmi panel in the cross passage, with dvarapalas on either side. The lotus tank in front of Lakshmi is a magnificant relief work.

Plate XXXVII—Ellora : Cave No. 16 (Kailasa)—Gajalakshmi panel in the lower level passage porch, with its lotus tank depiction in foreground.

Plate XXXVIII—Ellora : Cave No. 16 (Kailasa)—Southern court-figure of monolithic elephant and the barrel-vaulted cave front on the south wall scrap.

Plate XXXIX—Ellora : Cave No. 16 (Kailasa)—Detailed view of the southern wall of the front mandapa, showing the panel sculpture of Tandava Siva in the central part and shrine reliefs of smaller size on the sides.

Plate XL—Ellora Cave No. 16 (Kailasa)—Mid-level view of the emerging staircase with the mukhamandapa and the twin-bhumi level wall section on the plinth.

Plate XLI—Ellora : Cave No. 16 (Kailasa)—Axial view of the upper level set-up, from south-west, showing part of Nandimandapa, Mukhamandapa, Southern porch (bhadravalokana) and the superstructural tower and the *hara* system besides part of the monolithic banner pillar on the south-west courtyard.

Plate XLII—Ellora : Cave No. 16 (Kailasa)—South side porch (bhadra-valokana)—Details.

Plate XLIII—Ellora : Cave No. 16 (Kailasa)—Details of the massive plinth and the parivara monolith sub-shrines at the upper level on the northern side.

Plate XLIV—Ellora : Cave 16 (Kailasa)—General view from south-west, emphasizing the deep sheer pit, shaft sunk into the hill top, for carving out the central monolithic tower.

Plate XLV—Ellora : Cave No. 16 (Kailasa)—South court, south western corner showing monolithic column, door leading to the upper level, with planking Ramayana panel and the rise of the upper sides of the Nandimandapa porch and the corner wall shrine relief.

Plate XLVI—Ellora : Cave No. 16 (Kailasa)—General view from the north-western corner of the court.

Plate XLVII—Ellora : Cave No. 16 (Kailasa)—Mukhamandapa porch poised over the ground *tala* high plinth, with massive *hora* parapet, and gaja-munda vedi for the porch itself. Ramayana panel narration on the exterior of the hidden staircase south face, is also seen.

Plate XLVIII—Ellora : Cave No. 16 (Kailasa)—Full view of the main scheme from top to bottom, from the south-western side showing monolith pillar, massive plinth, upper mandapa porch and the tower above.

Plate XLIX—Ellora : Cave No. 16 (Kailasa)—Nandimandapa exterior north-west corner showing supporting pillar scheme wall details and the monolithic banner column in the north-west court, side wing.

Plate L—Ellora : Cave No. 16, (Kailasa)—Roof centre of the Nandi-mandapa showing inter-locking mahanasika **barrel in a** *tri-ratha* layout carrying divinilty within the ***kudu.***

Plate LI—Ellora : Cave No. 16 (Kailasa)—Close view of the main shrine tower and its *sukanasa*.

Plate LII—Ellora : Cave No. 16 (Kailasa)—Main *vimana* **tower-south** face, showing the liner storeyed pattern and **the well-** projected *sukanasa* on front.

Plate LIII—Ellora : Cave No. 16 (Kailasa)—Parivara shrine monolith on the north-east corner-frontal view.

Plate LIV—Ellora : Cave No. 16 (Kailasa)—General view of the monolithic parivara sub-shrine on the north-west corner which faces south.

Plate LV—Ellora : Cave No. 16 (Kailasa)—Inner cloister—details of the lower part of Andhakasura vadha murti, with seven *matrs* and ganas-the foot of Siva planted on two gana heads; Kalabhairava (emaciated) dancing near by.

Plate LVI—Ellora : Cave No. 16 (Kailasa)—Panel of Somaskanda seated on Nandi Bull, with attendants.

Plate LVII—Ellora : Cave No. 16 (Kailasa)—Eastern court of the monolith at ground level, with the running sides of square sectioned pillars fringing the cloister walk, over a vedi parapet relief.

Plate LVIII—Ellora : Cave No. 16 (Kailasa)—Wall panels of the Sabhamandapa exterior showing also the hara above and the frowning lion on the mukhamandapa roof edge. The major panel here is of Jatayu's fight with Ravana.

Plate LIX—Ellora : Cave No. 16 (Kailasa)—Wall details on the main mandapa exterior, south side, showing panels of Lakulisa (in niche shrine), Ravana fighting Jatayu etc. and the south side porch and the *hara* scheme above it.

Plate LX—Ellora : Cave No. 16 (Kailasa)—Main temple bridge porch below Nandimandapa, showing the Ramayana panel.

Plate LXI—Ellora : Cave No. 16 (Kailasa)—Panel figure of Surya with elaborate makara torana, with Aruna and attendants relieved out of the makara motif.

Plate LXII—Ellora : Cave No. 16 (Kailasa)—Side walls of the front porch in the court;-Parvati wearing *channavira* and mirror in left hand seen, with vidyadhara hovering above.

Plate LXIII—Ellora : Cave No. 16 (Kailasa)—Wall of sabhamandapa (exterior upper level) mithuna in 'direct kiss pose.

Plate LXIV—Ellora : Cave No. 16 (Kailasa)—Inner cloister—Wall face of the sabhamandapa exterior south—Mithuna in *kapola-chumbana* pose.